Come Back,
Como

Steven Winn

Come Back, Como

Winning the Heart of a Reluctant Dog

HARPER

HARPER

an imprint of
HarperCollins*Publishers*
77–85 Fulham Palace Road,
Hammersmith, London W6 8JB
www.harpercollins.co.uk

First published in the USA in 2009 by Harper,
an imprint of HarperCollins*Publishers*
This edition 2010

1 3 5 7 9 10 8 6 4 2

© 2009 Steven Winn

Steven Winn asserts the moral right to be
identified as the author of this work

A catalogue record of this book is
available from the British Library

ISBN 978-0-00-734399-7

Designed by Ashley Halsey

Printed and bound in Great Britain by
Clays Ltd, St Ives plc

Find out more about HarperCollins and the environment at
www.harpercollins.co.uk/green

For Sally, Phoebe and Z.

And for my parents,
Willis (1917–2002) and Lois (1917–2009)

Contents

Come Back, Como

On the Loose

It was a gorgeous September morning in San Francisco's Inner Sunset District, glowingly warm and bright. I was spending it on my knees in the middle of Eleventh Avenue, pleading with a dog.

'Como,' I called out in the most casually reassuring voice I could muster. 'Let's go back home. C'mon, boy. Let's just do it.' I inched a little closer to the cream-coloured terrier mutt who had just fled from our house a few blocks away and led me on a frantic chase that didn't show any signs of ending well. Como, his tawny ears lifted in high-alert mode and brown eyes widened, inched back. He kept a safe distance on the pavement, twenty yards off. His tail was raised and furled like a raffish feather over his back end.

This wasn't working any more than trying to outrun him had. At fifty-two, I wasn't about to win a footrace with a nimble, two-year-old terrier. The moment had arrived for a fresh approach if I ever hoped to recapture this scruffy shelter dog my wife and daughter and I had adopted ten days ago, which had been more than enough time to learn his distaste for men – notably me – and highly developed flair for escape.

'Hey, Como,' I said, ditching my phonily unrattled tone for

something even more phonily playful. 'Check it out.' I got off my knees but stayed down in a passive, nonthreatening crouch. He watched closely and came a few steps closer. Encouraged, I sat down, braced my hands behind me and stretched out my legs, as if I were settling in for a placid picnic in the park. I was careful to stay in profile to him, to keep him in sight while avoiding even the slightest hint of confrontation. I slowly extended a hand in his direction, rubbing my thumb and index finger together.

'C'mon, Como. C'mon, boy.' After a while it was clear I'd rub the skin off my fingers before he'd come all the way. I was rested now and considered springing up and making another direct dash at him. But as soon as I shifted my legs a little to get up, Como laid his ears back and retreated. So much for that plan.

At that point I was fresh out of human tactics. My next idea wasn't an idea at all but a kind of unformed impulse to act like another dog – something I'd probably last done forty years ago or more. I stood up, dusted the grit off my palms, crossed the street, and started up Eleventh Avenue on the opposite pavement. I was respecting Como's territory but claiming some for my own, just as dogs do. What a great idea, I meant to say in his language, to explore this stretch of town. You're the leader, natch, but let's do it together.

Como looked completely nonplussed when I gave him a quick glance. He watched, his shoulder blades suspiciously hoisted, as I started plodding up the hill. But soon enough he seemed to sign on to the deal and continued on his side. We both hit Moraga Street at about the same time and kept climbing. Oddly, on that choice morning, there wasn't a car moving or a person in sight. We had the Inner Sunset to ourselves.

Forcing myself not to look over at him, I stepped off the

pavement and started walking in the street on the next block, gradually narrowing the distance between us without seeming to. It was like an algebra problem about slowly but steadily converging lines destined to meet at a certain point on the graph. And it might have worked out that way if I wasn't running out of breath, with several more blocks of steep hill ahead. We were nearly at Ortega Street when a final, desperate inspiration hit. I let out a huge, resigned sigh and went down in a heap. I was counting on the sheer animal surprise of it to seize his interest – and I was right. Como lowered his nose in my direction and came out into the street to investigate.

I played along as best as I could, sinking from a propped elbow slump to a full-body collapse. I could sense him, almost hear and smell him creeping closer, but I had to stay in character if this was going to work. I had to be in the moment, as actors say, shut out everything else and become a helpless, incapacitated, fallen beast. It was a reckless gambit – a car might turn off a side street at any moment and come whipping down that hill straight at us – but there was something strangely peaceful about it, too. I was both giving up and giving it all to this last, best shot I had. I felt the heat rising from the tarmac. I heard the traffic whispering over on Nineteenth Avenue. I smelled the oil stains nearby and the rubber tyres of the cars parked beside me. I'd lived in this neighbourhood for twenty-two years and never experienced it this way – lying flat on my back in the middle of the street and gazing at the rooflines, telephone wires and cloud-studded sky.

As slowly as I could, I rolled my head sideways. There was Como, two feet from my face, his nose busily twitching. We looked right into each other's eyes. It may have been as close as we'd been in the tumultuous ten days he'd spent with us. With my fingers crooked to snare his collar, I arched my arm above his tail and back. I had him. He was hypnotized. He didn't move, still didn't move. It was over. We were going home, with both my arms wrapped around him.

That's just how it would have happened, I'm convinced of it, if at that very, perversely well-timed moment a gardener's truck hadn't clattered across Eleventh on Ortega. It was the first sign of other life we'd encountered all morning. The noise of it startled both of us – the snarly engine, banging suspension, and rakes and hoes rattling in the back. I flinched. Como sprang free. I sprang after him and ran.

❦

As I went thudding up Eleventh Avenue, a leaden certainty that I'd never catch Como settled in my chest. I knew that I'd soon be telling my wife, Sally, and daughter, Phoebe, that our new dog was gone. That I'd let him loose and that he'd run up the hill away from me and out of sight and that he was never coming back. That it was all my fault. That I would understand if they never forgave me. The air felt poisonously hot and acrid as I gulped it in.

But there was also something fitting, even a little weirdly thrilling, about this maniacal morning run through the neighbourhood that kept me running as hard as I could. One way or another, we'd been chasing the elusive Como for a very long time. Hopeless as my chances looked, I wasn't going to give up now. My feet slammed the pavement. After all we'd been through, I kept running, ran until that leaden certainty melted into a burning physical pain that flowed across my rib cage, up into my throat, and down through my thighs. And then, with Como running ahead of me, I ran some more.

CHAPTER ONE

How It Didn't Begin

I wanted Ecstasy.

That, it seemed clear to me, was the direct route to the other things I wanted, too. I wanted family harmony and companionship. I wanted laughs now and stories to tell later. I wanted rituals and something new to photograph on holidays. A reason to be outdoors and a potential bond with neighbours and strangers.

I wanted a twelve-year-old daughter made happy and fulfilled beyond all she had patiently imagined and a wife beaming back at me in the mutual glow of a marital mission accomplished. I wanted reunions and separations – and more joyful reunions. A counter to my own bouts of loneliness and isolation. An end to this endless search.

But most of all, and for all those reasons and more, I wanted Ecstasy – suddenly, unmistakably, irrefutably.

And there it was, in matchless canine form, gazing up at me from a cement floor on the other side of a hurricane fence at an animal adoption shelter in Redwood City, California. Part beagle and part corgi, Ecstasy was the dog, I instantly felt certain, that we had been looking for all along. For a long, soulful moment we communed through the diamond-shaped openings between us. A little shiver, a tremor of cross-species connection, ran up my spine as our eyes locked through the fence. This was it. This animal would soon become part of our family.

She was, first of all, a delight to behold. Saucer-eyed and crowned with perfect isosceles triangle ears, she had a soft white coat touched here and there with irregular brown spots, like morsels of chocolate melting into a creamy dough. She was exactly the size and weight we were looking for – lap-sittable at something under twenty pounds. She looked healthy and untraumatized, holding my avid, appraising stare without going into some needy spasm or fearful cringe or one of those teeth-baring, cage-rattling fits that had startled and alarmed us on numerous occasions during our quest to adopt a pet.

This dog did none of it. To her great credit, in my estimation, she did nothing much at all. Seated about two-thirds of the way back in her narrow enclosure, she looked serenely untroubled by me, by the starkness of her environment (bare floor, dim overhead lighting, battered metal food and water dishes, ratty-looking blanket and stippled rubber barbell), or by the tumult of wild howls, frantic barking and claws scrabbling on cement that lent this perfectly respectable shelter, like the many other respectable and some not-so ones we'd visited over the past three months, the air of an asylum for the four-footed criminally insane.

In the midst of it all, this dog – 'our dog' – remained comfortably seated. Very comfortably, in fact, with a rounded haunch tucked under on one side and her two back paws casually lolling on the other. She looked as if she were sunbathing out on some warm California beach, half hypnotized by the waves rustling in the distance. As if dimly aware of an admirer, the object of my new affections blinked softly and stood up on her stubby little corgi legs. She moves, I marvelled, and remembered Phoebe's first wobbly steps on her aunt Judy's front lawn in Milwaukee ten years before. Like that sublime waddle, this was poetic locomotion – leisurely and stress-free, a casual stroll around her confines. As those short legs scissored back and forth beneath her plumply rounded form, a slightly over-size head bobbing as she went, I was freshly enchanted. There were none of the distressing behaviours we'd seen so often – no fretful pacing or sudden lunges at potential adopters, no leaping up on the fence or sad-eyed sulking at the back of the cage. Here was a dog so calmly self-possessed that nothing would rattle her. What could be better for a family that had never had a dog and a daughter whose shyness and quiet disposition had made Sally and me uneasy in the first place about the unpredictable havoc a pet can wreak? Plus, this one was cute and sort of comically disproportionate, now that she was up and in motion – beagle bigger in some places, corgi smaller in others.

I smiled and started calling out to her: 'Here, girl. Here, girl. Come on, girl.' She declined my invitations, went back to where she'd been sitting when I found her, and sat back down. That was endearing, too, in a way. She seemed to know her own comfort zone and how to find it. Even as I was being charmed, that reflexively sceptical part of me did wonder for a moment: If this dog is so great, why hasn't anyone adopted her? But I throttled that impulse and went on adding up all her positive attributes.

Maybe she'd just arrived at the shelter, I told myself, and we would be the lucky family that got her. She was beautiful. She was kind. She was loyal. All that shone through. I pictured her in our house, resting on the carpet in the living room, plodding into the kitchen to be fed, resting some more on the carpet. Her name, 'Ecstasy', was hand-written on a sign wired to the door of her cage. Below that was another captivating line: 'House-trained. Gentle. Good with children.'

'Phoebe. Over here. Quick!' I called out to my daughter in an urgent, stagy whisper calculated to rise above the barking, braying and choral whimpering of the other dogs and still not attract the attention of any other potentially competitive dog seekers. This was our third visit to this shelter, located twenty-five miles south of our home in San Francisco, and we knew the way things worked here. You had to act briskly and furtively when a promising dog bobbed up in the sea of snarling pit bulls and broken-down setters that looked as if they'd been through the animal equivalent of the Crimean War and held out no hope for a happy conclusion. Good dogs went fast, as we always said. One day we'd be here to catch one. Now here it was.

Phoebe came around the corner from the next row of cages and stood next to me. She was silent for a long time, staring in at the dog of our dreams. Finally I couldn't contain myself. 'So, what do you think?' I asked. 'Isn't she adorable? See if she'll come to you.'

Phoebe crouched down and waggled her slender fingers through the fence. Sure enough, Ecstasy arose and ambled over. Her tail, which I hadn't noticed before, switched back and forth a few times as she walked. After stretching forward to sniff my daughter's hand, Ecstasy came a few steps closer and allowed her short muzzle to be stroked. Sally should be here, I thought. She should be seeing this. Just as I was about to go off in search of her, Phoebe stood up. A recent growth spurt had added several inches to her height. Taller than some of her friends' mothers already, with a face and body that seemed to be morphing into something lovelier and more limber every day, our daughter could give me the woozy, time-spanning sense that she was already fully grown. But she was actually only twelve, still very much our soft-spoken but single-minded child. She locked her arms at her sides and stared at the ground.

'I don't like her, Daddy,' she said of Ecstasy.

'Why not? You just met her. She likes you.'

'I just don't. She feels funny.'

'What do you mean, she feels funny? Kristof had that weird springy fur, and you liked him.'

Mentioning Kristof was a mistake. I knew it as soon as the words left my mouth. I could see it in Phoebe's face, in her narrowed eyes and the combative set of her jaw. Kristof was a dog we'd found at the SPCA in San Francisco several months back, a poodle-mix puppy that Sally and I vetoed on the grounds of house-training issues and his likely size (thirty to forty pounds) as a full-grown dog. Phoebe had been furious at the time, accusing us of denying her the one and only thing she truly wanted and not ever meaning to get a dog in the first place. As a father, her bleak, accusatory look hadn't been easy to forget.

That was early on in our search, and we'd told her – and really thought it – that there would be plenty of other dogs. We were right about that: there were plenty of other dogs, hundreds and hundreds of them. The problem was that almost all of them were either too manic, too menacing, too unruly, too big, too old, or too hideous to consider. And the ones that weren't any of those things were snapped up so quickly that I became convinced insider trading was a bigger problem in the California dog market than it was on Wall Street.

After promising Phoebe on her twelfth birthday that she could finally have the dog she'd been campaigning for since the time she could talk (and she was an early talker), we'd entered into our search with a blithe, even slightly smug attitude. Think of all the terrific unwanted shelter dogs out there that would be happy to have a home with us, we told ourselves. Just think of what we offered – a decent-size house with a small fenced garden out back, proximity to Golden Gate Park and its acres of open space, a daughter who regarded dogs as semi-divine beings, and two adults whose flexible work schedules as a community college teacher (Sally) and a journalist (me) would facilitate regular walks and plenty of daytime attention. What dog wouldn't want to sign up for all that? As a karmic bonus, we'd be saving some animal from a premature demise if he or she weren't adopted. The idea of finding a shelter dog, instead of laying down five hundred or a thousand dollars or more for one of the boutique breeds that had become so popular, added a self-anointed sheen of virtue.

None of that counted for much with Phoebe. All she knew, as the summer wore on, was that she still didn't have a dog to come home to. For a while, as part of her sustained lobbying effort, she'd made a point of reminding us which of her friends and classmates had or were about to get a dog. She'd go and spend the afternoon with Laurie after their Saturday soccer practice or game and come home with stories of romping through the house with Laurie's Airedale, Spencer. Emily had a frisky white terrier named Popcorn. Molly had Lola, an immense, affectionate hound of some kind. Lily, whose parents were divorced, had Bagel the dog at her mother's house and a cat at her father's apartment, with a promised dog on the way there as well.

And then there was the troublesome case of Tobias, whose chocolate Labrador, Mia, died when the kids were in fifth grade. Minutes later, it seemed, Mia was replaced by Oscar, a dachshund puppy who made an appearance at school one afternoon when I was there to pick up Phoebe. As a swarm of kids crowded around the squirming, undeniably adorable Oscar on the playground, my daughter walked stoically by and headed for the car.

'Don't you want to . . . ,' I started to ask, and then realized that I was the intended audience for her performance. We drove home in a well-orchestrated silence.

From time to time Sally and I would enter into discussions with Phoebe – actually, they were more like inquisitions – about our dogless state. Did she really think she was ready to handle the responsibility? Would she feed him and bathe him and walk him, even if it was raining or she had too much homework or she just didn't feel like it? Did she realize that a dog wasn't just something you could pay attention to when you wanted to and ignore the rest of the time? Did she know it was a lifelong commitment?

Yes, yes, a thousand impassioned, ardent and ultimately weary yeses to all those questions. I can remember Phoebe rolling her eyes once about that lifelong commitment line. She knew perfectly well, by the age of five, that a dog didn't live forever. You had it and loved it with all your heart for a while and then it died, and that was that. For all her romantic fixation on the subject – the dog posters on her walls and sheets on her bed, the dog calendars and sweaters, her ceramic collection, and stuffed dogs of all breeds and sizes – Phoebe may have been more grounded and realistic about having a pet in the house than we were.

Sally and I would sometimes lie in bed with the lights out and confide all our worries and worst-case scenarios to each other as Phoebe slept soundly, dreaming of dogs, no doubt, down the hall.

My conversations with Phoebe took on a different, quasi-legal cast. When she was working the evidence of her canine-enriched peers especially hard, I would sometimes cross-examine her and introduce conflicting testimony. I'd name all the families we knew that didn't have dogs.

'What about Jeanne?' I said. 'Or Camille? They don't have dogs.'

'Jeanne's dad's allergic,' Phoebe answered. 'Camille's family lives in an apartment. They're not allowed to have dogs.'

'And Sophie?' I continued. 'They've got a big house.'

'Sophie doesn't want a dog. She likes birds.' There was a pointed pause. 'And she's *got* a bird.' She added the name for emphasis: 'Fellini.'

'Well,' I said, 'we're not like other families. We do things our own way, in our own time.'

'I know,' Phoebe said. 'I know.'

❧

Ecstasy was almost certainly a lost cause once Phoebe had declared her aversion to the way the dog felt to her. But I wasn't ready to give up.

'Wait here,' I told her. 'I'm going to find Mommy.' I glanced over my shoulder at Ecstasy as I left. She had resumed her customary spot in the cage, lying down now on the bare floor. It seemed a little odd that she avoided her blanket.

Sally was outside, taking one of her frequent breaks from the animal-shelter chaos that tended to produce a headache and/or hay fever attack. She stood at the edge of the car park, looking through a hedge at the back of a 7-Eleven.

'Come back inside,' I said. 'I think we may have found one.' At some level I must have thought that if I just didn't mention that Phoebe had already spurned her, Ecstasy still might have a chance. After Sally said something back to me that I didn't hear, we walked in past the front desk, where a family with three small children was rejoicing over the big grungy Akita mix they'd just adopted, and headed for Ecstasy's aisle. Phoebe was nowhere in sight.

Sally did pretty much exactly what Phoebe had. She peered into the cage, leaned down and got the dog to come over and inspect her hand. I leaned down too, and made my first physical contact with Ecstasy. I noticed that her nose was a little warm, but her fur felt smooth, not 'funny' at all.

'She's nice,' I murmured, trying not to disturb the intimacy the three of us had achieved down there by the base of the cage. The shelter was strangely quiet at that moment. 'Her sign says she's gentle and good with children,' I said. 'You can tell that. She's not skittish at all.'

Sally went on petting Ecstasy's head and neck and even got a finger behind one of her large pointy ears to scratch. The dog looked blissfully contented, as if she'd been drugged. Her eyes lolled upward. Even as she kept scratching, my wife threw a sceptical look in my direction.

Sally had come into this dog search as hesitantly, probably more so than I had. She knew going in, as she does about most things in our life together, just about what would happen. I'd talk up the limitless glories of something (a vacation, a remodelling project, now a dog), and she'd end up handling the bulk of phone calls and e-mails (to hotels, plumbers, the vet), not to mention the worrying and fretting that followed. No matter how much Phoebe and I insisted otherwise, a dog was going to be one more huge responsibility of which Sally would shoulder more than her share. It wasn't fair and it wasn't right, but there it was.

It was also only part of the pattern. For all her pragmatic, work-saving reservations about adopting a dog, Sally and I both knew what else was coming with a pet. No matter what kind of dog we found, she would fall hopelessly, heedlessly in love with it. Despite her practically toiling efficiency, my wife is far more swooningly romantic than I, with all my swashbuckling pronouncements, will ever be. Movies (both sad and funny), Springsteen power ballads, a family photo album, Olympic athletes looking solemn on the podium – they can all bring on Sally's readily flowing tears. Fifteen years into our marriage, long after I was accustomed to this trait of hers, even I was startled to witness Sally's giddy laughter turn to tears when her father, on his eightieth birthday, spontaneously sang a Pepsi-Cola jingle from his youth. She was crying for his childhood, for hers, for her mother who had died suddenly in her fifties, for the bittersweet rush of it all. A dog was going to conquer her completely.

'Has Phoebe seen her?' Sally asked, withdrawing her hand from Ecstasy's cage.

There was no point in lying outright about that, although I

was tempted. 'Just for a minute,' I said. 'She didn't really spend any time with her.'

'What did she say?'

'Not much. Something about her fur being a little weird. But that's just something to get used to. Real dogs don't feel like Dakta,' I said, referring to the stuffed Alaskan husky puppy Phoebe had been sleeping with every night for years.

'I know what she means,' Sally said. 'Her coat feels dry. You wonder how well they really take care of these animals.' She looked down the row of prisonlike cages and mouthed something else I didn't catch.

'What did you say?' I asked her. As often as I genuinely don't hear what my soft-spoken, at-times-inaudible wife says, my incomprehension is sometimes a delaying tactic to gather my thoughts.

'Of course they take care of them,' I said to Sally's prior remark. 'They'd get shut down if they didn't.'

'How do you know that?' Sally challenged, her voice ratcheting up now. 'Nobody shuts down those awful puppy farms that turn out sick dogs.'

'What are you talking about? This isn't some puppy farm. We wouldn't have come back here if that's what we thought.'

Just then, as if he'd been set off by the rising pitch and tension in my voice, a bulldog unleashed a fusillade of barking in one of the cages behind us. I turned around and gave him a tough look, which only increased his fury. Soon enough some of the other dogs joined in. It got so noisy that Sally and I, mercifully, had to stop arguing. A staff member from the shelter showed up and asked us if everything was okay.

'Great,' I shouted. 'Everything's fine. You've got a lot of great dogs here.'

He didn't respond to that and went over to calm down the bulldog.

'Where's Phoebe?' Sally asked. 'I thought she was with you.' Now her voice had an edge. We took off in opposite directions. I found Phoebe by the bulletin board in the lobby. She was studying, as she had on our previous visits, the snapshots of families with the pets they had adopted. Everyone in the photographs – even the dogs and cats and an occasional rabbit this shelter doled out – seemed to be smiling.

'That'll be us someday, sweetie. I promise.'

She looked up at me. Her hazel eyes were wet and ready to spill over. 'Why were you and Mommy yelling?' she asked me.

'We weren't yelling. Did you hear us?'

She went back to looking at the bulletin board. Sally slipped in beside her and put a hand on our daughter's head and stroked her fine-filament blonde hair. It was one of those moments when I realize how much my wife and daughter resemble each other – their fair hair and sea green eyes, slim shoulders, soft voices, upright posture, and an uncanny way of expressing defiance, uncertainty, or tenderness with the slightest shift of their chins.

'What kind of dog is that one?' Sally asked Phoebe, who had made a study of breeds from the books she'd got for Christmas and birthdays over the years.

'I'm not sure,' she said. 'It might be part Portuguese cattle dog. Or maybe a laika.' And then, still looking at the bulletin board, she said in a softer voice, 'I don't want that dog, Daddy. Estasy.' She pronounced it without the hard *c*, so it came out 'Ess-tuh-see.' It was like the sound of air slowly hissing out of a party balloon.

I knew how hard it must have been for Phoebe to tell me

that. She was passing, once again, on a chance to have a dog. She didn't really know what she didn't like about this one. She didn't know when, if ever, the right dog would come along. And she felt bad about disappointing me. She was trying very hard not to cry. I was both terribly proud of her and miserable about what she and all of us were going through. Sally and I exchanged a short, helpless look over our daughter's head.

'Let's get out of here,' I said. 'Who wants ice cream on the way home?'

'I do, I do,' Sally said. We often did this when our daughter, an only child, turned sombre. We acted like children ourselves in an attempt to jolly her out of moods that frightened us a little with their black totality. Phoebe walked behind us to the car and then positioned herself in the backseat right where I couldn't catch her face in the rearview mirror.

We stood outside the ice cream store with our cones and dishes and watched the aeroplanes slant down over the bay to the San Francisco International Airport. 'That was us a few weeks back,' I said, recalling our flight home from a visit to my relatives in Missouri. No response. 'This is pretty good,' I tried again, motioning at my Caramel Pecan Swirl with a plastic spoon. 'But it's no Winstead's malt.'

'Why do we always have to go there?' Phoebe asked, of Kansas City's famous 'steakburger' joint.

'Like you mind,' I said. 'I never hear you complain about the French fries.'

'The onion rings are really where it's at,' Sally put in.

'That's so wrong,' Phoebe answered.

They went at each other cheerfully for a little while on that inexhaustible topic. Then they started in on me for the time I almost made us miss our flight by insisting on a last-minute Winstead's run. This was good. We were done with dogs for the day and putting this latest failed attempt behind us. On the ride home Sally and Phoebe hatched a plan to go swimming at the YMCA later on.

I was glad the gloomy, defeated mood had lifted, glad to be headed home with my wife and daughter chattering away. There were some decent leftovers in the refrigerator for dinner, which meant we wouldn't have to hurry up and cook something before they changed into their swimsuits and took off for the Y. But as I drove north past the airport and headed across 380 towards the white hood of fog that often looms over San Francisco in the summer months, my thoughts sailed back to that docile, slightly vacant-eyed dog we'd just left behind.

I suppose I knew Ecstasy wasn't right for us. Maybe she wasn't right for anyone. 'Gentle with children', I realized, could just as easily mean 'Catatonic with everyone'. 'Nearly brain dead.' 'Requires regular resuscitation.' And still, somehow, it did seem that something had slipped away.

Maybe we were the one family that could have coaxed Ecstasy out of her shell, found the core of love and loyalty that lies inside even the most unlikely dog. Maybe her peculiarly ill-suited name was a kind of clue, inviting us to find the buoyancy and joy buried in this decidedly unecstatic animal. We re-entered the fog at the Stonestown shopping centre and started the climb up Nineteenth Avenue.

None of us would have guessed it that afternoon, as the clammy wet air swirled around us and the parti-coloured houses streamed by, but we would soon be heading to Redwood City again. Back we would go, just a few weeks later, to the same shelter, hopeful but far from certain that anything would come of it. There was no way to have known it, but the Ecstasy that didn't happen that day was a prelude to the madness that did.

CHAPTER TWO

Life Cycles

P hoebe was born on 14 June 1991. By the Fourth of July she'd started working on us to get her a dog. I know that's not really possible. Our daughter didn't even roll over for another six weeks, and her first steps came when she was already close to her first birthday. But in retrospect, I think she was just marshalling her energy for the nonstop pursuit of dogs that would begin as soon as she could get around on her own. Once she was walking, no setter, spaniel, or terrier, no bulldog, Chihuahua, or Great Dane was safe from Phoebe's determination to pet it, pull its tail, or throw her arms around its neck and hang on as tightly as she could. It's a minor miracle she wasn't carried off from us by some mutually affectionate mastiff or golden retriever.

Her psychological tactics began even earlier. Phoebe didn't employ the obvious strategy of only liking dog picture books or story books. She was devoted to *Goodnight Moon*, which featured a mouse and kittens, three bears and a cow – but no dog. Beatrix Potter's canine-free *Tale of Peter Rabbit* was a big favourite. So were the *Ant and Bee* books and *The Runaway Bunny*, which she wanted to hear over and over again. That story about a furry little thing determined to flee his family and home, as we'd later realize, foreshadowed our own animal future only too well.

Before her full-fledged dog obsession emerged, Phoebe had convinced us of her healthily well-rounded interest in other animals. She played with Beanie Babies, and not only the ones that looked like dogs. She liked to go to the San Francisco Zoo and gaze up from her buggy at the giraffes and elephants and apes. She even showed a fondness for her aunt Nancy's ginger-coloured tabby cat, Angus, when we visited Seattle. We didn't think we had a problem.

But there were also signs that dogs occupied a disproportionately large share of Phoebe's inner life. Certain stuffed animals began making more frequent appearances in her bed at night. First it was a beagle that squeaked when you squeezed him. Then came an enormous black Lab she named Charcoal. And finally, definitively, there was Dakta, the plush husky puppy whose tag name ('Dakota') she misconstrued the first time and refused to correct.

'Calling Doctor Dakta,' Sally and I would say. 'Is Doctor Dakta in the house? Can Doctor Dakta please report to the room of Miss Phoebe Ann Winn?'

'You sillies. He's right here,' she'd call back at us, standing in a doorway and hugging the little grey-and-white husky to her chest.

Meanwhile, our daughter was cultivating her interests as a collector. After someone gave her a china German shepherd for an early birthday, she kept requesting more little dogs to keep the shepherd company on a shelf in her room. The china pack multiplied faster than her friend Marlena's pet mice reproduced, expanding from one shelf to two and then three. Rearrangements of the collection could take hours.

Phoebe's favourite Disney video, by far, was *One Hundred and One Dalmatians*. There was a long period when we left that tape in the VCR and switched it on wherever we happened to have stopped it the time before. Phoebe didn't mind the interruptions; the film was like a continuous loop in her imagination. 'Doll-may-shuns,' she would say, before she could say a whole lot of other words. More often than we should have, we pressed play. That was guaranteed to quell whatever difficult mood our daughter might have been in at the moment.

Sally and I used to joke that we'd probably watched that movie once for every Dalmatian in it. After more than a year of repeated viewings, we stopped kidding about it. 'I honestly do think she's watched it a hundred times,' Sally said to me one evening, while we were making dinner and Phoebe was transfixed once again by the 'Twilight Bark' scene.

'Minimum,' I said, and went on chopping an onion. We were having fusilli with marinara sauce, a dish that our pasta-loving child preferred above all others. It occurred to me that we were like – too much like – Roger and Anita, the mild-mannered London couple that allows their house to be overrun by all those Dalmatians in the story. I mentioned that to Sally when we were getting ready for bed.

'I don't know,' she replied. 'Phoebe may think we're more like Cruella De Vil.' That's Anita's demonic old school friend, a fur-fixated monster who cosies up to the dogs in the hope of killing them off for their spotted pelts.

'What are you talking about?' I said, knowing exactly what she was saying. We were Phoebe's enemy when it came to dogs. We were the sinister bad guys who wouldn't get her one. We could pretend she was talking to God and not to us when she whispered a wish for a puppy – 'some day' – in her prayers. We could pretend we didn't know what it meant when she staged elaborate tea parties for her china dogs or clung to Dakta in bed at night. But of course we knew. We knew we were the ones who wouldn't get her a dog.

'She's much too young,' I said after we turned out the lights, returning to our regular topic of self-justification for why we couldn't get our four-year-old a dog. 'She doesn't know what's involved. All the walks in the rain and the feeding.'

'How would we ever travel?' Sally said, lying on her back in the darkness. 'Who would stay home with him if something happened?'

It was like a litany in church. We'd been through these lines countless times before. We traded off. Sometimes Sally brought up the vacation problem or the rainy walks, and sometimes I did. Guiltily, with those very solvable questions left unanswered, we tried to sleep.

❧

Eventually, as we continued to feel bad about ourselves, Sally and I decided to address the family pet problem at first with fish. When Phoebe was five, we bought a small, globe-shaped glass bowl and put it on the table beside her bed. It was big enough for one goldfish at a time. The first two died so quickly that none of us can remember if it was Claro or Hako who came first. Phoebe had a mysterious streak when it came to naming pets – she smiled enigmatically when we asked where 'Hako' had come from – but she was faithful about sprinkling a few flakes of fish food on the water twice a day and helping to clean the bowl on weekends.

Either Sally or I had to lift it off the table and carry it downstairs, but Phoebe scooped out every last grain of coloured gravel herself and put them in a sieve to be washed. She stood on a stool at the kitchen sink to scrub off the little ceramic castle. And then, with the care of a surgeon, she netted Claro or Hako from the water-filled peanut butter jar and returned him to his now glistening home.

We certainly couldn't fault Phoebe for those early, hasty deaths. She'd been responsible and done everything right. 'It happens, sweetie,' I told her, after we found one of the fish upside down on the surface one Saturday morning. Phoebe was sitting on the edge of her bed in her pyjamas and peering intently at the empty bowl after a quick toilet funeral. She looked serious but not terribly upset. It was as if she could see past this transitory demise to a distant future, which involved something more evolved than fish. The bowl was like her crystal ball, in which she could conjure up visions of herself romping on a wide green lawn with a puppy.

When it came to Rosie, the next fish in the line of succession, Sally and I had only ourselves to blame. Convinced, for some reason, that the bowl needed a thorough post-Claro-and-Hako cleaning, we took it downstairs and added a capful of bleach to the water and scrubbed the glass walls inside and out. We rinsed thoroughly, refilled the bowl, and let the water sit overnight, as the goldfish book advised, before we let Phoebe pick out a new resident. This one had a reddish tint and seemed especially perky in her pet-store tank. But a few days after we got her home, Rosie began to wilt. She hovered listlessly above the castle, fins gamely fluttering for another week or so, before submitting to her fate.

When I returned to the pet store to complain, the assistant listened to my story, then asked if anything 'unusual' could have got into the water. 'Did your kid maybe put something in the bowl? They do that sometimes, 7Up or salt or something, just to see what happens. Or detergent. You didn't use dish-washing detergent to clean the bowl, by any chance? It's just about impossible to wash out the residue, and goldfish can't take it.' He didn't mention bleach, but he didn't have to. I brought Phoebe back the next day to pick out another fish and a new bowl.

These various watery deaths and replacements brought back my own experiences with the animal life cycle when I was growing up. Like Sally and me, my parents held firm whenever my sister, Judy, and I badgered them for a dog. Our early pet impulses had to be satisfied in other, more primitive ways. I kept tropical fish, their luminous colours and reproductive fervour offset by a general lack of personality and high mortality rates. Judy had a series of pet-shop turtles, their chief function being the opportunity to stage elaborate funerals after the determined little reptiles had crawled out of their plastic island-paradise home and plunged off the pink bookshelf in her room.

Judy was under the spell of Billy Graham during her turtle years. Stirred by his televised sermons, she fashioned high-flown homilies for Christopher or Luke or Mark or John, who were placed in cotton-padded jewellery boxes for their final journey. With me assigned the role of gravedigger, and whatever neighbourhood kids she could round up for the procession, my sister sombrely led the way into the backyard. Dressed in a coral-pink bathrobe that served as her preacher's vestments, she presided over lengthy services under the magnolia tree. I was always afraid, when I sunk my father's garden trowel into the ground the next time, that it would hit a rotting jewellery box from a prior funeral.

If the turtles were all about the social rituals of death and public mourning, the fish I kept in the basement were a solitary pursuit. Every day after school I'd go down and check on my two tanks in the basement. One of them held a transfixing assortment of neon tetras, zebras, angelfish, black mollies, swordtails and at least one whiskered catfish busily vacuuming the coloured gravel and silently rustling plastic plant leaves. The other, smaller tank, where I kept guppies, was more problematic. I always went there last, half dreading that one of my fragile, fan-tailed beauties would either have contracted some furry white fungus overnight or, as they often did with no warning, simply died and floated, swollen belly up, to the surface.

By the time I reached seventh grade, I'd begun to lose interest in fish. My parents had to remind me to feed them. The tank walls grew thick scums of green algae, which I delayed cleaning until I could barely see signs of life behind them. One day, when my father was downstairs doing something at his basement workbench, he happened to notice how bad the tanks looked and threatened to drain them if I wouldn't keep them clean. 'How could we *possibly* have a dog and expect you to be responsible,' my father asked, 'if you can't even take care of a few *guppies*?'

I can still feel the sting of his scorn and disappointment and the murky, guilt-laced anger it raised like a welt. Remembering it, I had to wonder what squalls of feeling stormed through Phoebe as she stared into that glass bowl beside her bed and wondered if a dog would ever replace it.

🐾

Nibbler, the last of Phoebe's fish, lived the longest – well over a year. Our daughter continued to be a good caretaker. She fed Nibbler and changed his water and arranged for our neighbours, Pam and Cheryl, to look after him when we were away.

She wrote out long, detailed instructions and carried the bowl over to their house herself, now that she was old enough to lift it. Phoebe also wrote a poem for a school assignment around that time. Titled 'My Wish', it began:

Whenever I see a dog go by I close my eyes and wish
That I could have a dog of my own instead of just a fish.

All those passing dogs, she continued a few lines down:

look as if they've been invited to a party and I wish they'd in-
vited me.

The poem ended with a resigned sigh of social responsibility:

But then I think of those kids in countries that are poor
And I don't believe I would wish for anything more.

'Did you see this?' I asked Sally. She nodded. 'I'm not sure if we should go out and get her a dog tomorrow,' I said, 'or award her the Nobel Peace Prize.'

Sally had a better idea. 'Let's get a bird,' she said. 'I've been doing some reading. Lovebirds are supposed to be really gentle and have lots of personality. They'll sit on your finger and crawl up your arm and nuzzle your ear. She'd love that. They're kind of cute, too.'

Because it came out of nowhere, and because I tend to trust Sally's instincts and bow to her research, I immediately agreed. We told Phoebe, who was ten, at dinner that night. A fifth-grader, she had learned to mask her feelings somewhat, while reading ours perfectly. I thought she was happy about the bird idea, but I also figured she must have seen it for what it was – a dog dream once again deferred by some other creature. 'That sounds great,' she said, and dug her fork back into her spaghetti carbonara. Her tastes in pasta, along with her skills at handling us, had grown more sophisticated over the years.

We had to wait a few weeks for a fresh shipment of lovebirds to arrive at the pet store Sally had chosen. We made several trips across town and spent a long time pointing at various very green birds, all of whom looked alike to me and let out identical piercing screeches. Phoebe finally settled on one, who was boxed up like Chinese leftovers in a small white box. We took him home and released him into a spacious cage we'd set up in the dining room. Our new family member hopped around from one wooden perch to another for a while, pecked briefly at his cuttle stone, and landed on the swing. After a little more exploring, he wrapped his claws around two of the wire cage struts and stared at us out of one white-rimmed eye. Suddenly, frantically, he began thrusting himself up and down and up and down.

'It looks like he's doing push-ups,' said Phoebe, who was standing back a few feet from the cage. To me it looked more graphic than that. Is that the way lovebirds love each other? I wondered.

Sally reached out a finger to stroke the bird's head. He held still for it at first, then abruptly flung himself to the opposite side of the cage. We watched for a while longer. There was something both fascinating and a little alarming about the way he lunged around, noisily ruffled his wings, hauled himself up by his curved beak, or suddenly posed in place. We draped a towel over the cage and went upstairs to bed.

The next day Phoebe had a name for him: 'Kewi,' she declared.

'Like the fruit,' I said. 'That's good. They're both so green.'

'No,' she replied firmly. 'It's different. You spell it with an "e". K-e-w-i.'

Phoebe seemed to sense right from the start that there was something distinctive about this bird. Instead of hopping onto a finger or even a stick held out in front of him, Kewi shot off in the other direction when anyone approached. Sally, exhibiting a patient confidence that Phoebe and I lacked, kept at it. She changed Kewi's water twice a day, sprinkled seeds into his feeding dish, relined the bottom of his cage with pages of the *San Francisco Chronicle* (my employer), and spent a lot of time talking to him in a soft voice. He did seem to screech a little less when she was around.

One afternoon, when Phoebe was at school, it was Sally who made the shrill noise. I ran out from the study to see what had happened. Sally was pressing a paper towel to the back of her hand. 'He got me,' she said, sounding more wounded than she was. 'I was changing the paper, and he just dive-bombed me with his beak.'

We agreed not to tell Phoebe what had happened, although we did instruct her to keep her fingers away from the cage. In a show of solidarity, I joined her in the hands-off method. Sally refused to give in. She continued to brave the cage to change the water, food tray and paper. Kewi didn't nail her every time; he was too sly for that. But after a half dozen bloody encounters, Sally took to wearing thick long sleeves and heavy garden gloves when she was on bird duty. Even then she'd still pull her breath in sharply at times; Kewi's beak could go right through the padding.

After we'd had him for about six months, a strange thing happened one night while we slept: Kewi laid an egg. This bird, whose bellicose manner made us assume he was brimming with testosterone, turned out to be a she. The eggs, delicate little off-white things that lay in the *Chronicle* sections Kewi shredded at the bottom of the cage, continued on an irregular basis. This unexpected maternal turn of events recommitted Sally to the cause of calming our savage feathered beast. She went on plunging into the cage in her semi-useless armour to maintain order and retrieve the eggs. She started a collection on a shallow dish, piercing the eggs with a pin at both ends and blowing out the contents, as if preparing to dye them for a lovebird Easter. From the study I would hear Sally murmuring to Kewi, without ever making out what she found to say to her sharp-beaked tormenter.

Everything about this bird experiment was confounding. Both Phoebe and I – and Sally, too, for that matter – often referred to Kewi as 'he' or 'him' when we weren't thinking, even after biology had decisively told us otherwise. Call it sexist, but none of us could entirely get used to this bright green borderline-personality brute being female. The truth is, we never quite got used to having a bird in the house at all.

The end, when it came, was sudden and entirely unforeseen. Returning from a week's vacation, we set our suitcases down in the front hall and walked back to the kitchen. We'd left the cage on a newspaper-covered counter to make things easier for the friends who had agreed to feed and water him/her while we were gone. It didn't quite register when we saw the cage was empty and silent. Could our friends have taken Kewi back to their house to look after her? But why would they do that and not take the cage? And then we saw her: stretched out on the guano-streaked newspapers at the bottom of the cage, Kewi lay on her side with one long wing covering half her tiny breast, like a blanket that had started to slip off. Her staring eye stared at nothing now. She was plainly, emphatically dead.

After we recovered from the initial shock, Sally and I had the same reaction. We pulled Phoebe away from the cage and started comforting her.

'What happened?' she said, her voice hushed in genuine wonder. It was the first air-breathing creature she'd ever seen dead.

'It's okay,' Sally said, taking Phoebe in her arms. 'Birds just get sick sometimes.'

'I'm sure she didn't suffer,' I added.

Phoebe looked dazed, but she didn't cry. She came up close to the cage and peeked in briefly again, backed away and told us she wanted to go upstairs. I waited until she was out of sight to let my own feelings fly.

'How could those jerks do this?' I erupted, trying to tamp down my rage so Phoebe didn't hear it from her bedroom above us. 'What the hell's the matter with them? Look,' I snarled, pointing out the obvious failing of our bird-sitting friends. 'The water and food are both empty. They never even came over.' I crumpled up some of the newspaper on the counter, including a section with one of my own bylines, and stomped around the kitchen. 'I can't wait to hear their excuse.'

Sally, I finally noticed, hadn't said a thing. She stood perfectly still, gazing into the cage, with one hand resting on the latch. Her head was down, so I didn't get it for a moment. She was crying, the tears streaming down both cheeks. The anger welled up in me one more time and then collapsed. Sally loved Kewi. She cared about her more than Phoebe did, and certainly more than I ever had. She'd tried, she'd tried as hard as she could, to make Kewi belong to us and us to Kewi. Sally's hands alone, which looked as if she'd spent the last year in a canning factory instead of a classroom, proved it. This was a loss for her. It was a loss for all of us.

Right then, in the heat of that miserable moment, I knew what we would do. We would get Phoebe a dog. We would get us all a dog. We'd failed with fish, and now we'd failed dreadfully with a bird. We wouldn't fail with a dog. We wouldn't. We just wouldn't. I felt like an inconsolable child and a determined husband and father all at once. We would get a dog. It's what we needed to do for our solitary only child and for us as a family, for now and for the future. I didn't say any of this to Sally, as I pulled her away from the cage and held her and felt her sobs through my chest. But somehow I sensed that she knew it and had decided it, too. I leaned back and looked her in the face. Maybe not right away, we said to each other, without saying a word. But yes, we were going to do it.

I was still royally steamed at our friends, but even as I continued to hold on to Sally, I began to let my righteous anger go. Maybe there was a misunderstanding, I told myself – which turned out to be true. Sheila and Todd had thought they were supposed to come the following week. They looked stricken when we told them what happened, and apologized over and over, although I did think I saw a small, conspiratorial glimmer in Todd's eyes at one point. Wasn't it sort of okay, he seemed to be confirming with me, that our nutcase bird was out of the picture? That would be several days later, when we'd got past the first jolt of coming home to a dead pet.

After Sally got control of herself and washed her face, we went upstairs to see how Phoebe was doing. She was sitting on her bed cross-legged, with Dakta in her lap. Both of them were looking out into the hall, as if they were waiting to tell us something. 'I don't want to get another bird, Mommy,' she said. 'I know you're sad that Kewi died. But can you just promise me one thing? Promise me you won't get another bird.'

I was standing behind Sally, but I knew, by the way her shoulders shifted up, that she was about to cry again. It took her a moment to get the words out. When they came they were faint but clear. 'We promise,' Sally said. 'We promise.'

CHAPTER THREE

The Other Dogs
in the Room

There were two very good reasons why we didn't have to think about getting a dog for a long time. The reasons were named Jessie and Riley.

Of all the things that made us grateful to have Pam and Cheryl as neighbours – their buoyant greetings on the street, the easy exchange of reciprocal favours, their political fervour, their festive parties, and the tin of Pam's sublime ginger and dark chocolate cookies at Christmas – we were especially thankful for their two Welsh springer spaniels. A mother-and-son team, the dogs were both exuberantly friendly and exceptionally pleasing to look at, with their striking brown-and-white colouring, craggily handsome faces and lustrous brown eyes. I liked them but couldn't tell them apart, whenever one or both of them rushed me on the pavement and wedged his or her snout between my legs. Phoebe had no trouble at all distinguishing them.

'That's Jessie,' she'd lecture me, with a six-year-old's certainty. 'Her face is completely different. She looks like a mother.'

'What's different?' I'd ask.

'Oh, Daddy,' she'd answer, holding Jessie's lightly freckled and supposedly more feminine mug up for inspection. 'Just look.'

After a few months of observing Phoebe's excitement every time she encountered the dogs, Cheryl asked me if we might like to have Riley and Jessie come over to our house for a trial visit. We accepted. For Phoebe it was like a dream playdate, with the dogs loping up the stairs to her room and tearing back down for a romp around the main floor and then back upstairs again. The playdates continued in the months and years ahead. For Sally and me they served a dual purpose. It was both fun to have a couple of lively and thrillingly large animals in the house (for a limited time) and very effective as a dog-delaying strategy.

'It's good practice,' Sally or I would say, watching Phoebe roll around with the two spaniels on the living room floor or put them through their sit-and-stay routines. 'She's learning what dogs are really like.' Left unsaid was our shared assumption that the practice and learning phase could go on indefinitely. In effect we were stalling our daughter by playing rent-a-dog with the neighbours.

Over time, we all grew fond of Riley and Jessie and started phoning Pam and Cheryl's house fairly regularly. 'Can the dogs come over this afternoon?' one of us would ask, then go down the back steps to unlock the gate between our two houses. Let out of their back door, Riley and Jessie would charge down one set of stairs and pound up ours into the kitchen. Food, no doubt, was a primary motivation. Phoebe was pretty free about offering our visitors the apparently addictive dog chews we now kept in our pantry. But the dogs also seemed to enjoy being in a different place and finding new mischief to get into. Jessie was fond of transporting Phoebe's stuffed animals around the house in her mouth. If we were cooking, Riley kept a vigilant watch for anything that might drop to the floor. His unbridled appetite appealed to me enough – so frank and forthright; so essentially, unapologetically male – that I began to let bits of bread or cooked chicken, raw vegetables, even a pickle slide off the counter. Riley would inhale anything and everything and lift his huge head up hopefully for more.

That probably laid the groundwork for one of our favourite episodes. It happened on a Sunday morning when Phoebe and I were getting ready to meet Sally at a picnic. We were bringing a pasta salad, which I was preparing with Riley underfoot. Running late, I nearly tripped over him when I went to get the pesto out of the refrigerator. 'Watch out, big guy,' I said, as I stepped around him to take the colander of drained fusilli from the sink. Quickly I mixed it with the green beans, pesto, cheese and walnuts and went upstairs to tell Phoebe to get ready. I couldn't have been out of the kitchen for more than a minute and a half. That's how long it took Riley to plant his front paws on the kitchen table and gobble down half the salad from the bowl. He was still licking the green smears from around his mouth when I returned to cover the salad bowl with plastic wrap.

I stayed mad for about ten seconds. When Phoebe came in and I showed her the half-empty bowl, she checked my face to see how I was reacting. Both of us burst out laughing and began telling the story to each other as if it were an old folktale. 'Riley's Pesto Salad', we christened the dish, a name it proudly retains.

Riley and Jessie's visits bracketed and buffered our years of futile attempts with assorted fish and one feathered pet. After

Kewi was gone, the tenor changed. We still liked and looked forward to the neighbour dogs' visits, but they also seemed tinged with our own animal inadequacies. Why did we have to sponge off Pam and Cheryl for this part of our lives and not manage it ourselves? Why, really, were we denying our daughter the one thing she did seem to want above anything else and that we'd already, albeit tacitly, decided to do? Why were we still holding out, when we had both known that with Kewi's death we had turned a corner?

Several months after we put the birdcage away in the garage, I broached the subject with Sally when we were alone in the kitchen. 'You know, we can't keep having Riley and Jessie over here forever,' I said.

'Why not?' she replied defensively. But I could see in my wife's face that she agreed.

Without ever saying it, we knew we were finally giving in. We were letting go of our pet pasts. We were bidding farewell to Claro and Hako, Rosie and Nibbler. We were saying our last good-bye to Kewi. Further back, all those buried turtles and fungus-prone guppies of my boyhood were becoming history. So were the assorted cats and one ill-starred duck Sally's family had had as pets over the years while she was growing up.

Sally and I had to put another part of our own stories behind us as well. We tried not to talk about it around Phoebe, in part to avoid the inevitable comparisons she would draw to her own dogless state, but we had each had a family dog when we were about her age. Both of them, by coincidence purebred miniatures with European names and volatile dispositions, left their marks in more ways than one. Neither Sally nor I had chosen to live with an animal of any kind since. Our first-and-only dog experiences had pretty well cured us of any such longings.

In my case, a dog was sprung on me long after I'd given up hoping for one. I was in seventh grade, and my sister, Judy, was a sophomore in high school, when our parents casually announced one evening that we were going to look at a puppy after dinner. For reasons that were unclear to me at the time – and I avoided probing, in order not to jinx the plan – my mother and father had decided we should have a dog. It later turned out that Judy had been engaging in some back-channel negotiations with our parents to win them over to the cause.

After dessert all four of us drove over to the house of a miniature dachshund breeder in our suburban Philadelphia town and stood around an improvised pen in the living room. The mother dog was lying on her side on a sheet of clear plastic as six tiny tan things no bigger than small mice wriggled at her distended grey belly. The breeder picked up one of the puppies and placed it in my sister's cupped hand and then in mine. Careful not to apply more than the slightest pressure, I ran my index finger down the puppy's back. He felt slick and smooth, like a fish freshly out of water. I couldn't believe how small and helpless he seemed.

Six weeks later, when the littermates were deemed old enough to leave their mother, Gengy came home with us. His name was a shortened form of my mother's maiden name – Gengelbach. My sister took credit for the idea of giving our German dog a German name and declared that he would take up residence in her bedroom.

'Nothing doing,' said my mother, whose Midwestern common sense prevailed. Raised on a Missouri farm, where dogs and cats were left to fend for themselves outdoors, she believed in letting animals know their place right off. She slid a heavy piece of hardboard across the open doorway between the kitchen and dining room, held up one finger and commanded Gengy, 'Stay!' and hustled us off to bed.

For over an hour the puppy whimpered and scrabbled his little claws against the barrier. 'Don't you dare go out to him,' my mother called from across the hall, astutely reading both my mind and my sister's. 'He's got to get used to his own bed. He's got to know who's boss.' When the noise finally did stop, an hour or so later, I was still awake and excited and unable to contain my curiosity. Tiptoeing past the rattly dining room hatch, I peeked over the new kitchen fence. There, stretched out with his back against a cabinet door and the dog curled up in the lap of his black-and-yellow striped bathrobe, was my father. Both of them were asleep.

From day one there was no mistaking it: Gengy was first, foremost and forever my father's dog. Stepping through the back door in the evening, he would greet Gengy with the kind of animated, singsong voice he reserved for dogs, infants and children too young to speak back to him and say something unexpected. With us or even with my parents' friends, my father was generally taciturn, bordering on dour. It was as if he had two personalities, or at least this second, childlike shadow self that was set free by the sight of a baby or an eleven-pound miniature dachshund.

Gengy, who was always highly adept at getting what he wanted, eagerly reciprocated my father's affections. On car rides long or short, he hopped up on the seat back and wrapped himself around my father's neck, like some prized fur collar on an elegant coat. At dinner he loyally took his place beneath my father's chair, resting his head on the rung, snapping up surreptitiously dropped morsels of meat, or cosily chewing on the tongues of my father's shoes. One night my mother noticed a fresh hole in one of his pricey new Corfams when he stood up. 'Oh, never mind,' my father said. 'Now they're worn in.' Gengy no longer slept in the kitchen – that ended as soon as he was house-trained. From that point on he spent his nights curled up on my father's side of the bed.

The rest of us liked Gengy well enough. I suppose we loved him. But we were also wary of him, especially during the unpredictable rages that came over him when one of us was holding him and a friend or neighbour approached. Most times nothing happened. Gengy would flick his switchlike tail and greet people happily. But every once in a while he would tense up and, before we could react, snarl and clamp down on an extended finger or hand with his teeth. What made it particularly scary was the way he bit and held on. He wouldn't nip or snap and be done with it, but grip like a fox trap that had unexpectedly sprung shut.

When it happened with Jennifer, the little girl who lived next door, she looked startled for a moment, her own mouth opened in a little 'o'. Then, as Gengy held on and I tried to pry his jaws open, tears rolled from her eyes and ran down her cheeks. She never cried out or said a thing. After that, Jennifer kept her distance. Mrs Corwin, from up the street, reacted differently. I happened to be in the front yard with my mother, who was holding the dog. Something about our neighbour – the way she moved or held out her hand to pet him – rubbed Gengy the wrong way. He lunged out and bit into the meat of her wrist.

'Jesus Christ!' our neighbour shouted. 'Get him off me!' My mother did her best and finally freed Mrs Corwin's arm. The woman stared down at her wound, and then at us. 'What the hell's wrong with that dog?' she demanded, and stormed back up the street. We hurried back inside and shut the door, my mother angrily scolding the dog as we went. I replayed the scene over and over in my head, ashamed and thrilled. I'm not sure I'd ever heard an adult swear so freely. I kept seeing the twisted, raw look on Mrs Corwin's face and hearing her voice as it rang out by the dogwood tree in our front yard: 'Jesus Christ!' 'What the hell?'

That night, when my father got home from work, he and my mother went into his study and shut the door. Judy and I could hear them arguing. We guessed but didn't want to know if they were talking about getting rid of our violent dog. 'We could get sued,' Judy warned me. 'The Corwins could maybe get our house.' The study door stayed shut for a long time. At dinner nothing more was said about the incident. Gengy was back under my father's chair, gnawing on his shoes and waiting for something delicious to fall in front of his long, thin snout.

I told Sally my Tale of Gengy in 1975, when we were first getting to know each other. That was in Seattle, where I was working on a start-up weekly newspaper after bailing out of the graduate English programme at the University of Washington. Sally had a job tracking down overdue books for the King County library system. Her boss, Karen, introduced us.

Sally and I were attracted to each other right away but pretended we weren't. She was still in a long-term relationship, with a high-school-vintage boyfriend, that was fraying but officially intact. Newly flattered by a woman who had sent me a fan letter about a photography review I'd written, I was wondering if that letter might lead to something more (which it subsequently did). By tacitly agreeing we were off limits to each other, Sally and I were free to be friendly and also flirt a little without putting ourselves on the line. Another eleven years would pass before we got together again and started dating. When we did, it was that long-ago history of easygoing friendship (and repressed romance) that proved to be such combustible stored fuel. As soon as I saw her name on a phone message at work in June 1986, as soon as I saw her face in the *Chronicle* lobby, as soon as our fingers knitted together on one of the grubby, initial-gouged wooden tables at the M&M Bar down the street from my office, the flutters kicked in and kicked up. I barely noticed that I didn't hear a lot of things she said. Our first kiss, a few hours later, left me so woozy I almost felt nauseated. We laughed about it later – how falling in love is a lot like motion sickness, with everything lurching uncontrollably along.

To be entirely, technically truthful about it, that first kiss actually wasn't our first. That had happened on Halloween night in 1975, at a fancy-dress party in West Seattle. Sally went as Marlene Dietrich. I was Groucho Marx. We both paraded around the place with unlit cigars, ate barbecued squid and drank a little too much ouzo. Later on, we sat on the drooping wooden steps of the front porch, just out of the rain, and let our knees bump together. We were travelling in opposite directions and knew it, Sally on her way out of a long love affair and me on my way into one. But with a soft rain falling, smoke drifting off from the grill and an aimless flow of conversation between us, our paths were briefly, perfectly aligned that night. The kiss was unplanned and effortless and seemed to happen inside a silent, singular bubble. We turned to each other, tasted sticky ouzo, Groucho greasepaint and damp cigar leaves on each other's lips, and stood up. One kiss, and we were ready to leave.

On the drive back from West Seattle, we talked about our families. We each had hardworking fathers, housewife mothers and an older sister. Both of us had roots in the Midwest – mine in Missouri, where both my parents were born and raised, and Sally's in Kansas, her mother's home state. We didn't realize it, at least not consciously, but we were exploring each other's foundations. The conversation turned to pets at some point – her childhood cats and one doomed duck, my fish and turtles. Then I told her about Gengy. She laughed about my father's fixation on the dog and listened intently when I described Gengy's antisocial streak.

'Your dog bit people?' she asked.

'Well, I'm not proud of it. But yes, that's right.'

'Did he ever bite you?' she asked.

'No,' I said. 'Why do you ask?'

She took a deep breath and told me about Beau.

A few years after Gengy arrived in our house, Sally's mother, Marty, abruptly decided to get a dog. Family theories differ as to exactly how and why this came about, as Sally told me, but homesickness must have been a factor. Of the various places the Noble family had lived over the years (her husband was a Boeing engineer), Marty had apparently been happiest in New Orleans. That's where she turned, as if to reclaim some of the good times she'd had there, to find a pet. One of her old Big Easy friends knew someone who bred miniature French poodles. 'The next thing we knew,' Sally remembered, 'Mom had us driving out to the airport to pick up Beau.'

Beau was short for Beauregard. Which was short for Pierre Beauregard. Which was short for Pierre LaPierre Beauregard.

Beau was the real deal, a purebred pedigreed poodle with all the papers to prove it, as French as the Eiffel Tower or a *croque-monsieur*. He was decked out in ribbons and bows when he landed at the Seattle-Tacoma International Airport. The trip from New Orleans hadn't been easy. Once he'd been de-crated, Beau got into the backseat of the car with Sally, who tried to calm a very nervous dog down as they drove home to Bellevue, a suburb across Lake Washington from Seattle.

Since Sally's sister, Nancy, was already away at college by then, Sally had the luxury of being the new family member's unrivalled playmate. But just as Gengy was unmistakably my father's dog, Beau belonged to Marty. She was the one who fed him, house-trained him and walked him most of the time. Sally, like Judy and me, was already old enough (ninth grade) when their dog arrived that she had other things on her mind, not the least of which was a pretty serious boyfriend – the very one she'd still be hanging on to when we met.

For Marty, gregarious by nature, the dog was company during the long days in a place where she hadn't yet made the kind of friends she had in New Orleans. In one of Sally's prized family photographs, her mother is dressed in a navy blue polka-dot blouse and reaching out her arm to Beau, who is standing on his hind legs and focusing his attention on her tightly closed hand, which must have held a treat. I was never introduced to Sally's mother; she died in 1977, less than two years after Sally and I met. But I have a distinct sense of Marty from this snapshot. The look of affectionate absorption in the dog and the delight she took in the poodle's thick grey coat, softly mottled ears and large alert eyes are unmistakable.

But Beau also had his dark side. Unlike Gengy, who turned his wrath on visitors, Sally's family dog did his damage closer to home, biting every member of the family at one time or another. Sally still bears a slight scar on her small right toe as a battle wound; Beau got her when she happened to walk by and rouse him from a nap. Her sister and her father both had their turns on the wrong side of the dog's temper. But it was Marty who suffered the most dramatic indignity.

'He jumped up and bit her on the breast,' Sally told me, as we drove up Aurora Avenue that Halloween night. I assumed that her mother must have been leaning down over Beau, perhaps when he was sleeping, and startled him so much that he leaped up from wherever he was lying with teeth bared. Much later, when I came across a faded photograph I'd never seen before, I began to consider another possibility. In this particular shot, Beau is posing on a picnic table, with his front legs widely spaced and what looks unnervingly like a smirk on his face. It's the front left paw that stands out. What ought to be a padded furry foot looks more like a bird of prey's menacing bare talons. The longer I looked at the photograph, the more Beau's long, wide ears began to resemble wings that might have shot out to the sides at any moment and sent him airborne.

Sally's rationally inclined sister, Nancy, rejects any such fanciful ideas. To her Beau's bad behaviour has a simple explanation: he was mercilessly teased by the neighbouring children. Sally remembers that, too, and agrees that it must have played a part in Beau's outbursts. But she also takes a longer view, speculating that the dog was already a little unhinged by the time he arrived in Seattle. Could it have been her own history with a traumatized dog, I would come to wonder, that led us to the damaged dog we wound up adopting ourselves?

'That long flight couldn't have done him any good,' Sally told me years later, in another one of our dogs-of-our-youth dialogues. 'Plus, he was a poodle, for Pete's sake. A *French* poodle.' Having spent her junior year of college abroad in Aix-en-Provence, and a later stretch of her life in Paris, Sally feels entitled to cast the occasional aspersion on any and all things French.

'Pete the Pete's sake,' I corrected her. 'Pierre LaPierre.'

Sally offered a wan smile in return. Even after all these years, Pierre LaPierre Beauregard is still not a particularly amusing subject to her.

Did that failure to find much humour in the Beau chapter of her life suggest a more deeply ingrained aversion to getting a dog? I wondered. And what about my own less-than-sunny recollections of Gengy? Maybe our own dog pasts were just too stained and tattered to promise much success for us as dog-owning adults. How, I fretted, might those shortcomings play out with an actual, undoubtedly imperfect dog in the house? Were we just setting up Phoebe and all of us for disappointment and inevitable failure?

Like anyone who has ever lived with a dog, Sally and I both knew that complications were bound to cloud the idealized picture a child paints. We feared for the multiple forms of deflation and pain Phoebe might face when her dog dream finally came true. But perhaps we had learned that lesson too well, with those childhood dogs who bonded more strongly to one of our parents than to us and who had erratic and sometimes vicious natures.

'We've got to be in this all the way,' I said to Sally in bed one night. 'If we're going to do this, we have to really commit to it.'

She kept reading, as if she hadn't heard me or was choosing to ignore my remark. I was about to repeat myself, with emphasis, when Sally laid her book down on her stomach and looked off towards our daughter's bedroom at the far end of the hall. 'What we can do is try,' she said. 'I'm in if you are.'

I slid my hand across the sheet and rested it on her hip. I'd asked her about getting a dog, and she'd answered by doing a pretty good job of describing marriage and parenthood in two short sentences.

CHAPTER FOUR

Buon Compleanno
– *Happy Birthday*

In June 2003, Sally, Phoebe and I took a long-planned trip to Italy. We were in Venice, in the midst of a record heat wave, on our daughter's twelfth birthday. That was the date we'd chosen to tell her we would look for a dog when we got home. We were all in pretty foul spirits from the heat, not to mention the mosquitoes that kept us up at night and the not-very-good birthday dinner we'd just eaten at a restaurant in the Dosoduro district. Phoebe sat on a scratchy couch in her shorts and tried to look pleased by the book, Italian clothes and Murano glass beads we gave her.

'Oh,' Sally said, playing it for maximum understated effect, 'I almost forgot the card.'

Phoebe opened the envelope, noted the dog picture on her birthday card, and read our vow inside twice before it registered. She looked up and saw us both nodding our confirmation. Even then she didn't trust her eyes.

'Really?' she said. 'Are we really getting a dog? Like, really?'

'We really are,' I said.

'Really?'

'Really.'

'Really?'

Sally ran over and thudded her head into Phoebe's mid-section. 'Would you two please stop saying "Really?" It's really driving me crazy.' She rolled over on her back and kicked her legs in the air in a mock tantrum.

'Your mother's lost it,' I said. 'Better send the carabinieri for her.'

Phoebe paused, as if the word for the Italian police force might be sinking in. Not a chance. Her mind was fully dog-occupied, with no room for a new Italian word or phrase. 'So we're actually getting one,' she said, staring me down like a prosecutor. 'And not a stuffed dog or some joke dog or something like that. We're getting a dog when we go home. When, exactly? I mean, like right away?'

It went on like that through the evening, the next morning, and the three more days we spent in Venice. I'm not sure Phoebe realized she was getting on and off the water-bus vaporettos, spooning chocolate-hazelnut gelato into her mouth, getting lost over by the fish market, or tagging along with us to churches and museums. Her head was so full of dogs – her dog, really and truly hers – that the canal-laced city that might have enraptured her became a kind of blurry backdrop. We took the long flight home to San Francisco on a Wednesday. The next morning she was up at seven and ready to begin the search.

'Can you let us sleep a *little* longer?' I pleaded, trying to open my jet-lagged eyes without letting any light in.

'How much is a little?' she asked.

'I'll get up,' Sally groaned from her side of the bed. 'I can't go back to sleep now anyway.'

By the time I got downstairs, the two of them were hunched over the computer, combing through dog adoption websites. While Phoebe had initially hoped for a puppy, we had all agreed, in a discussion on the aeroplane, that finding a shelter dog was the right thing to do. Phoebe, an avowed champion of animal rights, was persuaded on the grounds that she'd be saving a dog that might otherwise be put down. Soaring across the Atlantic, we had told each other how exciting and fun this was going to be. All those unwanted dogs out there, waiting to be wanted by us. All those breeds and choices. We'd search out the best, most lovable pooch we could find.

From the start we were overwhelmed. Dozens of sites bore pictures of dogs that ranged from the occasionally cute to the decidedly peculiar to the downright menacing, along with elaborate terms and conditions for getting a look at them and proceeding through an adoption. Phone calls to these various shelters in the Bay Area, and some as far away as Monterey, Sacramento and Redding, almost invariably led to a recorded announcement. Sometimes we could leave a plaintive message on voice mail, but few were returned. When they were, the dogs that might conceivably have attracted our attention were already gone. I began to wonder if those dogs had ever been available in the first place. Maybe it was all a game of bait and switch. The shelters lured you in, put you off, and wore you down, with a sinister plan to palm off the mangiest, least desirable dogs they had left.

Frustrated by our cyber-search, we began driving around to shelters, dog fairs and special events. The SPCA was an obvious first stop. There, in a handsomely remodelled facility, we encountered a memorable collection of pit bulls. It's possible that there were other breeds on offer that day. It's also possible that our experience was not at all representative of the charm and ingratiating qualities pit bulls can demonstrate. But all I remember is walking down a hallway of horrors, with one burly, blunt-nosed dog after another in some state of distress. Some of them barked and howled at the sight of us. Others smeared the glass windows with their mouths and tongues. A few of them showed their teeth and snarled. One paced back and forth in his den, apparently oblivious to being watched.

Neither Sally nor Phoebe nor I said much as we made the rounds. On the way out, the attendant asked us if we'd seen anything we liked. Phoebe, to my surprise, spoke up. 'Not today,' she said. 'But we'll be back.'

And so we were, a few days later. Amazingly, after the pit bull extravaganza, the SPCA's adoptable population had gained a number of new and more promising members. There were a variety of smaller dogs along with a few puppies – a long-haired collie, a Dalmatian or two, and the poodle mix Kristof, to whom Phoebe took an instant shine. We asked to meet him in the visiting area. He was a lively and friendly dog, almost buoyant, with a coat of spongy black coils that bounced when he trotted. As Phoebe was scratching Kristof behind the ears and bonding with him nose to nose, Sally and I asked a few questions and learned that he was not house-trained and might reach forty pounds. Both things were deal breakers.

'Let's go, sweetheart,' I said. 'Lots more dogs to look at.'

Phoebe instantly saw that it was hopeless to put up a fight. She shot us one poisonous look, turned and walked away from Kristof, and headed for the car. For most of the ride home she was silent. As we pulled into the driveway, she let us have it.

'You don't want a dog at all,' she accused, leaning forward from the backseat to speak directly into our ears. 'You didn't even mean it.' She got out of the car and slammed the door. Sally and I sat staring through the windscreen for several minutes, listening to the engine tick and then go silent. No one promised us this was going to be easy.

The search wore on, from a boisterous pet fair that crowded a pavement in San Francisco's Noe Valley neighbourhood with dog walkers, cyclists and coffee drinkers (and precious few dogs) to a dreary place near the Oakland International Airport that had the feel of a smuggling operation. We gave the San Francisco SPCA a rest but checked out the branches in other communities. Sally kept up the Web and phone search and had us primed to drive thirty miles north to Novato one afternoon, only to learn that the dog she had in mind was now 'quarantined' for unspecified reasons.

After another call, to Redwood City, we inched down Highway 101 in rush-hour traffic to visit a vaguely promising set of so-called Turlock terriers. Neither of them panned out, but over sodas and a Slurpee in the adjacent 7-Eleven car park, we agreed that we all had a good feeling about this particular shelter. 'I can see us coming back here,' said Phoebe, who now seemed to be hunkered down for a long campaign. She took a pull on her Slurpee straw and settled back in her seat.

Patient as Phoebe was – as we all were – there were plenty of discouraging moments along the way. Days, whole weeks, would go by when nothing turned up on the Web sites and none of our phone messages was returned. Many of the dogs we saw, in person or online, made even our daughter shudder. It didn't help matters when Phoebe's good friend Marlena stopped by one day to introduce us to Lizzy, the toy poodle her parents had had waiting for her as a surprise when she came home from summer camp. Plopped down on our carpet, this impossibly tiny, ink-black puppy whirred around the house like some maniacal windup toy. Phoebe was enchanted. We all were. But Sally and I could also feel a fog of misery seep into the room as we watched Lizzy spring into Marlena's lap. Phoebe went upstairs to her room after her friend was gone and shut the door.

Later that night, Sally called Marlena's mother and quizzed her. Lizzy, it turned out, had been a relatively easy, if fairly expensive, acquisition. People looking for purebred or hybrid speciality dogs, like Labradoodles, Yoranians, or Pugaliers, contacted breeders directly, waited for a litter, and paid up. Marlena's parents had driven to Las Vegas over a weekend and driven home with Lizzy in the backseat.

'Maybe we should forget this shelter-dog business,' I said to Sally that night. 'It really isn't working.'

'Which would be teaching her two things,' she replied. 'That you can give up on your principles and buy your way out of any problem. We agreed we would get a shelter dog.' I tried not to show my annoyance at her being right. 'And by the way,' Sally added, sensing an advantage, 'you can take over the computer search tomorrow. I'm sick of doing it all myself.' That I heard loud and clear.

Sally was right. Like Phoebe, I'd been half-waiting for a dog to magically appear. It was time for me to pitch in a little harder, even if that meant adding a little more tension and drama. Two days later I spotted a Boston terrier and a semi-schnauzer on the Redwood City site. We called Phoebe at a friend's house where she was spending the day and told her we'd pick her up in half an hour. By the time we arrived at the shelter, both those dogs were gone. We were about to leave when I took one last walk along the cages. That was when I laid eyes on Ecstasy. I was sure, as I called Phoebe over to meet this precious corgi-beagle mix, that our search was over. Phoebe and the fates had other ideas.

A week later, after she was sick of listening to me curse the computer screen for not delivering up a dog, Sally took over the search again. The house turned noticeably calmer. As more than a few of our friends have pointed out, my wife's patient and becalmed nature makes her about as close as she could be to my biochemical opposite. Sally can spend an hour or more on a task – marking papers, ironing shirts, or trolling dog sites – and not utter a word. When she does have something to say in the middle of a chore, it usually deserves attention. Even a muttered 'possible' about some dog on her screen would have me peering over her shoulder.

'What do you think about this one?' she called out one hot September afternoon shortly after Phoebe had started back at school. I came over from my desk as Sally moved her cursor onto a thumbnail image on the now familiar Redwood City site and clicked. A swarm of dull-white fur, two dark eyes and a bulbous nose, which looked too big for his terrier face, popped into full view. The dog was looking back at us with his neck jutting forward, as if he had just heard something alarming. He looked ready to bolt right out of the picture frame.

'Where are his ears?' I said.

'Right there,' Sally said, brushing the cursor across the tangled top of his head. 'I guess.'

His fur flared out in a kind of mandala around his face, with swooping mutton chop curves at either side, a shaggy crown that shot straight up in spots, obscuring his ears, and a long fringe over one eye. The ragged fur below his chin was like some '50s beatnik's poorly groomed goatee.

'He's one year old and house trained,' Sally read from the text below his mug shot. 'He weighs twelve pounds, and his shots are up to date. His name's Gandalf, and he's looking for a good home with children.'

'He needs more than one?' I asked. 'We've only got one child. Isn't that the wizard in *The Lord of the Rings*?'

'What?'

'Gandalf. His name.'

'Stop stalling,' Sally said. 'We've got to get s*ome* dog. *Some* day. I think he's kind of appealing. A little startled-looking, maybe, but pretty cute.'

I looked at the picture some more and tried to imagine this being the dog that could come and live with us, that would go for walks with us and get washed (which he looked like he desperately needed) and curl up in Phoebe's lap. I couldn't imagine any of it. But then I'm not sure I had ever fully imagined our search coming to an end and resulting in an actual dog in the house. Really.

'All right,' I said, then felt an impulse to change the subject. 'What day is it, anyway?' I asked Sally.

September 11, 2003, she told me. It was not a date we would have any trouble remembering.

CHAPTER FIVE

A Spirit Possession

Sally and I were waiting outside Phoebe's school that Thursday afternoon ten minutes before the final bell. As soon as the first kids started drifting into the courtyard, Sally hopped out to grab our daughter. It's a good thing we were known around the place – Phoebe had been a student there since kindergarten and was now in seventh grade. Otherwise a call to the police might have been in order. We were behaving like hired kidnappers, with Sally combing the crowd of milling children and me gunning the getaway car out on the street.

Unaware that we had a potential dog in our sights and needed to act fast, Phoebe had stayed inside to talk to a teacher and then gossip with friends. Sally found her in a side hallway near the front desk and hauled her outside. She was up to speed by the time they got to the car.

'What's he look like?' she wanted to know. 'What colour? How big? What kind of terrier is he?'

Sally and I glanced at each other. Neither of us had any idea.

'A mutt,' I said, hanging a right on Turk Street and heading for the freeway. 'The best of all breeds.'

Sally, in her sensible way, offered the necessary disclaimers. 'We've got to wait and see,' she said. 'Don't forget we've had our hopes up before.'

But somehow, even as she said it, memories of the Ecstasy misfire and the other dead ends in Redwood City melted away. Today would be our dog day there. Sally was feeling it, too. She glanced over and shot me a quick, nodding grin.

The traffic cooperated. We zipped onto Highway 101 and sped by the football stadium at Candlestick Point and then past the airport with no delays. Phoebe chattered a little about her new seventh-grade teachers and classes, mostly to keep her mind occupied and tamp down her anticipation. The car air conditioner was on full blast up front, which meant I caught about a tenth of what she was saying. It didn't matter. She was just killing time until we arrived.

We turned in past the 7-Eleven and parked in the shelter's half-filled car park. Phoebe bolted out of the car before I had my seat belt off. When Sally and I came through the door, our daughter was requesting directions to Gandalf's cage. That alone was a testament to her determination. Phoebe has always been especially reluctant to speak to strangers.

'Are you here by yourself?' the woman at the front desk asked her.

'No,' she said, gesturing in our direction. 'I'm with them.'

Them. As if we were anonymous bit players in her story. Which, in a sense, we were. A good deal of Phoebe's wishful life had been aimed towards this moment. We'd been the drag on her sails.

The woman at the desk punched a few numbers on her phone and asked someone to come out and meet us. A young woman showed up promptly and politely looked us over.

'They're interested in Gandalf,' the desk woman told her, in a voice that must have required some effort to sound that neutral. I may have imagined it, but I thought I caught a knowing look pass briefly between the two shelter staffers. The younger one, whose distinguishing feature was a notably long and narrow nose, led us back into the barking, howling maze. She stopped at a corner and gave us a quizzical small smile.

'Isn't he adorable?' she said.

For a moment I didn't know what she was talking about. The only dogs in our vicinity were large, wine-coloured hounds. And then I saw him, or what I had to guess was him. Pressed into the farthest, darkest corner of his cage, a sand-toned shag writhed against the fence. It required some faith to perceive him as a dog. His shoulders hunched up, and his claws dug at the floor as he tried to press himself into the cement wall behind him. His tail was tucked out of sight. 'Scrawny' would have been a compliment to his stature, or what we could make out of it. With a little less fur he could have passed for a large rodent that had just spent six months scouring for food and water in the desert without much success. His eyes were two dark circles of alarm.

When our guide called his name, Gandalf charged straight at us and began leaping at the fence – once, twice, . . . eight or ten times without stopping. Sally and I instinctively stepped back. I caught her eye and mouthed my reaction: 'Is that really him?'

'I guess so,' she mimed back at me with a shrug.

Phoebe hadn't flinched. Standing close to the long-nosed woman, she watched calmly as the dog continued his trampoline act. 'Why does he do that?' she asked.

'He's excited to see you,' Needle Nose replied. 'Can't you tell?'

'Yes,' Phoebe said in a dreamy half-whisper.

'Do you want to meet him?'

'Yes,' our fearless daughter said again. Needle Nose extracted a key from a big clump of them attached to her belt.

'Wait a second,' I said. 'Are you sure it's okay? I mean, he doesn't know her.' I'd noticed, on one of Gandalf's grimacing rocket leaps, two curved and sharp-looking canine teeth. Phoebe and Katarina – I finally read the name on the badge pinned to her shirt – turned to look at me.

'Dad,' Phoebe said.

'Steven,' said Sally.

Katarina, who didn't have anything to call me, followed up by gently raising her eyebrows and jingling her keys. I couldn't help feeling a little pulse of injustice. No one had offered to let us meet Ecstasy. Maybe that would have made the difference, and we could have been a happily dog-enhanced family by now. But that was then. The tide was pulling in another direction now.

'All right,' I conceded. 'Go on.'

'Actually I have to bring him to the visiting room,' Katarina said. 'They'll tell you where to go out front. We'll meet you there.'

The visiting room was a long, wedge-shaped area upstairs, with old desks and chairs stacked along one wall and a distressed-looking fake leather couch at the far end. The only natural light came from a row of frosted windows along the room's bare wall. We sat down in the gloom and waited. I felt as if a doctor were going to come in and give us some bad news. A few minutes later the door opened, and Katarina brought Gandalf in on a leash. She shut the door behind her before letting him loose. The dog did a quick sprint around the perimeter of the room, keeping himself as low to the ground as possible, veered away from us, and scurried under a desk.

'Terriers always do that,' Katarina said calmly. 'They like to tunnel down into things. It's their hunting instinct.' She could have been hosting a documentary on the Discovery Channel. When she crouched down and held out an inviting hand (which turned out to be concealing a treat), Phoebe went over and crouched down beside her. They stayed that way for quite a while, until Gandalf crept out from under the desk, eyed and sniffed both hands, and decided to go for it. He grabbed the treat from Katarina and sped back to his hiding place.

'Now you try it,' Katarina said, planting a treat in Phoebe's hand before coming over to stand beside her dubious parents. Phoebe copied Katarina's technique exactly, with one arm fully extended as she patiently waited.

'He's not coming out,' I muttered to Sally. 'This isn't going to work.'

Sally didn't respond. Watching our daughter closely, my wife was seeing what I couldn't yet: Gandalf was going to come home with us. Phoebe had already made up her mind and, more importantly, her heart.

It didn't matter that this dog was about as wild, elusive and unapproachable as anything this side of a coyote. It didn't matter that he was hiding under a metal desk and wouldn't come out. It didn't matter that he looked like he'd just been ejected from a street sweeper or that he wasn't the doe-eyed, floppy-pawed puppy Phoebe had drawn in crayon a thousand times since she was two.

None of it mattered. He was going to be her dog. She was going to rescue him from whatever it was that had made him like this.

Gandalf's thin feet were like little white blades when he finally darted out, grabbed the treat from Phoebe's hand and escaped again in a spring-loaded crouch. Our daughter stood up and looked us both, one after the other, directly in the eye. 'Can we have him?' she said. 'Can we? I really, really want him.' Then, after an expertly timed pause, she delivered the knockout punch: 'Please?'

Showing his own flair for timing, the dog chose that moment to make another circuit of the visiting room. Even Katarina looked a little startled as he barrelled along the bare wall towards the door and angled past her. His ears were swept back and lay flat against his head, as if he were charging through a wind tunnel. Phoebe got out of his way and came to sit with us.

'Is this typical?' I asked, as Gandalf completed another lap and reversed course.

'Sometimes,' Katarina replied noncommittally. 'He's a very lively dog. That's good.'

Good for what, exactly? I wanted to ask, but managed to keep that to myself.

'Maybe we should think of another name for him,' Sally said. I looked over at her in amazement.

'What did you say?'

Sally stared back at me for a moment. 'You heard me.' Her suggestion, or rather, a decision disguised as a suggestion, came with the clear assumption that we had already agreed to adopt this dog. What difference would another name make? I wondered. He'd still be just as crazy.

Phoebe picked up on the opening right away. 'Yeah, Mom, that's a cool idea. It should be something Italian.'

'Like Lasagna,' Sally said, which got them both giggling.

Gandalf zoomed past again, this time with Katarina shifting position to snare him.

'Or Fettuccine,' Phoebe said. 'How about Provolone? Or Prosciutto? His full name could be Prosciutto with Melon.'

Bent over laughing, she and Sally were having a grand time. I was completely lost. I didn't understand why my wife and daughter were working on a stand-up comedy routine based on an Italian menu. I didn't understand how we had managed to get ourselves trapped inside this weird room with a lunatic dog and a woman who was trying to lure us into taking him home. I didn't get any of it. Katarina had Gandalf in her arms now and was carrying him towards us.

'Make your lap flat,' she told Phoebe, and set the dog down on her legs. 'Don't worry. He's very gentle.' For a moment he lay still, as Phoebe lightly stroked the back of his neck. But then he lunged. Instinctively Sally and I both reached out to hold him in place. I thought later how stupid it was to contain him like that. We were taking Katarina at her word about a dog that could easily be vicious if he felt trapped or scared.

Sally had hooked her fingers under his collar, so he couldn't get away. Beneath his coarse long fur, I could feel Gandalf's shoulder and back muscles tense. There was a force in him that rippled up through my hand, even as Sally and Phoebe made soothing, tender sounds and went on petting him.

'He seems strong,' I said. 'Can you feel that?'

'He feels great,' Phoebe said. 'He's so soft.'

It was hard not to object. Compared to Ecstasy's plush coat, which felt 'funny' to Phoebe, or even to Kristof's springy, oily coils (which she didn't mind), this one was almost repellent. It was like a worn hall carpet that got a lot of traffic and hadn't been cleaned in a very long time. Phoebe seemed to adore the sensation, running her hand down his back over and over again.

'Try scratching him just above his tail,' Katarina suggested. 'He really likes that.' And so he did, thrusting his hind end up to prove it.

'Here, Daddy. You try it.'

I put my hand right where Phoebe's had been and scratched. Gandalf sensed the difference. He whipped his head around to see what had happened and tried to wriggle free.

'Terriers are very sensitive,' Katarina said, reaching down to take Gandalf from Phoebe's lap. 'I'll leave you guys alone with him now, if you like. That way you can get to know him a little better. You get used to him, and he gets used to you.' She was good, that Needle Nose was. She knew just how to play out these visits for optimal effect.

Katarina set Gandalf down in the middle of the room and slipped away. I noticed again how careful she was to shut the door quickly behind her. The dog sniffed back and forth along the bottom of the door, finally gave up, and headed for his dark, safe hiding place under the desk.

'Hey, Prosciutto,' Sally called out softly to him. 'Come back out here. We want to see you.' She got up and copied Katarina's crouched-down, hand-out method. Sure enough, the dog ventured out, warily approached, and took something from her hand.

'What was that?' I said.

'A treat. Katarina left a little pouch of them,' said Sally, waggling it in her other hand. That bit of the shelter's trickery had escaped me.

'Don't you think you're just buying him off?' I challenged. 'Try it without the treat.'

Sally gave me a quick caustic look. 'Maybe *you* should try,' she said.

'That's okay. I'll watch from here for now. Be careful, dear. We don't actually know anything about him or what he might do.'

Phoebe had got up and was peering under the desk, where the dog had once again retreated. The waiting game went on for a while. I thought she would get discouraged, but that didn't happen. Gandalf – or Manicotti or Mortadella or whatever we were calling him – got quite a few treats out of the deal. Phoebe kept watch by the desk cave entrance and tried everything she could to connect with the mutt inside, with and without the shelter's crunchy little pellets as bait. But as far as I could see he wasn't giving an inch or getting used to us, as Katarina put it, in the slightest. Sally came back to the couch and sat down beside me.

'You know, you're really not helping by just sitting over here,' she whispered. 'Can't you see how excited she is? Can't you see how much she loves him?'

'*Loves* him?' I whispered back. 'How in the world do you love a dog you just met who doesn't want anything to do with you?'

'Look,' Sally said.

Dressed in bright red jeans and a patterned T-shirt, her tawny blonde hair pulled back in a ponytail, our daughter looked her true age of twelve, but she also looked two or twenty, ten or sixteen. She was bigger and smarter and faster now. She was growing up. But there was this thing that had never changed in her and maybe never would, this powerful pull that dogs held for her, the need to be near them and to be needed by them. She was kneeling, peering into the dark place where the Italian scamp was hiding.

Sally was right, of course. Loving dogs – loving this dog –

wasn't something conscious or considered for Phoebe. It was a total-body impulse, a spirit possession that took hold of her and made her deaf and blind to any cautions or misgivings. I had no idea where that had come from and only a faint glimmering of what it might mean about her deeper capacity to love others and care about a wider world. But I knew it was real. I stood up and went over to stand guard with her.

'Where is he, Skidge?' I said, using one of the nicknames we'd pinned on Phoebe over the years.

'Right in there,' she said in her softest voice, trying not to rattle the dog. 'See?'

All I could make out were three dark circles – two eyes and a nose – in the furry haze of a face. 'Do you have one of those things,' I asked, 'the treats?'

Without taking her eyes off him, she reached down into the pouch and handed me one. Just as Katarina and Sally and Phoebe had, I crouched and held a little morsel of pressed chicken-flavoured sawdust in my hand. The dog didn't budge. I waved the treat around a little to see if that made a difference.

'What are you doing?' Phoebe said. 'You're freaking him out.' She took the treat out of my hand and held it low and steady near the floor. Finally, about the time I thought her arm must be ready to fall off, the dog poked his nose into view. His head and half of his scraggly body followed. He sniffed the air for danger, apparently determined I was it, and slid back out of sight.

'C'm'here, boy. Come on, little guy. No one's going to hurt you.' Phoebe crept forward on her knees. Once again he inched forward. Instead of giving him the treat, Phoebe used it to draw him out and back towards where I was sitting on the floor. She held out her other hand for the dog to smell and told me to do the same, all the while keeping his attention by holding the treat just out of his reach. How did she know to do this?

'You see, Daddy? He's getting used to you.'

I didn't see anything of the kind. He looked positively miserable, with his desire for the treat just barely keeping his impulse to bolt in check. 'I guess so,' I offered.

Phoebe manoeuvred him a little closer and made a nifty move to get a finger under his collar. She immediately rewarded him with the treat, then slowly tugged the dog between us. 'You should pet him. He needs to know your touch.' I followed her instructions, patting the shag rug on his back a few times. Phoebe, meanwhile, had found a spot on his neck to scratch. That's how Katarina found us when she returned.

'Hey, way to go,' she said. 'He really likes you two.' The sound of the door opening panicked the dog, who struggled to break free. When Phoebe let go of his collar, he made a run at the door and repeated his close inspection of it. Maybe all dogs are big on doors, I thought, but this one's fascination with the way out of the room seemed particularly intent.

'So what do you guys think?' Katarina went on, in her congenial, saleswomanly way, ignoring the dog's snuffling scrutiny of the door behind her. 'I've never seen him like this,' she said, by which she might have meant either this friendly or this manic.

Before I could ask what the point of comparison was, Sally came over and put her arm around Phoebe's shoulders. They were about the same height now, my wife and daughter, and they presented a united front. 'Do we need to talk about this?' Sally said to me, with the clear conviction that we didn't.

'So what happens now?' I asked, turning to Katarina. 'I mean, what would the next step be?' I was trying to keep one last, rapidly disappearing escape route in sight.

Katarina bent down to hook Gandalf back on his leash and then stood up briskly. 'We can go over all the details at the front desk,' she said, and left us to find our way there without her.

The shelter's paperwork was ready for us when we got there. That seemed a little presumptuous, but maybe they knew from experience that once a family is upstairs in the visiting room, it's all over. I asked Sally to fill out the forms, on the premise that her handwriting was neater than mine. She and Phoebe went to work on them together on a couch across the waiting room, where the two of them promptly began conferring sotto voce. I hung around the desk and tried to do a little more probing.

'So how many dogs get adopted here on, say, a daily or weekly basis?' I asked the woman who'd greeted us when we came in. Katarina and Gandalf were nowhere to be seen.

'It varies. Some days we get a real run, and six or eight dogs – and cats – may go out the door. Other days it's real slow.'

'Because . . . ?'

The woman paused, trying to gauge what I was really asking. 'You know, I just think there's a natural rhythm to it. Personally, I'd love to take every single one of these little monkeys home with me if I could. That Gandalf is something special.'

'Yes,' I said, 'he seems to be. Do you have pets yourself?'

The woman had to answer a phone call. She held a finger up to me and raised her eyebrows as she listened. With her hand over the receiver, she mouthed, 'They're asking about *him*. About *Gandalf!*' She told the caller that she was so sorry, but that wonderful dog had just been taken. 'How about that?' she said after she'd hung up. 'Another half hour, and you would have missed out.' I was beginning to get the slightly queasy feeling I have in car showrooms. Was this whole thing an elaborately contrived hustle? Could my wife and daughter be in on the pitch to get me sold? I knew I was getting a little paranoid and tried to retrieve my sanity and composure.

'So, do you have any advice for us?' I asked. 'Like what we should look for right away?'

'Well, there are lots of things to think about. Where the dog is going to sleep and who's going to feed him and walk him and all that. Establishing a routine is very important. We want this to be successful for you and for the animal. That's why we're here. And you know, if for any reason it really isn't working out, there is our thirty-day policy.'

'I don't know anything about a thirty-day policy. What's that?'

'Oh, no one told you? Well, it's kind of a safeguard, in the very rare cases where it's not a good match. You have thirty days to return the animal to us for a full refund with no questions asked.'

'And after that? After the thirty days, what happens?' I asked, eager to know the specifics of the policy. She was downplaying it, but it sounded important to me. A commotion behind us cut off further discussion. Katarina was leading Gandalf into the lobby. Actually it was a combination of leading and dragging. Every few feet the dog would start yanking in a different direction. I noticed that he was wearing a harness, which was presumably more secure than the ordinary neck collar he'd had on before.

'There he is!' the woman behind the desk exclaimed.

Phoebe rushed over to greet her new dog. It wasn't exactly a made-for-video encounter. He flinched and yanked away when she approached. Katarina said something reassuring under her breath and handed Phoebe the leash. 'Why don't you walk him around a little bit, just inside for now, and I'll go and talk to your parents. Congratulations.' Phoebe looked a little awed and bewildered, as if someone had just put her behind the wheel of a car and told her to drive to Los Angeles. She held the leash out in front of her and waited for the dog to do something. As soon as Katarina moved away, he pulled towards her.

'It's okay,' Sally said, crossing over from the couch now. 'We're right here.'

Katarina motioned us over to another desk, where the shelter's assistant director, an exhausted-looking woman in her fifties, joined us. We all went over the paperwork together. Then we got still more sheets from a file, with information about Gandalf's up-to-date shots, his reproductive status (neutered), estimated age (about a year), and the tiny computer chip implanted in his neck, which would allow him to be traced back to this shelter and then to us in case he got lost. We were given a small sample bag of dry food and offered some boilerplate advice about nutrition and finding a good vet in San Francisco. I wrote out a cheque for one hundred dollars, and the soon-to-be-renamed Gandalf was ours.

'Do you have a good book about living with a dog?' Katarina asked. 'There's lots of good advice out there.'

We nodded, and they were ready to let us go with all their good wishes. Before we went, I raised the issue of the thirty-day policy.

The assistant director let out a small sigh. 'It's all there in the agreement,' she said, nodding at a clasped envelope that was now in Sally's hand. 'But really, it comes up so infrequently that we almost forget to mention it. We tend to find good matches here.'

'How infrequently?' I asked.

At that, both women lost eye contact with us for a moment. 'Well, it's kind of funny that you ask,' the assistant director said, her weary aspect brightening as she warmed to her story. 'The only dog that's been returned in the last month happened to be Gandalf. An older woman took him, and all that terrier zip and energy were not quite what she needed. I thought all along she would have been happier with a cat.' She served up a raconteur's smile. 'But look at it this way,' she said. 'If that woman hadn't returned him, you wouldn't be going home with this great dog today.'

I glanced over at Sally to see if she was looking at it that way. But her attention was elsewhere. She was watching Phoebe weave around the lobby with the dog.

'Is there anything else we ought to know?' I asked.

To this day I give Katarina credit for answering truthfully. Nose or not, she was finally no Pinocchio. 'We don't really know what may have happened,' she began. 'Gandalf was on the streets in Santa Clara County and spent some time in another shelter down there before he came here. Somebody – some man – must not have treated him so well somewhere along the line. Maybe it was an owner or somebody on the streets. You can see it: he's definitely wary around men. But he's a sweetheart. I know you'll all give him plenty of love,' she said. 'And patience.'

Ten minutes later we were in the car, driving home. Phoebe was in the backseat, cuddling the dog in the blue blanket she'd picked out months ago specifically for this purpose. Sally was sitting in the passenger seat, lost in whatever busy thoughts she was lost in. Knowing her, she was probably planning exactly where we were going to put the dog's crate and where his bowl and water dish should be.

And I, somehow, had mutely agreed to adopt a dog that had already been adopted and returned and had probably been abused, who knows how badly, by at least one man and maybe others. From the dog's point of view, it seemed likely, one man was as suspicious as the next. He didn't like any of them, and for perfectly good reasons. I glanced up at the rearview mirror. Phoebe and her new love were snuggled down in the far corner of the backseat, out of my sight. They both seemed very far away, cordoned off in some private kingdom whose roads and gates and secrets were barred to me.

Once again the traffic on 101 was uncannily light. We were speeding towards our new life, whatever it might hold, with nothing to slow us down.

CHAPTER SIX

Home Makeover

S ally and I knew everything there was to know about adopting a dog and bringing him home. We'd read the books, talked to friends and relatives, and gleaned whatever wisdom we could on our dog-hunting visits to various SPCAs and shelters. No matter how the advice was presented, fancied-up and elaborated, it pretty much boiled down to this: Love with Limits.

Dogs want and need to be loved. They're sensitive creatures keenly attuned to humans and eager to bond with us and love us back. But if you don't establish dominance and a clear chain of command early on, both you and your dog are likely to be locked in a miserable, endless power struggle that can drain you both. Dogs want to please us, we kept hearing, and they want a consistent set of rules for how to do that. It's in their interests and in their natures. So one of the most important ways of loving a dog and showing you care is to show that you're the boss. A benevolent one, but the boss all the same.

The problem with all this is that dogs don't read, watch public television programmes about dog-training methods, or listen to the pronouncements of the experts. It's every bit as much in dogs' interests and their natures to run wild, eat anything and everything they can find, and do precisely what they want as it is for them to toe the line and please us. And that doesn't even account for the particularly strong determination that a traumatized animal might have to do things his own way.

The moment we brought him into the house, the no-longer-Gandalf but still unnamed dog we'd just acquired set out to claim his new territory. That was one way of looking at it, as he dropped his nose to the ground and began vacuuming the living room, dining room and hallway for scents, bits of food and who knows what else. But natural curiosity about a new place seemed only a small part of what was driving him. From the frantic way he was going about it, angling across one room and doubling back, sweeping along a wall and suddenly stopping in place, glaring in our direction if any of us moved and otherwise ignoring us, he was behaving like a wild beast caged up with his captors and desperately searching for a way out.

I could identify. If our newest family member felt trapped by his strange new surroundings, I shared the feeling. The more the dog nervously patrolled the downstairs, the smaller and more confining our house seemed. I felt more than a little cornered myself.

'How long do you think he's going to do this?' I asked. It was like watching a pinball career around without racking up any points.

Phoebe plugged into her sympathetic instincts and got down on the floor. 'It's okay, boy,' she soothed, as the dog zoomed by and headed upstairs. 'That's right. Look around. This is your new house.' She clambered after him, a look of serious purpose fixed on her face. Our daughter, who had surprised us with her interest in seventh-grade science after previously despising anything involving a test tube or a number, was taking a methodical, orderly approach to the dog's adjustment. She seemed to regard it as a real-world environmental challenge. That was fine, but I was feeling panicked about what we'd just done. As soon as Phoebe followed not-Gandalf upstairs, Sally and I had our first chance to talk freely. First I confirmed that she'd heard what the people at the shelter had said about the dog's history with men.

'I heard,' she said. 'I heard all of it. Getting any dog is taking a chance. We knew that going in.'

'Easy for you to say. You're not a man.'

'And you are,' she shot back. 'Get over it. Here, help me with this.'

She was unfolding the clear plastic drop cloth we'd got at the hardware store. The plan was to line the dining room floor with it and make that room the dog's mistake-proof zone in the house. We attached the plastic to the bare floor beyond the carpet with blue tape. I'd brought the old folding wooden gates from Phoebe's toddler years up from the garage and stretched them across all three doorways. Once used to prevent our daughter from tumbling downstairs, they'd now keep the dog confined to quarters. Sally put the dog's heavy-duty plastic sleeping crate in what she thought was the cosiest nook of the room, behind the cabinet we use to store lightbulbs, half-used rolls of tape and takeaway menus.

'Phoebe!' she called upstairs. 'Bring him down so we can show him his bedroom.'

Our daughter arrived with the dog in her arms.

'See how he likes it,' Sally coached.

Phoebe set the dog down as gently as possible. For a moment he froze in place. Then he unfroze all at once, tearing at the plastic with his front and back paws and barrelling straight at one of the gates, just as he had done at the shelter. But instead of jumping up on it, he shied away at the last moment, as if the gate were electrified and sending off some warning sizzle. The same thing happened with the other two gates he approached.

'It's pretty weird,' I said, 'but I guess it's going to work. I don't know about the plastic, though. Looks like we're going to need something thicker.'

As he continued to circle the room, the dog was making quick work of our temporary flooring. The plastic was soon bunched up in some spots and shredded in others. The blue tape was the next target. He clawed at one corner of it by the kitchen and tried to pull it loose with his teeth.

'Hey, stop that,' I called. That earned me a brief, sidelong look before he went right back to work.

'He must like the smell of it,' Phoebe said. 'Or maybe it's something about the colour. It matches his blanket.' Phoebe was in full amateur scientist mode, observing, speculating, postulating. I liked imagining her in a white lab coat, even if her hypotheses made no sense to me. But then I was already getting used to feeling disoriented by having this animal in the house.

'Do we have any of that black electrical tape?' Sally wondered. 'That might work better.'

She was about to look for it in the cabinet drawer when the dog, in a sudden burst of inspiration, left off gnawing at the blue tape, gathered himself, and took another run at the gate that closed off the wide entrance to the living room. This time he kept going and cleared it with room to spare in a great arching leap. It left us speechless for a moment, the way a pole vaulter does when he snaps skyward and soars over the bar. We stood there on the tattered plastic and watched him go, his thick tail lifted in triumphant salute.

❖

Several hours later, after we'd had dinner and Phoebe had taken the dog for a walk and we'd tried unsuccessfully to feed him – he was apparently too stressed to eat or even drink any water – we gathered in the dining room again to settle him down for the night. Sally thought it might be a good idea if we all sat on the floor.

'We must look gigantic to him,' she said.

'We are,' I agreed. 'Aren't we supposed to be?'

'Dogs are just like us, Daddy,' Phoebe instructed me. 'They need to feel confident and feel good about themselves. We have to do everything we can to help.' She'd been hearing that sort of message about the values of empathy and community since kindergarten and apparently learned it well. If it was true about people, why not about dogs?

'You're right, sweetie.' I crawled over towards the dog, who was lurking behind Sally's outstretched leg. He was watching me closely but didn't seem too perturbed by my approach until my hand got snagged in the torn plastic and I freed it with a tug. That made him start and pull back.

'No sudden movements,' Sally scolded, as the dog skittered away.

Phoebe had arranged his blue blanket inside the crate and left the door of the little compartment open. She went over to gather the dog up in her arms and introduce him to his sleeping space. A few pats on his tail end induced him to enter.

'Wow, look at that,' I said. 'He likes it. It must feel reassuring to him, like that place under the desk in the visiting room. Remember what Katarina said about terriers burrowing into holes?'

The dog's tail and then the rest of him popped into view. He backed out of the crate a lot more quickly than he'd gone in. 'What happened?' I asked.

'He found the treat,' Phoebe said.

'You put a treat in there for him?' I said, signalling my disapproval of more food bribery.

'That's right, Steven,' Sally said. 'How do you suggest we get him in there?' I knew to back off when she used my name like that. It had been a long, eventful day, and we were all worn out by the excitement and the stress. I changed the subject.

'So what are we going to call him? He needs a name if he's not going to be Gandalf.'

Sally suggested Prosecco, in tribute to the sparkling wine we'd liked in Italy. 'Since he's so bubbly and full of life.'

'I didn't have any of it,' Phoebe objected. 'Anyway, I decided I don't want to name him after something you eat or drink.'

'What's the Italian word for "jump"?' I mused. 'He really can fly for a little dog.' He was roaming around again at the moment, and it looked to me as if he might be considering another steeplechase run over one of the gates.

'Or what about some famous Italians?' said Sally. 'There's Dante and Michelangelo and Leonardo da Vinci. And Pavarotti – Luciano Pavarotti.'

'Isn't he that fat guy?' asked Phoebe. 'We can't name a little dog after a big fat guy who sings opera.' Her face scrunched up.

'Palladio,' Sally tried. 'Remember? We visited all those big houses he built on the way into Venice. His nickname could be Pal.'

Phoebe seemed to consider that for a moment. It was in Venice, after all, that we'd told her she could have a dog. That had to mean something. I thought about suggesting Gondola or Marco (for Piazza San Marco) or Doge the Dog. But I could see she didn't need any help. Phoebe's face had got that still, inward look it gets when she's made up her mind. Her lower lip pulls in under her front teeth, and her eyes seem to turn a little greener and more focused. She got up, cornered the dog by the hutch, and stood facing us with him in her arms.

'Como,' she said.

'Perry?' I asked, without thinking that a twelve-year-old couldn't possibly remember that old crooner in the cardigan sweater.

Sally understood. 'No, like the lake.'

Phoebe nodded. We had spent a couple of days at Lake Como on our trip, including one when we took a boat ride out of Bellagio at dusk. The silky water, the mountains rising on either side of the lake, the idea of the Swiss Alps being so close, the other boats like great gift boxes of floating light – it had all enthralled her. One dream was merging with another. Sally and I smiled at each other and then at her.

'Perfect,' one of us said.

'Como it is,' said the other. It was time for bed.

Phoebe did the honours of settling him in for his first night at home. She set Como down by the crate and held on to his collar with one hand while she fluffed up the blanket with the other. He went in reluctantly but without putting up a fight. Phoebe got him turned around so he was facing forwards, then shut and latched the door. Each one of us took a turn looking in through the metal-grate window in the door.

'Lie down, Como,' Phoebe told him. 'Be a good boy and go to sleep. That's a good boy. Lie down.'

Sally was next. She went on in more or less the same vein. When I got down on my knees to peer in, the dog was still standing bolt upright, a look of pure astonishment on his harried face. His bony back grazed the top of the crate, and his slim front legs were firmly braced. He looked both miserable and determined to do something about it. I decided to act as if all was well.

'Good-night, Como,' I called out to him, as I backed away from the crate. 'We'll see you in the morning.' We turned out the lights and went upstairs.

Our house, which is located four blocks south of Golden Gate Park in the western part of San Francisco, is generally cool and comfortable at night, especially in summer, when the frequent heavy fogs act as a natural cooling system. We usually need a blanket or two in September. But not that year. The month had started out sunny and hot and stayed that way. With the windows wide open as we got ready for bed, the street noise of people and cars and passing buses distracted us from what was going on downstairs. Phoebe popped into our room three or four times to tell us exactly what to do with Como the next day, when she was at school. Sally, a teacher of English as a second language at San Francisco City College, had classes in the morning and got home by noon or one o'clock. I often worked on my *Chronicle* assignments at home.

'I'll take over at the weekend,' our proud new dog-owning daughter assured us. We said good night to her and turned out the lights.

Darkness magnifies everything. The moment Sally and I pulled the sheet up over us we heard it – a heavy rhythmic thumping. Since a dread of earthquakes is hardwired into every San Franciscan, I assumed the worst and waited for the bed to start shaking and the window glass over our heads to rattle. Sally caught on first.

'It's him,' she whispered. 'What's he doing?'

The thumping stopped. The house got very still. Then the noise started up again, this time accompanied by a songlike whining that went up and down a couple of octaves, guttural at the bottom and keening, eerily catlike, at the top. Thump. Bump. Thump-thump. I could hear what had to be the crate banging against the cabinet or the wall or both.

'What should we do?' Sally said, her own voice scaling up. She'd been the model of solidity and common sense all day, supporting Phoebe through her glorious Day of the Dog and reining in my own baulkiness and anxiety along the way. Almost immediately, as it often happens when she lies down at night, her own demons were set loose. There's something about being horizontal and poised on the lip of sleep and the unpredictable chaos of dreams that makes Sally helpless in the face of her own sprinting imagination. I heard it right away in her voice.

'Nothing,' I suggested, knowing that was an unlikely strategy. I was trying to sound as if I were in control when I was really just stalling for time to think of something better. The assault downstairs was escalating. The thuds and whimpers had taken on a purposeful if irregular pattern. It was like listening to an amateur carpenter who had taken on a job he couldn't handle, each hammer blow more futile and enraged than the last. The dog's half-strangled howls could have been the canine equivalent of him swearing under his breath.

'We can't just lie here,' Sally said. 'It's going to wake up Phoebe. She's got school tomorrow. She won't get any sleep, and she'll be completely exhausted, and she's just started all her new classes.' I hopped out of bed and told her I'd go and check. Whatever I found had to beat listening to more of that. 'Don't upset him,' she called after me.

Como must have heard me on the stairs. Things were quiet as I stood in the front hall in my underwear to wait him out. After a few minutes the thumping started up again, but there was also another sound now that we hadn't heard upstairs – a stubborn grinding that old gears or a stone mortar and pestle might make. It was persistent but not steady, and came in the lulls between thumps. I crept closer and listened some more. Once again the dog must have sensed my approach and stopped whatever he was doing.

When I finally peeked over the shortest of the three gates we'd rigged up, I could see that Como had thrust his crate out of the nook and had it angled six feet away from the wall and halfway under the dining room table. He must have done it by propelling himself against the sides of the crate, which didn't have much space inside to manoeuvre. It was alarming but also impressive in a way – all that willpower. I decided to take it up with him directly.

'Look at you,' I said, stepping over the gate and walking across the sticky plastic in my bare feet. 'That's a whole lot of noise you're making down here. What's the idea?' When I bent over to look into the crate, I didn't see him. I knew there was no way he could have got out – Houdini's dog couldn't have managed that – but it took a moment to register that the grey shadow pressed against the back wall was him.

'What's going on in there?' I asked him, sitting down to get acquainted. It was our first real time alone. Como didn't make a sound or a move of any kind. After a minute or two I put a hand on top of the crate and slid it back into the nook where we'd first placed it. I'd read the books; I was asserting my credentials as a firm but fair boss. 'Isn't that better?' I asked. That produced a quick rustle at the back of the crate. He'd turned around and had two dark, unblinking eyes trained on me.

'Okay,' I said after another five minutes of dominance-establishing silence. 'All set for the night.' I went back upstairs and got under the sheet. We'd dispensed with the blanket in the heat.

'What was it?' said Sally, who was wide awake. 'What did he do?'

I told her about the way he'd moved the crate out into the room and how I'd moved it back, then realized I hadn't determined anything about the grinding noise. We both lay there, staring at the ceiling and waiting to hear what would happen next. As soon as the thumping resumed, as we must have known it would, Sally propped herself up on her elbow and started in about school again. This time it was her own schedule she was thinking about. Her teaching load required her to be up and out the door by a little after seven a.m.

'I've *got* to get some sleep,' she said. 'What if it goes on like this all night? And tomorrow night? It's so hot,' she added, flinging off the sheet and flipping over on her stomach. 'Maybe that's the problem. Maybe he's just roasting inside that thing.'

'It's not that hot downstairs,' I said. 'It's always hotter up here.'

'We should have got the fans out,' said Sally. 'Phoebe's probably burning up in there.'

'Phoebe's sound asleep,' I said.

'How do you know that?'

'I don't know,' I admitted. 'But don't you think we'd know it if she wasn't?'

'I don't know if we'd know. She plays possum and pretends she's asleep.'

'Why would she be doing that tonight?'

'Why do you think?'

By this point it didn't matter what either of us said or what it was about. We were playing marital tennis, where the ball can change size, colour, weight and direction and even disappear when it's over the net.

'I'll go down and check on him again,' I volunteered, hoping to put an end to this particularly pointless rally.

'No,' Sally said. 'Don't do that. You'll just get him stirred up again.' She reached out and put a hand on my arm. 'Wait. What's that?'

'What's what?'

'That,' she said, and didn't have to explain. She was hearing the grinding now. We both were. It had become a steady, pronounced drone that continued for a minute or ninety seconds, paused, and started up again. The thumps and bumps had stopped. The grinding/drilling/sawing sound had taken over.

'What's he *doing*?' Sally whispered, her eyes widening like those of an actress in some straight-to-video horror film.

'We can't keep going down there,' I said. 'That's just giving in to him. He's got to get used to sleeping by himself.'

Once we'd agreed not to pay any further visits downstairs, there was nothing else to do but try to get some sleep. I heard the 6 Parnassus go by a few times, the overheard wires zinging softly as the trolley bus crossed our street at the corner and continued up Ninth Avenue. The sound of it gradually merged with Como's wailing high notes, and at some point I drifted off. I don't know when or even if Sally fell asleep, but a few minutes after four a.m. – the alarm clock was inches from my face when she shoved my shoulder – she had news.

'He's gone,' she said. 'Wake up.'

'What? Who's gone?' I said, groping simultaneously for consciousness and my glasses. A couple of hours of sleep had momentarily wiped the dog from my memory.

'Listen!'

Sure enough, small clawed feet were on the loose downstairs. We could hear the clicking move towards the front door and back down the hallway to our study and then into the kitchen. I got up and put on my bathrobe. I needed to be at least semi-dressed to feel fully prepared. Sally was up, too, cinching the sash of her own robe. I followed her downstairs. When Como heard us, he shifted into high gear, scrabbling around in the kitchen and skidding on one of the throw rugs. I stepped in something wet and still a little warm at the bottom of the stairs and decided not to stop and confirm the obvious.

'You go that way,' I told Sally, pointing down the hallway. 'We'll try to corner him.' That meant me stepping over one gate into the dining room and another into the kitchen. Those were moves that proved to be trickier in a bathrobe than they had been earlier in shorts or my underwear. Landing in another puddle when I crossed the first gate, somehow, kept me from tripping. The surprise of it held me up.

'I've got him,' Sally called out.

'Did he pee in there, too?' I called back at her. I could see now, from the kitchen light she'd turned on, the wreckage of the crate. It looked as if it had been pried open with a giant can opener. I pulled back the top to get a closer look. Como, astoundingly, had gnawed through the thick plastic hinges to make his escape. That, apparently, was what all the grinding had been. The blue blanket was now a heap of fuzzy tangled strips and scraps; a mechanical shredder couldn't have done a more thorough job on it. I stood there and tried to take it in, to grasp what I could plainly see but still seemed incomprehensible. We were living with an alien.

'Yes, he peed,' Sally said. 'What are you doing in there? I can't hold on to him and clean it up.'

I stepped over the second gate into the kitchen and told her what I'd found. Sally had Como in her arms. With his face wrenched away, as if to see behind her out the window, he could have been a dusty old fur muff she'd found in a costume shop. The sky behind them was showing the first pale pink light of day. We spent the next twenty minutes finding the places where Como had decorated the carpets, throw rugs and hardwood floors. There were quite a few of them. Neither of us said much as we mopped up and moved on. Eventually, with the dog still riding around in Sally's arms, we went upstairs.

'Any ideas?' my wife asked me.

I was fresh out. She put the dog down on the floor of our bedroom to see what would happen. After one brief tour of the room, he picked out a spot near the bed on Sally's side and flopped down with his head between his front paws. It had been a long, busy night for all three of us. Sally and I crawled back under the sheet and tried to pretend the sun wasn't coming up. When my eyes popped open at one point, I was staring into Sally's. She stared back and blinked a few times. Then her eyes narrowed and glittered for a moment in the grey morning light.

'It's going to be him or us,' she said calmly. 'I think we've got to kill him.'

'I totally agree. How are we going to do it?'

'Pills,' she said. 'Poison his food.'

'Gas,' I proposed. 'Or stones in a canvas bag and into a pond. That's how my uncle got rid of extra kittens on the farm.'

'Horrid,' Sally said.

'True,' I concurred. 'But effective.'

Marlene Dietrich and Groucho Marx couldn't have played the scene better – half high-style melodrama and half absurdist comedy. Sally reached over and pawed my cheek. I returned the favour by scratching her behind the ear. It felt familiar and companionable, the two of us awake and loony for lack of sleep, just as we had been when our infant daughter needed to be nursed or changed or cuddled at three a.m. That's how we got through those nights, turning from misery to joking blackly as we hauled ourselves out of bed. With luck, it would see us through whatever Como had in store.

'I love you, you big lox,' Sally said, mauling me one last time with her hand.

'What, now I smell like smoked salmon?'

'Ox,' Sally clarified. 'I said "ox" – "I love you, you big ox."'

'I love you, too,' I answered, flopping over on my side. 'And it's a good thing. We're going to need a lot of it.' Drowsy at last, we slept.

As for any worries about Phoebe's next day in school, that wasn't an issue. A few hours later, when our daughter's alarm clock started beeping down the hall, she woke up rested and thrilled to start her first full day with a dog in the house.

CHAPTER SEVEN

Escape Clause

I t wasn't obvious at first. Como's behaviour was so thoroughly, chaotically demanding that it didn't occur to us he might be expressing any kind of embedded gender prejudice. If the dog had transferred his distaste for all men to me – the only male in his new environment – we either chose to ignore it or defer that problem until we had time to address it. The challenge of simply trying to contain him made anything above ground-level thinking irrelevant.

With Sally and Phoebe up and off to school the next morning, I decided to fortify the dining room security. He might have scaled the barriers I'd fashioned in the doorways and mangled his first crate, but I wasn't about to give Como the run of the house as a reward. 'Stay here,' I shouted to a dog who was nowhere in sight. I didn't have a clue where Como might be at that moment, but I mustered my sternest tone as I went off to the garage to forage for some sturdy cardboard boxes. My plan was to raise the height of the three gates by building up the boxes below them. Even the most athletic terriers, I figured, must have their leaping limits.

When I came back upstairs with the first set of boxes, Como

still didn't make his presence known. But I had a feeling, as I collapsed one gate, wedged in a row of boxes and refixed the gate above, that I was being watched. I couldn't swear to it; after a night of minimal sleep my perceptions were probably a little hazy. But when I stood up and made a move back towards the front door, I did hear something scoot up the stairs. Okay, I thought, that's fine. If Como had been spying on me through the banisters, maybe he could see that I meant business. This was going to be his spot in the house, and I was securing it. I went down to the garage for more boxes.

What happened next was both a warning and a stroke of dumb luck. Instead of running for cover when he heard me tromp back up the front steps with a new armload of boxes, Como was crowding the front door. Out, he'd clearly figured, was this way, and he didn't want to miss his chance for it. If I'd been empty-handed and simply pulled open the door as I normally do, he would have easily made his escape. But because I was balancing the boxes, I had to ease the door open slowly, nudging it lightly with my hip. I felt him before I saw him, something wriggly and furry at my feet (I was wearing shorts and sandals). Startled, I dumped the boxes on the floor. That sent Como into a fresh panic. He vanished down the hall and into the study.

I sat down on the floor of the front hall to get a grip. I'd just come very close to letting a cunning fugitive loose, the day after we'd brought him home. If it hadn't been for the boxes, he would already be on the run, heading back to Redwood City (not that he had seemed all that enamoured of life in a rescue shelter) or back to the streets of Santa Clara County or, for all I knew, Mexico. Now, whenever we came or went from the house, we'd have to be on high alert. Como was small, agile and fiercely determined. We were less than twenty-four hours into it, and this dog thing already had me in siege mode. I gathered up the scattered boxes and got back to work.

I was still at it when Sally came up the front steps around lunchtime. She stared at me over one of the five-foot walls I was erecting in each of the dining room doorways. 'How are we supposed to get in and out?' she asked.

I started to say something cutting to her, mostly because I hadn't thought of that problem myself, but caught myself before I did. We were both very tired from the previous night's ordeal and needed to go easy on each other. 'We'll figure that out when we get there,' I said, as if I were creating a moated castle on the spot and counting on spontaneous inspiration to see me through.

'Anyway, where is he?' she asked, taking the hall route down to the kitchen. I could smell the customary rice-and-bean taco she picks up on the way home from school at Gordo's in our neighbourhood.

'Not sure,' I said. I started to come in to join her at the kitchen table. But as she'd pointed out, I was walled into the dining room. That's when I discovered an essential design flaw in my new barricades. Stepping back to survey the shortest of the three, I bumped into the one behind me. The boxes gave way, and the gate clattered open and slid down the doorjamb. What had looked pretty formidable was in fact as flimsy as a puppet theatre set.

'What was that?' Sally called. 'Was that him?'

'No. Never mind,' I said, stepping over my downed battlement. 'I'll work on this later. We ought to go back to the pet store and get him a better crate. The one we got must have been made for puppies.'

Sally finished her taco and Diet Coke, rounded up the dog, who had managed to slink back upstairs without my noticing, and took him for a walk before we left. When we showed up at the pet store with the gnawed crate as evidence of our consumer dissatisfaction, the assistant widened his eyes and waved his supervisor over.

'What kind of dog did you say this was?' the store manager asked us. He was short and very thin, with dyed black hair, and seemed guarded and wary of us. It occurred to me that spending a lot of time around pets and pet owners might produce such a temperament. He inspected the crate's destroyed hinges closely.

'A terrier,' Sally said. 'We think he might be a mix of cairn and Westy.' That was news to me. She must have heard that at the shelter at some point when I wasn't listening.

'We've never seen this,' the manager said. 'I don't know what to tell you.' He handed the crate back to us, as if it were something that might implicate him in a crime.

'It must be defective,' I said, reaching into my pocket for the receipt. 'As you said, this just doesn't happen.'

'I didn't say it *doesn't* happen,' he corrected me. 'I said we've never *seen* it happen.'

'Same thing,' I countered. His shoe-polish black hair, which I took as an act of cosmetic aggression, was getting to me.

Sally stepped in to prevent any further escalation. She asked if a sturdier crate were available.

'Nope,' the manager said. 'That's the strongest one we've got. Unless you want to go to a wire cage, which I don't recommend for a dog like this.'

'A dog like what?' I asked.

He paused a moment and took a gentler tack. 'I have to ask

you something: have you looked at your dog's teeth?'

'What do you mean?' Sally asked.

'Any dog who could do that in one night,' he said, glancing down at the crate that was now sitting on the floor between us, 'must either have steel teeth or real ones that are worn down to nubs. He'd destroy his whole mouth on a wire cage, because I'd be willing to bet he'd go after it just like he did that one.'

Sally and I thanked him for his advice and stepped away for a private conference. We stood there in the cat toy aisle reconceiving our containment plans and how we might manage a dog who had spent his first night with us breaking out of jail and depositing puddles all over the house. 'Maybe he could sleep in our room,' Sally suggested. 'Or in Phoebe's. We could close him in one room or the other and shut the door.'

'How does that solve anything?' I asked. 'How does that keep him from peeing on the rugs?'

'Maybe he won't do that if he's not penned up.'

'But you just said we should close him in. Isn't that penning him up?'

'Maybe he won't see it that way,' Sally answered. 'Without the crate. And that gummy plastic stuff on the floor.'

There were an awful lot of maybes in her scheme, not to mention an overall sense of capitulation. After one night she was prepared to give up on the policy, laid out in several of the books we'd read and also endorsed by the shelter, to crate-train the dog. The potential benefits were numerous. Dogs who learned to like their crates were said to be more secure, more easily housebroken, less likely to destroy the furniture and more easily acclimatized to travelling. And here we were losing this battle before we'd ever really joined it.

But it was also hard to argue with the pet store manager's

view of Como as very possibly crate-proof. He was not some impressionable, malleable puppy, after all, but a year-old dog with some apparently gritty street experience and a case-hardened set of teeth as well. And it wasn't as if I had any terrific ideas of my own to offer. Once again, standing there in the whir of customer babble, soft music, parakeet twitter and the occasional lovebird shriek, I felt the walls closing in. What in the world had we done to ourselves?

'Let's get out of here,' I said. 'It's almost time to pick up Phoebe.' I grabbed the remains of our useless and clearly non-refundable crate and led the way to the car.

On the drive back across town to our daughter's school, we decided to tell Phoebe that Como could sleep in her room that night, on a strictly trial basis. We both pretended it would be preferable to test the dog out in the quieter back room, away from the street noise in our bedroom. And we knew that Phoebe would be thrilled by the news. Only grudgingly had she accepted the idea of keeping Como in 'prison' downstairs in the first place. 'Dogs shouldn't live in boxes,' as she'd put it. Left unspoken by all of us was the assumption that Como was more likely to settle down for the night in a room that didn't have another male, namely me, in it.

Phoebe was disappointed we hadn't brought her new treasure along to show off in the school courtyard. 'One thing at a time,' I said. 'Anyway, I don't think he'd do so well here.' Kids were surging around us, shouting and chasing each other and jumping off the benches. None of this seemed to faze the various dogs who'd been brought to school for Friday-afternoon reunions with their carefree young masters. I recognized Spencer, Laurie's exuberant Airedale, tugging towards a crowd of third-graders on his leash. And there was Oscar, Tobias's now fully grown dachshund, who had induced such a chill between Phoebe and me the day he made his first showstopping appearance here. It all looked so lively, so normal, and so absolutely inconceivable for the dog we'd adopted.

Phoebe shrugged off the small letdown of Como's absence and hurried out to the car. She was eager to get home. She and Sally discussed logistics, a fraction of which I heard, as I drove. They decided to make a sleeping nest for Como out of worn blankets and towels. 'They like the smell of old things,' declared Phoebe. 'It's very comforting to them.' Her knowledge of dog behaviour seemed confident, comprehensive and strangely intimidating. How did she know all these things?

As we pulled into the driveway, I issued an emphatic warning about going into the house. 'Let Mommy or me go first,' I said. 'He could be waiting right there by the door and get out in a flash. And that would be it.' I wanted to be very clear about the high danger of escape. Phoebe pulled her backpack out of the boot and ran up the steps. Sally unlocked the door, and the two of them went into the house without breaking stride. They were already hooking Como onto his leash when I came inside.

'We're taking him for a walk,' Phoebe chirped. She and the dog waltzed by me in the hall.

'Right back,' said Sally, following close behind.

Alone in the house, I took the opportunity to demolish our failed barriers. I collapsed the gates and stored them back in the garage with the cardboard boxes, then ripped up the blue tape and shredded plastic, wadded it into a huge ball and stuffed it in the rubbish. When Sally, Phoebe and Como returned, all three of them panting from a romp around the baseball fields in Golden Gate Park, the dining room was a dining room again, with no evidence of our attempt to incarcerate a dog there.

Round One belonged to Como. If it had been a boxing match, the judges would have scored it unanimously in his favour.

There was no letup in the heat when we went to bed that night. Sleeping would have been hard even if we hadn't had a maniac dog to contend with. We thought about setting up the floor fans but figured Como's presence made that impossible.

'Can't you just see him running right into one?' I said.

'Or getting his tail caught,' said Sally, with a little shudder.

'Or jumping right over it.' He'd become a kind of Superdog in our minds, able to leap large obstacles in a single bound or escape any confinement and simultaneously reckless enough to destroy himself trying.

Sally and Phoebe had made a gigantic sleeping spot for Como in a corner of Phoebe's room. Roaming around both floors of the house, he appeared to have no intention of using it. The only notice he gave it was a peremptory sniff or two in the midst of his swerving, high-speed explorations. But when we finally got him shut inside Phoebe's room for the night, we didn't hear a sound. Sally and I whispered our good-nights to each other – anything louder risked disturbing the fragile peace and setting the dog off – and turned out the lights. I'd rolled over on my side and was nearly asleep when Sally cupped a hand on my shoulder.

'Are you awake?'

'I am now,' I said, turning over. 'What's wrong?'

'Her light's still on.'

I squinted down the hall and saw the glow under Phoebe's door. 'And?'

'Go and see what they're doing,' she said.

'Why would I do that?'

'Shh,' Sally warned me. 'You're going to get him going.'

'Which is exactly what I'd do if I went in there. Relax. Get some sleep.'

Telling my wife to relax and get some sleep when her mind gets going is a pointless exercise. But after fourteen years of marriage, useless behaviour of all kinds gets repeated every day. I knew from experience that this conversation, such as it was, wasn't over.

'Do you see how he looks at us?' Sally said. I knew it wasn't really a question and waited for her to continue. 'Those dark little beady eyes. It's like he's staring right through us. Really, I think he's kind of terrifying. And the way he ripped through those hinges – he's demonic.'

I didn't know how to respond. It seemed to me that Sally had been having a whole lot smoother time with Como than I had. And besides, I thought we'd already dismissed the idea, by kidding about it the night before, of rubbing the dog out. But apparently he was getting to Sally in ways that hadn't quite sunk in for me yet. I was afraid of him, too, but that had more to do with my fear that he'd get out of the house on my watch or continue peeing everywhere or both. Now that she mentioned it, the dog did have beady eyes and a kind of pitiless expression.

'Well,' I said, trying to sound as soothingly bland as I could, 'I guess we'll just have to take it one day and night at a time and see how it goes.'

'Twenty-eight,' she said.

'Twenty-eight?'

Then it sunk in. For the first time, one of us had invoked the thirty-day escape clause the shelter had given us. Starting tomorrow we'd have twenty-eight days left to decide whether we could live with a monster – the one that was lurking down the hall with our daughter – or return him for a full refund, no questions asked.

'Oh,' I said. 'Yes. That's true, isn't it?' I tried to sound blithe about it. But I could hear the clock ticking.

❧

Phoebe looked pleased, if a little bleary-eyed, when she came down to breakfast the next morning. She was vague about how or exactly where Como had slept in her room, and she failed to mention the damage he had done to the pile of blankets and towels. But she insisted he hadn't kept her awake. Sally raised a sceptical eye from her cereal and announced she was going to the gym. Phoebe happily volunteered to take the dog for his morning walk and feed him his breakfast when they got back. I couldn't help wondering if she'd somehow heard us last night and knew that she had four weeks to earn Como a permanent place in the house. She would do everything in her twelve-year-old power to make it happen.

Considering what a wretched start we'd had with him, that first weekend with Como on the premises went pretty smoothly, a few puddled 'accidents' notwithstanding. Phoebe kept her promise to walk and feed him on schedule, and she undertook to give him his first sorely needed bath, with Sally's help. It took both of them to pin him down in the bathtub, douse him with water, and lather him up. I heard all kinds of alarming yelps, both human and canine, and at one point poked my head into the bathroom to see how things were going.

'Get out!' Sally shouted. An open door had given Como a fresh burst of inspiration, and he very nearly wriggled free from their four grasping, soapy hands. I yanked the door shut and retreated to the kitchen. After drying him off as well as they could with two striped beach towels, Sally and Phoebe let the dog loose. Maybe greyhounds can run faster on a track, but no dog could have made quicker sprints and sharper turns than Como did on his first post-bath run. I watched from a chair by the kitchen table. Sally and Phoebe looked on from the bathroom, peeking out like newcomers overwhelmed by the speed and engine roar at their first NASCAR race.

Up and down the stairs Como went, his feet pounding down the hall above our heads. Each return to the living room was like a crash landing, as he flung himself onto the carpet, neck-first, and rubbed first one side of his face and then the other. Suddenly he'd stop, his hind end raised to full height and head pressed firmly to the ground. Then, with a loud snuffle, he'd charge upstairs again, in search of more and drier carpet. It went on for quite a while, and we were all pretty entertained by it.

'Let's give him a bath every day,' I suggested. 'Maybe it would tire him out and make him sleep better at night.'

'Maybe you should give him the next bath, Daddy.'

'Yeah, Daddy,' Sally mocked.

We were having a good time, the three of us – the four of us – and it seemed as if we might be able to make this thing work after all. Carpets streaked with a watery residue of dog shampoo and a bathtub etched with claw marks were a small price to pay. Como burst back into the living room and gave us a look that defied us to catch him. His tail switched back and forth with pendulum precision. Phoebe made a lunge for him, but she didn't stand a chance. He was back upstairs before she, grinning happily, had picked herself up off the rug.

On Monday, Sally had a meeting after school and wouldn't be home before three. I had to go downtown myself for part of the morning, and when I returned, carefully inching through the front door, I realized I'd have to take Como for his midday walk on my own. Up till then, either Sally or Phoebe had been around to get him on his leash.

'Como,' I called. 'Time for a walk. C'mon, boy. Let's go for a walk now. C'mon, Como.'

Silence.

I searched downstairs first, checking under the kitchen and dining room tables and both desks in the study. Upstairs, thinking he might have found sanctuary in the heap of towels and blankets, I checked Phoebe's room first. Bad guess. As soon as the way was clear, Como zipped out of the front bedroom and down the stairs. I took up the chase, trying to make it seem as casual as possible. 'CO-mo,' I singsonged. 'Wanna go for a walk?' My feet tromping after him worked against whatever airy lightness I manufactured in my voice.

Our house is laid out to guarantee a dog's advantage in a game like this. If I went after him through the dining room, Como took the hall route. When I tried the hall, he had an open pathway through the dining room to the entryway and back upstairs. On one downstairs circuit I did manage to close him off briefly in the kitchen. But the floor plan did me in again. Dodging one way and then the other around the butcher block cabinet in the centre of the room, Como easily eluded me. Trotting off through the living room, he gave me a farewell look over his shoulder as he headed for the stairs.

This time I followed in defeat. I made no attempt to find or track him down and went to flop down on the bed and make a conscious effort not to think about anything to do with dogs for a few minutes. I had a writing deadline to meet, and there was only so much time I could give to chasing Como around the house. Maybe he could 'hold it' (as we used to tell Phoebe when she was making the transition out of nappies) until Sally got home. I was testing out an opening line for a story in my mind when I heard the soft jingling of the dog's licence and ID tags. I lifted my head very slowly and saw that he was watching me from the bedroom doorway. Here was my opening. I had to play it just right.

For a long time I did nothing, willing myself to be as still as possible. It worked. I could hear Como creeping across the carpet to inspect my inert mass. He came closer and closer, like a wolf towards a downed deer, venturing over towards my side of the bed for the first time. Feigned sleep, I thought, might reassure him. I affected a small yawnlike sigh, rolled onto my side as gradually as possible, and nuzzled the pillow with another smaller sigh. I hadn't tried this sleep-faking stunt in years. My childhood technique came right back to me. Como kept coming. I cracked open one eye to check on his progress. That stopped him. I shut my eye. More creeping. Closer. Closer. Closer. When I was sure he was close enough, I sprang, grabbing for his collar with my right hand and corralling his back end with the left.

I had him, as I'd tell Sally and Phoebe later. I felt two fingers slip under his collar, as I cradled his tail end in my other hand. He was like a fish on a line, thrashing and arching his back and hurtling himself three different ways at once. He didn't snap at me or make a sound, which turned out to be his secret weapon. That, and the sheer coiled strength that I had first felt when I petted him in the visiting room at the shelter. There was something unnervingly undoglike about this dog – his silence, his refusal to use those formidable teeth of his, his marlin-like fight that had turned my arms into poles and taut lines strained to the limit. I may have said his name a time or two, to try to calm him down. But whether I did or didn't, I knew I was going to have to let him go. Getting the best of him this way felt like a violation, a trick I had played on another powerfully driven creature. Our eyes locked for a second. With one last wrenching spasm Como broke free and shot off somewhere. I didn't try to find him.

Instead, half an hour later, he found me. I was on a bathroom break from the piece I was writing on my computer in the study. Comfortably seated, in a spot where good ideas sometimes arrive, I had just about solved a transition problem in my story when Como nosed open the bathroom door and stepped inside. We watched each other calmly for a bit. I'd given up on trying to catch him, which he seemed to know. He also may have sensed that I didn't pose a threat to him at the moment, with my trousers around my ankles. All in all, it was a fair and equitable truce. I reached out my hand. He came over and sniffed it. I waited a while to make a suggestion:

'Would you like to go for a walk?'

This time he put up no resistance, allowing my fingers to snag his collar. The tricky part came when I tried to make good on my offer. I lifted the dog and stashed him under my right arm, then tried to finish up and re-dress myself as best I could with my left hand. A good deal of the toilet paper roll unspooled onto the floor in the process. Belts, I discovered, aren't easy to buckle with a dog squirming around in one arm. But I did learn, should I happen to find my right hand incapacitated for any reason in the future, that it's possible to accomplish a whole lot more left-handed than I might have expected. Only later did it occur to me that I could have hopped over to the door once I'd snagged Como, shut him in our small bathroom before trying to make myself presentable, and then grabbed him again.

When Sally got home from school, the first thing she wanted

to know was if the dog had had his midday walk.

'He did,' I said.

'And how did that go?' She looked like she was prepared to grill me for details.

'Fine,' I said. 'Look, I've got a deadline. Can we talk about it later?' I wasn't quite ready to lay out the particulars of my bathroom gyrations.

That night, with Como settled down in Phoebe's room again, Sally noticed something when we were changing for bed. 'What is that?' she said, inspecting a spot on my lower back. 'Is that new?' We found some more of it – a red rash that I hadn't noticed – on my rib cage and upper arms. 'It looks bad,' she said. 'You'd better get that checked.'

Sally is often more attentive to my health than I am. I'm accustomed to her detecting something that I haven't or asking after some pain or discomfort that I may have mentioned and then forgotten when the symptom passed. She's not an alarm-ist, but she does tend to take a certain sane and sober approach to all things medical. I couldn't help noticing, then, that Sally's voice had a certain lilt that night, almost a bounce to it. 'Look at that,' she said, with the sort of admiring tone an impressive scenic vista or some striking artwork in a museum might pro-duce. 'It's all over both sides.' If I hadn't known better, I might have thought she was actually pleased by the appearance of my rash.

'It doesn't itch,' I told her.

'Doesn't matter,' she replied briskly. 'We have to find out what's causing it.'

What I didn't see, as I usually don't, was the move or three ahead Sally had already made as I was standing there with my shirt off. (It's a good thing we don't play chess; she'd cream me every time.) Suppose my rash was some kind of allergic reaction to Como, she was thinking. And suppose there was nothing to be done for it. Even Phoebe would see that we couldn't possibly keep a dog that was making her poor father suffer. My wife was shuttling Como and me around on the board inside her head, with a possible checkmate looming.

CHAPTER EIGHT

The Parable of the
PowerBar

My flight left San Francisco early Wednesday morning. With a stopover in Dallas, I didn't arrive in Tampa until evening. By the time I'd had dinner with friends and shared a cab to our hotel in St Petersburg, it was close to eleven o'clock. Normally such a long day of travelling would have worn me out. But as soon as I set my bags down in my room I felt a fresh burst of energy. I was two thousand four hundred miles from home. I was alone, untormented and unloathed in a room that bore no sign of canine life. The only sound was the soft cat purr of the air conditioner. I stretched out on the bed and soaked in the solitude for a few minutes, then took the lift down to explore the lobby and pool and a patio overlooking the Gulf of Mexico. I took off my shoes and socks and wandered into the moonlit sand. I went back inside and had a rum punch at the bar.

There was a perfectly legitimate reason for my being here. I was attending a journalism convention, where my duties included appearing on one panel and co-leading another. But it was also true that the timing of the trip couldn't have been sweeter. Just as the reality of adopting a lunatic, man-fearing shelter dog had started to sink in, I had a four-day Get Out of Jail Free card. I knew it wasn't going to last. I knew I'd have to go back home and face the choice to keep the dog (and live in a persistent state of anxiety and dread) or return him (and shatter Phoebe's freshly realized dream). I knew I was just pretending none of that counted while I was here at the beachside pink palace of the Don CeSar Beach Resort. But pretend is exactly what I intended to do.

First, as I'd promised, I called home. Sally answered on the second ring.

'Where have you been?' she asked.

'In the air,' I said. 'Flying.' Smart-aleck whimsy, under the circumstances, was probably not the right approach to take with her.

'You said you'd call.' I explained that I had tried earlier, from the restaurant in Tampa, and got no answer. 'You didn't leave a message.' A few lines of mumbling followed before I found an opening to concede her point about being out of touch.

'You're right,' I agreed, trying now to be as agreeable as possible. 'Sorry. I should have called sooner. So how's it going?' 'It', in this case, had an unambiguous meaning. It meant Como.

'Well, he got hold of a bath towel and ripped it to shreds. Then he ran around like he was going to choke to death. He must have swallowed half of the thing.'

'One of the towels in Phoebe's room?' I asked, thinking of the sleeping nest.

'He already destroyed those,' Sally reminded me. 'This was from your bathroom. It must have been the one you used this morning.' I felt a little chill, and it wasn't from the air-conditioning. The idea of Como yanking my wet towel off the rail and mangling it as soon as I left the house had a faintly predatory charge. Had he smelled me on the towel and gone after it for that reason? Or was he an equal-opportunity shredder, with anything in his path as fair game? Neither option held much appeal.

'What about peeing?' I asked.

'No, no more of that. For now.'

'Well, that's good.'

'Yes,' Sally said, 'the good news is that he *didn't* pee in the house. We're making great progress here.'

It was hard to combat her sarcasm, so I didn't try. I told her a little bit about the hotel, downplaying the gulfside location and large, plush bed with its sea-foam pillow covers. I didn't mention the moonlight or the rum punch. I told her I missed her and Phoebe and would talk to them again soon. Before we got off, Sally asked about my rash.

'It didn't bother me today,' I said. 'I'll check on it later.'

There was a pause on the other end of the line. 'You really have to be careful with things like that. It might just be a heat rash or something you ate. But it also could be an allergic reaction, and those things can be very hard to treat. Even impossible.'

'Okay,' I said.

'I mean it, Steven. You always ignore stuff like this until it's too late.' I sensed she might be plotting another chess move about the rash. But with all the miles between us, her strategy didn't register with me right away. Picking up my wife's conversational nuances by phone is next to impossible.

Phoebe got on the line to say good-night to me, and then we hung up. As I lay there in a room that was almost too quiet –

I missed the San Francisco buses huffing and wheezing outside – it finally began to dawn on me what Sally had meant. My rash had only turned up in the last few days – the days since we'd brought Como into the house. If it somehow turned out that I was allergic to the dog, our problem would be solved. We'd have no choice but to return him, and it wouldn't be our decision or our fault. I could almost hear Sally explaining it to Phoebe:

'We really, really wanted to keep him, sweetheart, but we just couldn't. Daddy's rash got so bad, and there was nothing to do about it. Maybe we can find another dog that he's not allergic to. Or maybe not. Maybe a dog is just not the right pet for us. Maybe we should think about a cat instead.' It made my rashy skin crawl to imagine the scene and the stony look on Phoebe's face. She despised cats, as I did. I must have spent an hour tossing and turning in my wonderful hotel bed before I got to sleep.

The conference sessions and panels started first thing the next morning. It was late afternoon before I had a chance to go back to my room, change into my bathing suit and get in a swim before dinner. That's when I noticed that the rash had spread to my chest, shins and ankles. As soon as I saw that, it started to itch after all. The more I rubbed and scratched, the redder it got.

Sally is only half right about the way I treat my body's irregularities. I do ignore them for as long as I can – and then leap directly to panic mode. If this was an allergic reaction to Como (which seemed logical enough), then why had it spread and worsened in Florida? What if I actually had some more serious skin condition that had nothing to do with the dog? Maybe my whole body was going to break out soon, and I'd have to hide out in my hotel room for the rest of the conference or submit myself to the care of some strange St Petersburg dermatologist. Maybe I'd have to fly home early, wedged into a middle seat and tortured by a need to tear off my clothes and scratch myself silly. I pulled a T-shirt on over my inflamed chest and paced in and out of the bathroom.

I told myself to calm down. I tried to call Sally, who wasn't home. In a way this was all her fault. I never would have noticed this stupid rash if she hadn't pointed it out. I probably had things like this all the time and never knew it. Ignorance really could be bliss. This was nothing, I decided – a harmless heat rash. It had been hot in San Francisco for a week, and Florida was hot, too (even if I'd spent virtually all my time there inside, in air-conditioned meeting rooms). Air-conditioning itself was bad. It could dry out your skin and aggravate even the mildest rash. A swim in the late-afternoon sun was what I needed, followed by a shower and some of the hotel's complimentary lotion. Lolling around in my Don CeSar robe, I reached Sally and briefed her on my day and my rash.

'I hope you didn't use their moisturizing lotion, or whatever they call it,' she said. 'That stuff is terrible. Talk about allergies. Now we'll never know what's going on.'

'How did this whole thing get to be about my skin?' I asked.

'What whole thing?'

'The dog,' I said.

The line went silent for a moment. I didn't know if that meant she was acknowledging my point or reloading for a fresh skirmish. 'Look,' she said, 'I just want it to clear up. I know how crazy you can get.'

I was relieved more by the soft retreat in her voice than by what she said. 'Okay, honey,' I said. 'We'll figure it out. Somehow.' We both knew we weren't just talking about the rash. We were talking, as hopefully as we could, about Como.

The conference went well, and all too quickly. Before I knew it I was sharing a shuttle van back to the airport with two writers from Boise and an editor from Odessa, Texas. I'd told the Idaho contingent a little about Como over the past few days, and they were asking me for any updates. I told them about the attack on my bath towel and a few other stunts the dog had pulled while I was away. They seemed to find it all pretty enjoyable. Finally the Texan spoke up.

'How big did you say that dog of yours is?' he asked.

'About twelve pounds.'

'And what breed?'

'A terrier mix. Really a mutt,' I said.

He considered the information for a while as the van rattled over a bridge. I thought he was going to give me some Lone Star speech about roping and branding and getting tough with your animals. Instead he told us about an incorrigible Lhasa apso he and his wife had had and how they hired a trainer to housebreak him and keep him from jumping up on guests. 'Little dogs,' he said, 'can have very big personalities. I suggest you call in an expert and save yourself a lot of trouble. You'll spend some money, but you'll be glad you did.'

That was something to think about on the long flight home. Phoebe might not welcome the idea of outside help, but I thought Sally might be ready and willing to try anything. My wife and daughter were both there to meet me, along with Como, when I wheeled my bag out to the curb at the San Francisco airport.

They'd had the best day yet with the dog – no accidents, no blanket or towel chewing, and a limited amount of roaming around during the night.

'Look at him, Daddy. He's getting used to us.'

Phoebe, who was dressed in her soccer gear, had Como on her lap in the backseat. He did look borderline normal, without that penetrating stare that Sally and I both found so unsettling.

'That's great, Skidge,' I said. 'Let's keep it going.'

She propped the dog up to look out the window, which seemed to interest him not in the least. He was like that on walks, too – mostly indifferent to if not downright evasive of people and other dogs. I made a note to myself to ask Sally if she believed Como might have 'socialization issues'. That was a phrase I'd picked up from the Texas editor in the van.

Another uneventful night with the dog followed. That made four nights in a row, three of which I'd missed, without any overt acts of warfare. As peculiar as he was, I thought, Como might indeed be settling in with us.

The next morning I called the advice nurse at Kaiser, our health insurance company, and described my rash to her. She asked a few questions before starting me through the phone tree to my own doctor. Surprisingly, he picked up. 'Don't get used to it,' Dr Palacios said. 'It's only because two patients in a row didn't show. I'm catching up on paperwork.' I told him about my symptoms and how they'd developed.

'It could be an allergic reaction,' he said. 'I'd really have to take a look. How long have you had the dog?'

'Ten days. It seems like ten years.'

'What do you mean?'

I filled him in on the night of the gnawed crate, the multiple accidents and the shredded towels and blankets. I stopped short of telling him that Sally and I thought the dog might be a potent evil spirit. Dr Palacios might have been on the verge already of thinking this whole rash thing was psychosomatic. If so, he tactfully skirted that possibility.

'I'll call in a prescription for hydrocortisone cream,' he said. 'That covers a lot of sins. You can pick it up at the pharmacy in an hour or so. Let me know if it doesn't clear up in another ten years. That's ten days in dog time.'

I laughed gamely and hung up. Como made himself scarce while I caught up on e-mail, showered and got ready to go and pick up the prescription. I had some other things to do while I was out and must have spent close to an hour on my errands. I stopped at Kinko's, picked up the dry cleaning, spent a while finding a parking space near the post office, and swung by Andronico's to get something for dinner and a few other items on the list. There may be a thousand and one reasons for what happened next, most of them having to do with Como and me and the volatile chemistry between us. But in the end I blame the dry cleaning. If it hadn't been for those plastic-wrapped shirts and two pairs of trousers tugging and fluttering like a pin-striped flag in my hand as I climbed the front steps, the folly of that day might have been prevented. Or then again, given Como's stunning willpower and determination, maybe not.

I pulled into the driveway and unpacked the contents of the boot, tucking the prescription and photocopies into the grocery bag and getting the house keys ready in my other hand. Then, on a lazy impulse to manage it all in one trip, I added the clothes. What would have been a quick run up the steps became an ungainly wobble. A light breeze pulled at the plastic sheeting. The hangers turned uncomfortably on my fingers. I tried to keep the clean trousers from dragging on the steps and nearly dropped the keys. 'Damn,' I muttered, now focused on the business of getting the front door open and my things inside while completely forgetting what might well be waiting on the other side – a dog who had already demonstrated his cunning and world-class escape-artist skills.

Juggling keys and packages, I turned the knob and got the door open a fraction. As soon as I did, Como bolted. The tiniest wedge of daylight was all he needed to snake around the door and make his break. He must have been lurking just inside, crouched and poised to go, when he heard me pull into the driveway. And then – who knows? Did the headless, cellophane-sheathed figure of shirts and trousers push him over the edge? One man was alarming enough. A grotesque second one, if that's how he saw the clothes in my hand, was just too much for him to bear.

It's often said that physical calamities – collisions, falls, a prized and fully loaded family platter slipping out of your hands in front of a full house at Thanksgiving – happen in super-slow motion. And sometimes that's true. Every millisecond is stretched to a seeming infinitude as, helplessly, you witness the consequences of your blunder play out in deliberate, inevitable, excruciating sequence. And sometimes it works in just the opposite way, with the rickety acceleration of an old-fashioned newsreel or *Keystone Cops* episode. Nightmare-like, you're flung into the middle of a frantic chase scene before you even realize you're in the film. That's what happened when Como took off.

I cursed myself and him in a single breath, dropped the grocery bag, let the dry cleaning slump and double over on the floor, and whirled around to see how far Como had gone. For the briefest instant, we froze. A look of astonishment flashed between us: neither of us could quite believe he was out there on the pavement in front of the house, off leash and accomplished so easily. We'd conspired to bring it about, his craftiness and my carelessness perfectly joined. And then he was gone, loping west on Lawton Street at a surprisingly brisk clip.

I thundered down the steps in pursuit, conscious at every step of trying to be as quiet and graceful as possible and not alarm Como any more than he already was. I felt like a moose in high heels. The fugitive crossed Tenth Avenue and cantered ahead. I barrelled along behind, losing ground with every stride. The squares of bare pavement stretched out between us. Como seemed to know just where he was going, beelining towards Eleventh Avenue, where he made a sharp left across Lawton and headed up a steep hill. That's when I lost sight of him and felt a sickening lurch of panic.

He was lost. I was sure of it. There was no way I could outrun a fleeing terrier, especially one I couldn't even see. I'd ruined everything, destroyed my daughter's happiness, and let my wife and myself and the greater community of responsible dog adopters down. This was my unconscious flaming into action. I'd wanted to get rid of the dog, and now I'd done it. Phoebe would see right through me to my black little soul. Sally would say nothing, as an unindicted co-conspirator, our mutual silence as telling as a courtroom confession. I sprinted across Lawton and started hoofing it up the hill.

The good news was, I could see Como when I came around the corner. The bad news was, he was almost a block away, his thick tail now the size of a Q-tip. The odds were heavily, impossibly against me. But then Como did something that gave me a glint of hope: he looked back over his shoulder to see where I was. And it wasn't just a glance. He kept looking, trotting forwards and looking backwards. At one point he almost ran into a street sign in front of him.

I knew it was risky, but convinced that there was no chance whatsoever of catching him, I decided to try my bright idea out anyway: I stopped. Sure enough, after a few more steps, Como stopped, too. He turned around to face me, up there on his hill, to see what I'd do next. For as long as I could stand it, I did nothing. I held my ground and tried to look as casual and unthreatening as I could, arms dangling loosely at my sides and a contrived grin pasted on my face. What had started out as a flat-out footrace that I was doomed to lose had taken on the very slightly more promising aspect of a game, a free-form blend of tag and Capture the Flag and Simon Says, with Como cast in the rule-making role of Simon. I had no idea how he wanted to play this out – and he probably didn't either. But at least in a game there's a possibility, however slight, of finding a way to win.

I waited some more, taking advantage of the pause to catch my breath, before making my next move. It was another risky one. Instead of advancing any further on the dog, I turned and slowly walked away, hoping to provoke his curiosity and convert our standoff into a round of Follow the Leader. I slipped around the corner and held out for a minute or so before checking on him. When I did, he'd come halfway down the hill. My hope hitched up a notch.

'Como,' I called out to him in my chirpiest voice. 'You win. I give in. Let's go back to the house now. Bet I can find a treat for you there.'

Even in the midst of the crisis, that part galled me a little. He shouldn't be rewarded for running off. But character training was the least of my worries at the moment. Somehow I had to get my hands on him and haul him in. I considered going back to the house for some actual, smellable treats as a lure, but was afraid to let him out of my sight. At this point my best, my only, weapon was to convince him I was totally, unambiguously harmless. And so I did, right there on the spot, sinking to my knees in the middle of Eleventh Avenue.

The desperate dance that followed – my begging and full-body collapses, Como's maddeningly close approach, our parallel scampers up the hill, the gardener's truck banging across Ortega Street and scaring Como off for good – wasn't going to end well. It might have gone on a little longer, until my legs and lungs gave out entirely and I collapsed like the dry cleaning back at the house. But it couldn't possibly end well. It couldn't, that is, without some heaven-sent act of intervention.

'Get in,' someone said. A car door stood open beside me. I did as I was told. 'I saw the whole thing,' the driver told me. 'We'll drive up ahead and cut him off.'

Where had he been? Why hadn't I seen him? It didn't matter. He was my gruff Good Samaritan, who had arrived out of nowhere, as abruptly and unexpectedly as the gardener's truck had. We sped through the intersection and on towards Pacheco. I didn't know where Como was at this point, but the Samaritan did. 'There!' he huffed, pointing with one hand and yanking the steering wheel around with the other. Now it really was a *Keystone Cops* episode, or some James Bond parody, complete with a stuntman driver. He screeched to a halt in a driveway and leaped out of the car. Como was in the next driveway down, a sunken rectangle that had him penned in. The driver handed me something when I got out. 'Use this,' he said.

It was a partly eaten chocolate PowerBar, with the wrapper peeled down. The Samaritan must have been chomping on it when he picked me up. He was guarding one side of the driveway now and signalling for me to pull off pieces of the PowerBar as bait. I wasn't thinking or planning anymore. I was just doing what came to me. I tore off a sticky black hunk of PowerBar and waved it at Como. I didn't know if he was panicked or exhausted or starving. Or maybe, like me, he was just tapped out on strategy. Whatever the reason, Como came towards me like some well-trained circus animal responding to a command. I hadn't spoken a word to him. When the dog was almost close enough for me to grab, the Samaritan hopped down in the driveway behind him and stamped his feet. At that, Como rushed straight into my arms. I shoved the hunk of PowerBar in his mouth.

For a moment I didn't quite believe it. I had the dog clamped to my chest and could feel his sweaty trembling torso and softly padded front paws, but the whole filmlike unreality of the morning was still spinning along. 'Oh, my God, thank you, thank you, thank you so much,' I started blabbering to my rescuer. 'I never would have got him. This dog's insane. Thank you, thank you.'

He shrugged, playing his hero's role as the strong silent type, and motioned for me to get back in the car. 'Where do you live?' he asked, snapping his seat belt in place. I told him, he turned the car around, and we started back down Como's escape route. I must have babbled some more and remember offering him a cash reward or a box of PowerBars. He waved me off and flipped on his wipers. At some point, without my noticing it, a speckling rain had started to fall.

The Samaritan pulled up in front of the house. I thanked

him some more and was out of the car and halfway up the steps before I realized I'd never asked his name. He was Asian. He wore tan shorts and a dark T-shirt and never said more than a few tightly clipped words. He drove like a magician. He'd saved Como for us. He was gone, and I've never seen him since.

An open front door awaited us. My keys were still hanging from the lock where I'd left them and run when Como got out. My head was too full – and somehow too empty as well – to respond to any more surprises or twists of luck, good, bad, or indifferent. I stepped around the clothes and grocery bag in the front hall, carried Como straight upstairs to our bedroom, dropped him on the floor and shut the door firmly behind me. I came back downstairs long enough to put the milk in the refrigerator. Keys in hand, I left the house in a pinprick summer rain shower. I didn't know where I was going or why. I just knew I had to escape.

CHAPTER NINE

Starting to Surrender

By pure force of habit, I drove to our neighbourhood Chevron station on Irving Street. My mornings often begin here, with the first of several caffeine-infusing Diet Pepsis I get during the day from the self-service fountain. The staff are always cheerful, offering smiles, small talk and an occasional free refill on my repeat visits. This time no one said a word when I stormed in, sent the soda foaming over the top of the cup, and dug into my pocket for a dollar and change.

'No problem, man,' the assistant behind the cash register said, holding his palms up when I couldn't come up with the right coins. 'A dollar's good.' He looked over my shoulder. There was nobody behind me in line. I took the hint that I was behaving like a madman and went outside, where I stood pulling on my straw and watching the traffic stream by on Nineteenth Avenue. Since fuelling myself up seemed to be a good idea, I pulled the car over to the pump and did the same, topping off a tank that was already three-quarters full. I thought about how far I could go, following Nineteenth across the park to the Golden Gate Bridge, up through Marin County, and on to Sacramento, Red Bluff, Redding and the Oregon border. The brief rain had stopped. It was a great day for driving. I could be out of the state and untraceable by late afternoon.

Even thinking about it brought on a little pinch of guilt. There'd been enough running away already that morning. I got back in the car and drove downtown to Sally's school. We had to talk, the two of us, and right away. We had to figure out how we were going to live with a dog who couldn't stand to be in the same house with me.

Sally's colleagues looked even more alarmed than the people at the filling station. I almost never show up at her school unless we're having lunch or meeting for a movie, both of which are relatively rare occurrences. Arriving when Sally's in the middle of a class, as I did that day, was unprecedented. I ran into one of her colleagues, Shama, in the hall near the office.

'What's wrong, Steven? What happened?' she asked me.

I hadn't thought I looked all that stressed, but I suppose the strain of my morning footrace showed. I tried to downplay it with Shama. 'Nothing. Really nothing,' I said. 'Is Sally around?'

That seemed to dial up Shama's radar. 'She's teaching. Do I need to get her? Is it something about Phoebe?'

'No,' I said, 'nothing like that. I'll just wait.' I feigned interest in a bulletin board display about citizenship. Shama, looking dubious, turned and went upstairs. When the class hour ended, Sally beat most of the students down to the main floor. Shama must have alerted her that I was there.

'I'll tell you outside,' I said, not wanting to share my story in a crowd, even one with limited English skills. Sally was silent through my narration of the getaway, chase and recapture. I told her about the long run up Eleventh Avenue and the Samaritan and his PowerBar.

'You were so lucky,' she said, reaching out to squeeze my hand. 'He could have been run over.'

I nodded. 'Or run away and then been run over,' I said. 'Not that we ever would have known it. Or maybe they would have traced him through the computer chip.' I pictured Needle Nose getting a call at the shelter and learning that Como – still Gandalf to her – had been found somewhere in who-knows-what condition. I could see her face, her crinkled brow and rueful frown, and tried to put all that out of my mind.

'So where is he now?' Sally wanted to know. When I told her I'd stashed Como in our bedroom, she frowned. 'Why'd you put him there?'

'Where else was I supposed to put him? We've got to keep him away from the front door.'

She didn't have an answer for that, but I could see she still thought I hadn't handled it well. But Sally must have known I was in no mood for being second-guessed and didn't press it. 'Let me go get my stuff,' she said. 'I'll follow you home.'

I pulled into the driveway as she parked in the space in front of the house. I went in first and found papers scattered in the front hall. Seeing the mess pushed my panic button. 'He's out again,' I shouted, forgetting that I'd shut Como in the bedroom, and almost slammed the door in Sally's face as she came in behind me.

'For God's sake,' she said, stooping to pick up the post, which had been delivered while I was out. 'You're really losing it.'

'You didn't just have to chase him all over town,' I countered. 'That wasn't exactly a party. Anything for me?' We stood there for a while shuffling through bills, mail-order catalogues and flyers from house-painting companies and Chinese restaurants. Neither one of us was particularly anxious to go upstairs and encounter Como. When we did, Sally eased open the bedroom door and called his name. The dog was lying on his belly by her nightstand. His tail thumped a few times when he heard her voice. She started towards him and stopped.

'Oh,' she said softly, as if not to upset him. 'Look at this.'

A wide swatch of carpet inside the door looked as if it had been burned down to the underlay and, in spots, the bare floor. Wood slivers and white paint chips littered the scene. Sally swung back the door to confirm the evidence. Como had tried as hard as he could to tunnel out of the room, apparently tearing at the carpet and door with his claws and maybe his teeth. It was an intimidating feat of destruction. Given a little more time, he might have accomplished his goal. Any enclosure, no matter how big, was a cage to him. We could have lived in the grandest mansion in Pacific Heights or, for that matter, a bank vault in the Financial District, and Como would have been attacking the stoutest closed door or steel-plated wall to get out. Sally and I contemplated the mess in respectful silence.

'Poor thing,' she finally said, and crouched down to summon the suffering house-wrecker. Como slunk towards her a few steps and waited for her to come closer. I was in a muddle as I witnessed their meeting in the middle of the room. Sally was confiding things to Como at such a hush I couldn't imagine even he heard her. But I also knew that my judgement and probably my senses were not to be trusted at the moment.

Everything that had happened that morning, out on the streets and now in our bedroom, had wrung me out. Como and I were in full-scale combat, and he was winning handily. It ought to have made it worse that Sally was consorting with the enemy, gently stroking my rival's neck and cooing at him.

But as I stood there and watched Como roll onto his back to receive a stomach rub, his four white paws dangling in midair like still flags of surrender, I also saw what Sally saw and what was obvious to me, too, now that I stopped to think about it: Como was terrified. He was living in a totally new place with new people and smells and rugs and doors, some of which closed in around him and set off whatever fears of entrapment and full-bore survival mechanisms had been planted in him long before we ever met him.

I thought about him living on the streets of Santa Clara County and how that might have happened. Had someone owned his mother and not been able to handle a litter of puppies? Had he, and any brothers and sisters, been given away and then sorely neglected? Was he abandoned when he was still a pup and left to fend for himself? Or had he been born out in the wilds of Sunnyvale or Cupertino and learned the rough-hewn ropes in storm drains, suburban culs-de-sac and litter-strewn public picnic grounds?

He'd been in two different shelters that we knew of (there may have been others), and adopted at least once and returned by an older woman who couldn't manage his volcanic reactions to unfamiliar situations. It was impossible to reconstruct or even imagine what might have happened to him in that place or any others where he might have lived. Above all, it was beyond our knowing what some man or men had done to him along the way, what coldness or meanness or outright physical abuse he had endured. That was the crux of it, the deeply tangled knot that lay buried somewhere inside him. How would we – how would I – ever unravel it?

We'd probably got off to exactly the wrong start by bringing him home and locking him in a cramped plastic crate with a few slit windows and barely enough room to turn around. Then I'd bailed out on him for my four days in Florida, only to come back and let him loose so I could hunt him down like a fox and trap him inside a walled driveway with yet another strange man to help me do the dirty work. As a reward, I'd tossed him right back in prison, albeit a more spacious one, and fled the premises as fast as I could. No wonder he'd torn up the place. I almost couldn't blame him.

Sally was rocking Como back and forth on the floor, tickling and kneading him like a tube of cookie dough. 'Look at you, you big nutcase,' she teased him. 'What are we going to do with you?' She flipped the dog over on his tummy and ruffled the band of lightly caramel-coloured fur that ran down his spine. Suddenly she stopped. 'Hey. Come and look at this.'

Parting the fur on his right side, Sally showed me a hairless bare patch of grey skin, about the size of a coin. Normally hidden by the coat that grew over it, the spot looked tender and raw when exposed.

'What do you think it is?' I asked.

Sally was busy raking and pulling Como's fur against the grain all over him, checking to see if there were other spots like this one. 'Maybe an infection,' she murmured. 'Something that didn't get treated right. Could be a birthmark.' She paused. 'Or a burn.' Her fingers went back to the bare place. She looked up at me. Her voice got stronger. 'Couldn't a cigarette lighter do this?' she said. 'It's about the right size. That would explain it.'

Explain not only the bare place, she meant, but why Como might be the dog he was, scarred by some idle cruelty, some man's compulsion to press a glowing red coil into the flesh of an animal. Neither of us spoke for a while.

'Hold him there a minute, would you?' I said, and got down

on my knees beside her. Como tensed a little when I reached out to touch him, but Sally held him firmly. I smoothed down the tangle on top of his head and lightly waggled my fingers under his chin, then up behind both ears. He kept his eyes on me at first, then stretched out his neck to expose more scratching surface. I figured he might be confused by this two-stage massage; perhaps he thought Sally had three hands, one that was holding him and the other two working on his neck. It didn't matter. He was getting to know my touch, whether he knew it or not. And I was getting to know what it felt like to touch him without the ulterior motive of capturing him and bending him to my will.

Sally began to feel achy and had to stand up. She gathered the dog up with her. We stepped over the carnage on the carpet and went downstairs.

'I still need some lunch,' Sally told me, and went off to Gordo's for her taco. Como and I waited for her in separate rooms. While I sorted and opened post at the kitchen table, he kept vigil in the living room. When Sally came up the front steps, I sprinted out to make sure Como wasn't poised for another escape. There was no need to worry. She put her key in the lock and walked in. Como trotted over to greet her. It looked like something they'd been doing for years, a routine so natural that neither of them paused or wondered at it. Given what I'd been through that morning, it was hard not to feel a little envious of how easily the two of them got along.

I sat with Sally while she ate and waited until she was through to present my proposal. 'Did I tell you about this guy I met in Florida?' I began. 'He and his wife had some wacky little dog that kept giving them fits. They hired a professional trainer, and he said it really made a difference.' I threw in the

Texan dog's breed to make it sound more official: 'It was a Lhasa apso.'

'What's that?' Sally asked.

'I don't know. Those little things with long hair in their eyes.' I wondered if she was stalling me, to come up with some reason why we shouldn't call in a trainer.

Sally wadded up her plastic taco bag and tossed it in the bin. 'We could, I guess,' she said from the sink. 'I mean, if you think it would help.'

'I know his problem is mostly with me,' I said, feeling generous about making that concession, 'but we all have to live with him.'

'You're right,' she said. 'How much do they cost?'

'Probably not cheap,' I admitted. 'I'll make some calls tomorrow. See if anybody knows a good one.' I tried to project a frank, take-charge attitude, which was a bit of a performance. I was certainly hoping it might help, but I had no particular faith that a trainer could do us much good. Como's wounds, literally and figuratively, ran deep.

Sometime that afternoon, before Phoebe got home from soccer practice, Sally vacuumed up the door shreddings and tried to make the entrance to our bedroom look not quite so brutal. I brought up the tape we'd used in our brief experiment to hold down the plastic in the dining room. We sealed over the gashes in the carpet with it and stood back to admire our new interior decoration.

'Looks great, don't you think?' offered Sally.

'Maybe the design writer at the paper could come out and do a piece on it,' I said. 'Low-tech chic. We could run a whole loop of tape around the border of the room.'

'Don't forget it's Como's favorite colour,' Sally reminded me.

'Blue's a real turn-on for him. Blue tape, his blue blanket.'

'Right. I should offer him that light blue sweater of mine as a peace offering. He rips it up, and we're both happy.'

'Hey, that was a Christmas present from Phoebe and me. We looked all over for it.'

'All over what?' I asked. 'Blue-mingdale's?'

I don't usually resort to puns, but for some reason that one cracked us up. We must have needed some laughs pretty badly, and had a few more about Como's home remodelling work that evening. That was until we started padding around at bedtime and sobered up. There was something about the clammy surface of the tape on the bottoms of our bare feet that discouraged us both. Even more dismaying was something neither of us had noticed earlier on. I saw it on my way down to the kitchen for a glass of ice water – a corner of the skirting board in the hall that Como had gnawed off. It was one thing for him to mangle the carpet and door when he was locked inside a room. But why had he gone after the woodwork out in the hall, where he wasn't closed in? I wondered when that had happened and thought about the deeper and possibly insoluble problems it suggested. Was he some kind of canine termite, bent on systematically consuming the house? Or was he just so unmanageably compulsive that he'd take his urges out on anything? Did we have a dog who was just too broken ever to be fixed?

I thought about how bizarre and unpredictable his behaviour could be. Out on our walks, Como was a moving study in contradictions. Most men we encountered, whether they were with dogs or without, put him on guard. He'd shift to the other edge of the pavement, wrapping his leash around my back or nearly tripping me if he cut in front. Sometimes he'd get so spooked by something – the particular size and gait of a man coming our way, the scent of another dog, the sound of a skate-board clopping over a curb – that the leash would spring tight as he made a lunge in the opposite direction. But then every once in a while he'd take a shine to some stranger and approach with wagging tail and pert, inquisitive ears.

'What a cool dog,' a teenage boy said to me one night, when Como trotted over to strike up an acquaintance. The kid had just hopped off a skateboard under a streetlight when we passed by. 'Where'd you get him?'

'Down in Redwood City,' I said. 'He's a shelter dog and usu-ally doesn't like males.' I could have added that he was even less well disposed to those on skateboards, which, like buses and motorcycles, could easily sct him off. For several minutes Como submitted happily to the boy's fur ruffling and friendly grunts. When the teenager got back on his board and swerved away, I could have sworn the dog watched him go with a wist-ful, longing gaze.

Como could be just as odd in our own house. He rarely barked when strangers or guests knocked at the door. Instead he had a hierarchy of seemingly well-developed reactions. He ignored the postman, fled at the sound of the FedEx delivery-man's cheery voice, and rushed over to greet Phoebe's friend Jeanne whenever she arrived. When our friends Kenneth and Donna came over to go to a concert with us one night, Como retreated under the dining room table and wouldn't stop trem-bling. These were people who had met Como several times before on apparently friendly terms. It was impossible to know what to expect. There was something flickering inside this dog all the time, a combustible heat and friction that could glow warmly, flare up unpredictably, or send him running for cover.

The day of the great escape had been a long, bruising one,

which may not have fully registered until Sally and I finally stretched out that night between the cool sheets. Como was in Phoebe's room down the hall with the lights out. Sally and I read for quite a while, relieved to have our minds in our books instead of on the dog.

'Just one more page,' I said, when Sally switched off her bedside lamp. She waited until I finished my chapter and the room was dark. 'Good night,' she said, then leaned over to whisper something directly into my ear, so I was sure to get it: 'Nineteen.'

That's all she needed to say. We had less than three weeks left to decide whether Como was going or staying.

Jake the dog trainer came highly recommended from friends who said he could work wonders in a few visits. Their own dog, a schnauzer, had humped anyone who walked in the door before Jake took charge. 'I don't even know what he did, exactly,' our friend Tony said, 'but it sure worked. There was something about making Gerhard sit very still near the door and then tapping him lightly on the nose a few times when one of us knocked. Then we had to have someone he didn't know knock and come inside. It was about two hundred and fifty bucks for three visits, but Gerhard was cured. We're hump free.'

We hired Jake for a Saturday-afternoon session. I'd told him on the phone about Como's history with men, which hadn't concerned him in the least. 'Look,' he'd said, 'dogs get these bad raps for being this way or doing that. But they don't think in terms of categories or patterns. They're just responding to their environment in the most adaptive way they can. The whole idea is to break out of the cycle. Sometimes it means tweaking the environment a little. Sometimes it means channelling the behaviours in a more constructive way. It's about your dog and you finding a space where you can coexist, with dignity for both of you. We'll figure it out.'

It all sounded sane and sensible, if a little New Agey. A few days later Jake arrived, wearing jeans and a black leather vest over a faded Grateful Dead T-shirt, with his long brown hair pulled back in a snug ponytail. Squat and moon-faced, he moved with a liquid, noiseless tread and spoke in the same level, soothing tones he'd used on the phone. I was struck by the fact that he didn't turn his attention immediately to Como, who circled him before moving in for a few exploratory sniffs. He was letting the dog get used to him, not exerting any pressure or expectations, giving him his space, as he put it. Phoebe and Sally came downstairs and greeted him. We all walked into the kitchen together. Jake took a seat at the table, declined an offer of tea, and pulled a well-worn leather satchel from his back onto his lap.

'So,' he said, 'what's the problem?' It was unclear, from the way he aimed the question, whether he was speaking to Como or us. No one answered, which seemed not to bother him. He reached into his satchel and rustled around inside it. Como came over and sat in front of him.

'Cool,' Phoebe said. 'How'd you make him do that?'

'I don't *make* a dog do what he doesn't want to,' Jake answered, keeping his eyes fixed on Como. 'We're just trying to establish a connection here.' Their collegial staring match went on for a little while. Then Jake reached down, and Como gobbled something out of his hand.

'What was that?' asked Sally.

'Nothing. Just a little smoked turkey. All right, Como,' he

continued, 'let's see if you feel like sitting. Can you sit? Sit, please.' Como sat and got another morsel of turkey.

'Now, that's my problem,' I said. 'I just haven't been feeding him enough luncheon meat.'

Jake let my attempt at humour wither. 'Up, please. Up. Can you please up?' Como baulked at first but soon got the message, as Jake rubbed his turkey-scented fingers together in the air.

'Wow,' Phoebe whispered, so as not to dispel the magic. 'You're really good at this.' Como was balanced on his hind legs, a pose we'd never seen. Jake kept him up there, milking the moment. After he let Como down, he slipped him another morsel.

'The tricks are neat,' Sally said, 'and I'm sure we can have fun with them. But that's not our issue. Como really seems to be having trouble adjusting to Steven.' She explained about the front-door escape problem and delivered the damage report on our bedroom. Jake had shifted his posture now, to clearly direct his therapeutic attention at us.

'Do the three of you get along okay?' he asked, meaning Sally, Phoebe and me. 'Any friction Como might be picking up on? Dogs are highly attuned to that.' Phoebe snickered a little but shook her head when Jake raised his eyebrows at her. Who knew what tales of family dysfunction she was itching to tell?

'Right now Como's the source of our friction,' I said, and immediately felt Phoebe's eyes on me. 'I mean, we're glad to have him and all. We've just got to come up with some coping strategies. It's hard worrying that he's going to run away all the time. That or eat the house if we lock him up.'

Jake nodded and served up some generic advice that wasn't much different from what we'd read in the dog books. We had to be patient. We had to be clear and consistent. We had to repeat things and try to think like a dog. 'It's really very simple for them,' he said. 'We're the ones who make it too complicated.'

Listening to his smooth patter, I wondered how it played out with his own dog and asked him what breed he owned.

'I don't have one,' he said. 'I live in an apartment in the Haight, and the landlord won't allow them.' The surprise must have shown in my face. Wasn't this like a swimming teacher who never went in the water? Jake had a prepackaged answer ready for me: 'It's much better this way. Trainers who have their own dogs start projecting. I can be totally objective.' I'd only been half aware of it, but the whole time he spoke to us, Jake kept passing Como bits of smoked turkey with his left hand.

I was about to thank our latter-day hippie trainer for his time when he came up with a last insight. 'Como doesn't bark much,' he said, gazing down into our terrier's round brown eyes. 'And I haven't heard anything about biting or nipping or anything like that. He's a gentle spirit, this little guy.'

The thought floated there in our kitchen for a moment. Jake didn't try to wring any more wisdom or advice out of it. And none of us contradicted him. He was right, and we knew it. For all the grief he'd caused us in the two weeks we'd had him, Como was anything but aggressive or hostile. Unlike Gengy or Beau, the neurotic and sometimes vicious dogs Sally and I had grown up with, Como had a sweet, placid, tender nature in there somewhere. The question was whether we could hold on to him long enough to let it flower.

Phoebe picked Como up, and we all walked Jake to the front door. I wrote him out a cheque for eighty-five dollars and opened the door. It was pretty clear that we wouldn't have him back for another session; we'd got what we could from him. But Sally told him we had his number and would keep him posted.

Our dog, too, had taken his fill from the smoked-turkey-rich meeting. Twenty minutes after Jake left, Como went into the study and threw up under the piano stool.

Sally was already in bed when I came up that night, after watching the highlights of a Giants game on TV. I thought she was asleep and tried to slip in beside her as quietly as I could. A thick summer fog had finally cooled things off, muffling the street sounds outside.

'I can't believe this is happening,' said Sally after a few minutes.

'Oh. Did I wake you?'

'No. I can't sleep.'

'You can't believe what?' I asked.

Another pause. 'This was just what I was afraid of,' she said. 'I'm falling in love with that impossible dog. Now I have to care. I already care a whole lot more than I ever wanted to.'

A fog horn sent its deep low moan into the night. Once. Twice. It was the last sound we heard before we slept.

CHAPTER TEN

Basic Training

The best thing about enrolling a problem dog in an obedience class for adult dogs is that you almost certainly won't have the only problem dog in the class. At least that's what I told myself, in the misery-loves-company vein, as we drove through the Mission District on the way to Como's first session at the San Francisco SPCA one Sunday night. The ten-session Basic Training course wasn't actually advertised as a remedial programme for flawed dogs and their inept owners. But it was hard not to read between the lines. Any beginning-level class for non-puppies implies that something has gone wrong or gone undone in the owners' attempts to handle their dogs on their own.

Sally, Phoebe and I each had our own ideas for why this class was a good idea for us. Sally cited, among other things, the smoked turkey factor. After cleaning up Como's souvenir of Jake's one and only home visit, she declared her firm opposition to any further attempts at food-based training. 'I seriously doubt the SPCA will be providing deli trays,' she said. 'Let's get some professionals on the case.' Phoebe, the lover of any and all things canine, liked the prospect of hanging out with a roomful of dogs for the next ten weeks. She was also keen to show off Como and see how he stacked up against the competition.

My own motivations were decidedly less straightforward. While I did hope that the class might moderate Como's behaviour and improve my still-troubled relationship with him, another part of me was pulling for a catastrophe. If Como really couldn't cut it in the class, if he couldn't learn some basic commands and get along with the other dogs and people, then maybe that would be the acid test of whether he was actually capable of leading a normal, reasonably socialized life with us. We still had about ten days left, on the thirty-day clock, to return him to the shelter.

In some ways, things had started to improve slightly between Como and me. Except for a few close calls when my guard was down, the dog hadn't slipped out again when I came or went from the house. Most of the time we still shut him in the bedroom when we left the house, without incurring further damage. He may not have liked treading on that strip of blue tape by the door any more than we did, and decided to just avoid it. Or maybe he'd accomplished all he could and was giving his assault on the carpet and door a rest. Even my skin had calmed down. The hydrocortisone cream had done the trick on my rash. And even if it hadn't, Sally had almost certainly abandoned her strategy to get rid of the dog with my skin as an excuse. She'd fallen for Como, and there was probably no way for her to fall back up. Increasingly, when it came to making peace with the dog, I was on my own.

Whatever modest gains Como and I had made had to be measured against our ongoing, unresolved problems. The dog's policy of avoiding if not openly spurning me had remained in effect. Most of the time it wasn't really an issue. If I was on one floor of the house, Como remained on the other – or at the very least in another room. While he greeted Sally and Phoebe warmly at the front door, he ignored me. Even when I took my turn filling his dish with food, he tended to wait until I had left the kitchen before coming in to eat. The female feedings, by contrast, were exuberant social events, with Como rushing in joyfully to celebrate his latest meal with my wife or daughter.

For me, it was often like living with an imaginary dog, one that you sensed was there but never actually saw. The difficulty came when he needed a walk and neither Sally nor Phoebe was around to take him. That continued to require making myself as inert and passive as possible. He still preferred having me stretched out on the bed or perched on the toilet.

On the bed, at least, I could get in some rest or maybe a little reading while I waited for him to make a tentative approach. Sometimes twenty minutes or more would pass before I could finagle him onto the leash. When the bed didn't produce results and I had to resort to the bathroom, the tactics were more delicate. If I dared to take a book or magazine in there, Como would have nothing to do with me. I didn't necessarily have to drop my trousers, although that added signal of helplessness did seem to reduce the wait time. Eventually he'd poke his whiskered white face around the corner and peer in at me from the hall, then gradually make his way close enough for me to nab him.

Some days it didn't work at all. I could have conked out on the bed for an hour or put in as much time in the bathroom without luring him close enough to leash. Frustrated by his intermittent refusal to play by his own weird rules, I might try to track him down and take him by force. On the rare occasions that I could catch him – I was usually no match for his terrier agility – I felt bad about it afterward. I may have got Como out for his walk, but I'd probably hardened his inscrutable heart to me even more. In his eyes, as I saw him seeing me, I was still just another male trying to dominate him.

The trouble with letting him skip his noon walk came on the days when I had to be somewhere in the afternoon, Sally had a meeting after school, and Phoebe had soccer practice or a game. His 'accidents', on those occasions, weren't really accidents at all but a logical result of my failure to perform the basic function of getting him outside. Como and I might have been better candidates for couples therapy than an SPCA course, but I was willing to give this a chance and see where it led. Clearly we both needed some basic training.

That first class we all attended with Como was actually the second session of the course. The week before we'd been told to come without our dogs. The instructor, a blunt, short-haired, square-shouldered woman in her forties named Sarah, spent that introductory hour making the case that we, not our dogs, were the real students. 'Most of the trouble people have with their animals has nothing to do with the animals. It's you,' she said, flicking her gaze from one face to another around the circle where we had arranged ourselves. 'We could spend ten months instead of ten weeks in this room and still not cover all the things people do to screw up their dogs.'

Sarah then summoned her own dog, a muscular Labrador retriever with a thick, mocha-coloured coat. So precisely, martially perfected was that Lab's behaviour and appearance that the affectionate informality of a name seemed irrelevant. 'World's Best Trained Dog,' I whispered to Phoebe, as we watched him respond to a series of crisply issued commands to sit, stay, lie down, sit up again, stay some more, fetch, circle a pair of orange pylons that had been placed fifteen yards apart, and finally smoothly snake his way back and forth between Sarah's legs as she strode across the room. 'Now, we may not get your dogs up to full speed right away,' she said, with what seemed to me a slightly patronizing tone, 'but there's no reason why any one of them can't master these things. It's all up to you.'

I looked around the room to see if other people were rolling their eyes (as I was trying not to do, thinking about Como) or signalling even a hint of scepticism. Everyone else, especially Phoebe, seemed too impressed to move. Sarah had put us all on the spot and challenged us to bring our dogs to class the next week with a properly serious attitude. We were also told to come with a supply of bite-size treats – hot dogs or cheese cubes or salami. 'Something your dog really, really loves,' this business-like teacher told us, before dismissing us for the night.

So much for the deli-free programme Sally had envisioned. I asked her on the ride home if she thought all dog trainers travelled in prime meat and dairy products to accomplish their ends. 'Sort of seems that way, doesn't it?' she conceded.

Most but not all of the class members showed up the next week with their dogs. Only a few, apparently, had been sufficiently intimidated by Sarah's Captain Marvel Lab to retreat. The atmosphere was decidedly different with all the restless, barking, panting dogs in the circle. The group ran the gamut from a rambunctious border collie to a fearsome-looking shepherd mix to a pretty brown-and-white Cavalier King Charles spaniel who wore the same pensive expression as her owner, a woman who was there by herself. Como assumed a safe position under Phoebe's chair.

Sarah called the class to order and began by asking us all to introduce ourselves and our dogs. Some of the animals perked up at the sound of their own names and tugged excitedly towards their neighbours. Como never moved a muscle when our turn came, and Phoebe spoke for us. 'Look at him. He's really cute,' I heard someone nearby say, and felt the same pulse of irrational pride that I had when Phoebe was an infant and someone would lean into her buggy and exclaim about her looks. Dogs, like children, become emblems for who we are out in the world. We can't help letting it happen.

When the introductions were over, Sarah walked around the circle and greeted the dogs individually and handed each group of owners a metal clicker. She had explained this training method the week before. The idea was to elicit the behaviour you wanted and promptly reward the dog with a prized treat and simultaneous click. Very soon, she promised, our dogs would learn to associate the sound with something positive; then the metallic click itself would be enough to produce the desired results – sit, stay, heel, come. 'You saw my dog last week,' she bragged. 'He was completely clicker trained.'

I didn't quite see why a dog would be willing to settle for a click instead of a hunk of Italian salami, but I was willing to give Sarah the benefit of the doubt. Her Lab, after all, was a finely tooled obedience machine. For the rest of us, in practice, things got off to a pretty chaotic start. Positioned around the room with our treat containers and clickers, we tried to teach our dogs a complex reward system with a stereophonic clatter of other clicks all around us. It was like trying to concentrate in a classroom full of enormous crickets. Como kept jerking his head around in confusion and alarm. Getting him to sit or stay wasn't going to happen. Most of the other dogs didn't seem to be doing much better.

'Okay, that's enough. Stop. Stop!' Sarah shouted. She instructed us to return to our seats in the circle. We did as we were told. 'Let's try to make this simpler,' she said, as if we'd all complicated matters by bringing our dogs to class and trying to follow the steps. Sarah asked a couple dressed in matching San Francisco 49ers regalia to lead their boxer to the centre of the ring. There, with her careful coaching, hair-trigger clicking and plenty of Triscuits the boxer kept wolfing down, the dog started flopping his tail end on the floor on command. Sarah looked at us with a mixture of triumph and disappointment. Why, she seemed to be asking, couldn't we all master this simple exercise? 'You see how easy it is,' she said, making it sound like a self-evident statement instead of a question. She called another dog up for a demonstration.

Como never got a turn that night, which was probably just as well. His demeanour hadn't varied from saucer-eyed amazement bordering on panic. I couldn't imagine him performing in the spotlight. 'He looks like he just witnessed a crime,' I whispered to Sally, 'and doesn't want to testify.' Phoebe gave me a sour look. Como's behaviour hadn't discouraged her at all, as she told us on the way back to the car.

'He's taking it in first,' she said. 'You'll see. He'll get it next time.' I admired her patience and sense of faith in the dog she had chosen. I also realized something else for the first time: they were a lot alike, Como and she. That may have been what drew her to him and made her so sure about him in the first place.

As a young child and even now, aged twelve, Phoebe was cautious, rigorously observant, careful to measure out every possibility and implication of a situation before she felt comfortable enough to enter into it. We had worried early on that she might be hopelessly timid, a terrified wallflower who wouldn't go down a slide or join a skipping-rope game, strap on ice skates, or speak up in class until she felt completely confident about the outcome. And who can ever know how things will turn out in advance? You only find out when you risk yourself and discover your strengths and limitations. But as Sally and I had learned over the years, Phoebe wasn't actually so frightened or withdrawn that she lived inside some protective shell. She was actually quite powerfully engaged in the world around her, in her own highly attuned and calibrated way. She saw things, felt things, imagined things that fell outside the scope of our own circumscribed adult radar. The teachers who really knew her grasped that about Phoebe. So did her best friend, Jeanne, a naturally gregarious and physically impulsive girl who often bowed to Phoebe's quietly willful drive to control their games and activities. Como, quite possibly, was wired a lot like Phoebe.

'So do you think this is working at all?' I asked Sally after I switched off my bedside reading light that night. She was nearly out and had to haul herself back towards consciousness.

'You do know,' she said with groggy precision, 'that my alarm rings at six a.m.'

'Sorry. I know. I just hope we're not leading Phoebe on. You know, getting her hopes up with this class if Como just can't cut it.'

'If anything,' Sally said, 'she and the dog are leading us on. I think they're way ahead of us here.'

She was probably right, even if I wasn't quite ready to accept it. 'Don't you want to smack Sarah?' I asked. 'She acts so superior.'

'I think she's good at what she does,' Sally said levelly. 'Phoebe likes her. Good night.'

It seemed that not everyone shared our daughter's favourable opinion of Sarah. At the following week's class, attendance was down to about seven dogs, which actually made things more manageable. We sat in a tighter circle, and Sarah took on a friendlier, more intimate manner. She asked us all for an update. The boxer and his owners were doing well. The border collie loved the clicker, but his need for long, athletic walks was proving difficult. Then it was the single woman's turn to tell us about her Cavalier King Charles spaniel.

She began with a heavy sigh. Her dog, it seemed, barked incessantly whenever the television was on. The neighbours were complaining about the noise. She was afraid she might get kicked out of her apartment. It went on and on, all that yipping. Nothing would make her stop. We all leaned in closer, like supportive members of a twelve-step group. We wanted to share her pain. 'The thing is,' she said, 'I live alone. TV is company for me when I come home from work. This has been really, really hard.'

Sarah was transformed. All that gruff, no-nonsense manner dissolved as she invited the woman and her dog to come forward. 'We'll get there,' Sarah said, gently taking the leash. 'We'll figure this out.' Her idea was to condition the dog gradually to the TV, with a mixture of reinforcement for silence and firm but reasonable 'time-outs' for barking. The three of them – Sarah, the owner and the dog – role-played a scenario that would involve turning on the television with the sound off at first, then slowly increasing the volume.

'See if she can take it for five minutes,' coached Sarah, 'reward her for that, and turn off the set. Then try it again in half an hour or so. During the week you can build up the time.' Clickers, I noted, didn't figure in the plan. The woman looked simultaneously grateful, hopeful and deeply relieved as she and her spaniel sat back down. I saw her wipe away a happy tear as she reached down to stroke the back of her dog's small, sleek neck.

That therapeutic exchange must have inspired me. When our turn came, I found myself spilling out all the trouble I'd been having with Como. I talked about the time he got loose and how he avoided me in the house and forced me to wait for him on the bed (I didn't mention the toilet) to take him out. The border collie's owner, a man in his twenties with a purple streak in his hair and a silver stud in his ear, stifled a smile.

Sarah was a little more confrontational with me than she had been with the TV-phobic dog's owner. 'You're going to hand-feed him,' she told me. 'You're going to give him all the treats – and good stuff, too. The yummiest you can think of.' I was to do it in the house, first thing in the morning and late at night, out on walks when I got him to heel or sit at a corner, anywhere, all the time. I was to become our own in-house Jake, in other words, stuffing Como with meat and cheese as fast as I could. I looked over at Sally, who had declared her firm opposition to a food-based curriculum before we started the class. We both shrugged. Whenever we thought we'd drawn a line with the dog, it seemed, someone or something came along to erase it.

Between the drama of the TV dog and Sarah's set of marching orders to me, it had been a draining session. Even Phoebe, who lived, breathed and dreamed dogs, looked a little dazed as she stood up to pull on her sweatshirt. I decided to show my earnest good faith by walking Como out to the car myself. Sarah met me by the door.

'Terriers are hard,' she confided. 'They've got this very willful way about them. You seem to be familiar with that. But when they come around, they are just about the sweetest, most loyal and loving dogs on earth. Except for Labs, of course,' she added with a smile, and gave me a good sock on the arm. She was a peculiar, thorny woman with a distinctly bossy streak. But I had come to like Sarah and could see why she was good at what she did. Her way of cutting straight to the point and doing it with her empathy worn right out on her slobber-stained T-shirt sleeve could be tough for some people to take. But dogs clearly thrived on her blend of clarity and love. I knew I could never be like Sarah, but I hoped I might learn something from her in the weeks ahead. For the moment, I resolved to follow her treat-a-thon programme for Como and me, even if it meant more surprises to clean up under the piano stool.

❖

Later that week, on a morning when I was working on a column that wasn't coming easily as my deadline loomed, Como pulled an unprecedented stunt. He strolled into the study without food lures or any other apparent motivation. Staring at a half-empty computer screen, with my back to the door, I didn't notice him come in, slip under my chair and lie down. Only when I turned to pull some notes out of the printer did I spot his tail, stretched out like a rare feathered treasure, on the floor beside my desk chair.

I was sceptical at first, chalking up Como's approach to some phantom food smell he'd detected. But I was also astonished, pleased and, yes, downright flattered by the unprovoked audience he seemed to be granting me. This was an important moment, and I didn't want to foul it up. My sister, who's spent her life as a schoolteacher and professor of education, once told me that children often respond best when they're not pressured or even noticed too much, when they feel free and comfortable to come forward on their own terms. I thought of that as I sat in my chair, trying not to disturb whatever inviting calm Como had sensed. I locked my legs exactly where they'd been. I didn't budge in the chair. As carefully as I could, I put my hands back on the keyboard and tried to flutter out a few words. I tried to make everything flow along as gently as I could, as if to will Como's strange overture into something more substantial and perfectly normal. I kept typing. The dog didn't stir. I even managed to make a little real progress on that stubborn piece I was working on.

At last, after ten minutes or so of our delicate balance, I decided to risk it all by reaching down to touch him, acknowledge and welcome his presence in the room. 'Once they come around . . . ,' I heard Sarah saying in her terrier speech. Slowly, without daring to lean over and look, I stretched my right hand down and under the chair. Como's cool, damp nose grazed my fingers. We held that pose for a while before I paddled him under the chin. He let me do it. He didn't bolt. I curled my hand around to scratch behind his ears. Neither of us had made a sound. I went on scratching until my arm started to hurt. Then I scratched some more.

It can't be possible that Como knew what the calendar said. But the fact of the matter is, his office visit came two days before the end of our thirty-day agreement with the shelter. His timing, like so many things about him, seemed uncanny. Four weeks after he had ripped through the hinges of his plastic crate to roam the house like a burglar and thwart every scheme we had to confine him, our unstable, orphaned terrier had found a home for himself.

When Sally came home that afternoon, I met her in the

kitchen and told her I'd given up and given in. 'I guess we're going to keep him, if it's all right with you.'

For once it was she who wasn't sure she'd heard me. I nodded back at her when she raised her eyebrows quizzically. 'Oh, Steven,' she said at that, grinning and plucking the dog off the floor. 'You're always the last one to know. There was no way in the world we were taking him back.' Como watched me peacefully from his safe perch in her arms as I turned and went back to my desk.

🐾

On the Sunday nights that followed for the next seven weeks, Como finally made a few tentative appearances in the centre of Sarah's classroom ring. On one memorable rainy evening, Phoebe stood beaming as Sarah praised her and her dog for how well she had taught him a few basic commands. Sally and I took turns accompanying Phoebe and Como to the classes. I liked seeing our daughter and her dog working together, and I cared about Como's progress, fitful as it was. He learned some things, even if he never got over his general uneasiness with his unpredictable classmates and their owners.

There was something else that brought me back to the SPCA. I wanted to know how the woman and her Cavalier King Charles spaniel were doing. The news was mixed. Some nights the TV could stay on and the dog would sit contentedly in her lap, she reported. Other times, in the middle of some Showtime movie that was making her forget her long day at work or some man who never called back as he promised (okay, I imagined that part), the dog would start up again. Stiff-legged in the middle of the room, she'd bark and yowl until the woman had to turn off the TV, take her out for a last walk, and go to bed.

I identified with this owner and her struggles with a difficult, exasperating, quirkily appealing dog that seemed to keep thwarting her the harder she tried. Nothing she did was right, it seemed, which only made her want to try something else and then something else after that. It was the dog's resistance that made her so vital and absorbing a challenge. They were enmeshed, those two, the woman who wanted to relax with her sweet, soft pet in front of the TV at night and the dog who just couldn't bear it. Anybody could love an easily lovable dog. It was the hard ones, the thorny, bruised and highly amped dogs, who put you to the test of how far you were willing to go, how much of yourself you were able to give up, how much it meant to connect to another, flawed being.

Sarah kept coming up with new ideas for the TV-fearing spaniel from one week to the next. She and the owner tried withholding food. They tried making the dog stand outside the apartment door, leashed to the knob, with the TV on inside. They tried moving the set to another place and turning the screen to the wall. They tried everything. It was an unfinished story when the ten-week course was over, a work-in-progress with no clear conclusion in sight.

'I've had dogs my whole life, and I've been working with them professionally for twenty-two years,' Sarah said at the end of the next-to-the-last class. 'You think you know a lot about them, and then something comes along to keep you honest. But that's what's so great about them. You can't ever fully know what's going on inside a dog's head. You just never really know what to expect.'

CHAPTER ELEVEN

A Social Life

Como ran up a perfect attendance record in his SPCA course and received a certificate congratulating him for successful completion of Basic Training. While he may not have graduated with honours – his diploma came with a suggestion that we enroll him in a follow-up class called Real World Manners – he did pick up a few useful skills. His most notable achievement was learning to stay on command. Phoebe proved especially adept at getting him to freeze in place. Her proudest moment at the SPCA came when she positioned him at one end of the joyless cement room where the class was held and retreated to the other while Como obediently awaited his order, 'Come.'

I watched that particular demonstration with a mixture of admiration and nervous apprehension. I was proud of Phoebe for volunteering to put Como through his paces in front of the class and pleased that they both performed so well. But it also made me very uneasy to see Como off his leash in such a big open space. I kept checking the two doors in the room, both of which did open, and fairly often, as people and their dogs came and went. All it would take was one little thing to spook him,

I fretted, and Como would have been out of there in a flash. I didn't even want to imagine chasing him through the unfamiliar streets of the Mission District in the dark.

Glad as we all were about him making it through the class unscathed, his triumph at sitting still by himself also nagged at me a little. 'It was a perfect picture of him,' I said to Sally, after his great demonstration of staying power, 'Como all alone. Do you realize he's hardly had a thing to do with any other dog in the class? Even that crazy King Charles spaniel mixes it up a little. And that boxer's everybody's friend. Except Como's.'

'So what,' she said, 'you're worried about his social life?'

'I am,' I admitted. 'He needs to get along with other dogs.'

Sally reminded me about Lizzy's visits and waved me off. Lizzy was the whirlingly energetic toy poodle who belonged to Phoebe's friend Marlena and her parents, Margene and Hans. Tiny enough to fit inside a small handbag, Lizzy went everywhere with her family. When they came for dinner or stopped by after a soccer game, Lizzy would be deposited on the floor and immediately engage Como in a sprint around the house. It was an amazing spectacle, like something an inspired choreographer or sideshow manager might dream up.

Flank to flank, the two dogs would charge around the downstairs circuit of the house, loop the butcher block in the kitchen, leap the gap between the dining room and living room rugs and rocket upstairs. It wasn't so much a chase as an exercise in simultaneous athleticism, made all the more striking by the contrast of Lizzy's springy black fur and Como's shaggy off-white coat. They'd jump and corner together, make the hairpin turn at the bottom of the stairs and re-emerge from their run on the upper floor as if riveted together. Finally they'd collapse near the fireplace, panting and meeting their audience's delight with a contented nonchalance.

For Lizzy all this was business as usual. She was a regular user of parks and other open spaces, where she'd eagerly cavort with dogs five times her size and shrug off any indifference or hostility she encountered by seeking out another playmate. Como, by any measure, was a dud with other dogs. Those that didn't plainly terrify him and induce evasive tactics on his part, he either snubbed entirely or barely acknowledged. It was embarrassing to encounter a dog owner we knew or a friendly dog-walking stranger and have Como go into his social pariah act. 'Well, anyway, he's really cute,' people took to saying, as if that might be compensation for my dog's standoffish behaviour. I began to think that Como was indeed a prime candidate for the SPCA's Real World Manners course. He was a canine boor.

Part of the problem was our firm policy of never letting him off his leash. That meant that parks and even fenced-in dog areas were out of the question. We just couldn't risk letting our guard down with a master escape artist. It's generally accepted wisdom that dogs tend to fare best with other dogs when they're free to explore one another without too much intervention and control from their owners. Dogs meeting on leashes are constrained, literally and figuratively, from being their true selves. And then of course there's the problem of tangled leashes. Como, if his leash got snared in another, quickly resorted to the kind of yanking and thrashing that only made matters worse.

Whenever I groused about his conduct outside the house, Sally and Phoebe looked perplexed and recounted their own eventful and fruitful walks. They'd both made friends with other dogs and their owners in the neighbourhood and said that

Como had, too. Had I met the lop-eared basset hound puppy? they asked me. Or the pure white, possibly Samoyed Nicky? Como really liked them both, I was informed. Same thing with Molly, the lumbering but docile Saint Bernard at the corner by the school. And what about Max and Willie, the ancient yellow Labs who were owned by that very friendly woman on Twelfth Avenue?

Sally, who took Como on his early-morning walk, even managed to break through our dog's customary resistance to men. Absent a common language, she'd struck up a smiling friendship with an old Russian man who ambled along our street at 6:30 a.m. with what she described as a short-haired, midsize black dog of unknown breed as a companion. The man kept treats in his pockets and had won Como's devotion by dispensing them to him freely. 'You should see it,' Sally said. 'Como spots him two blocks off and starts pulling on the leash and wagging his tail like crazy. He likes the old guy's dog, too.'

'It sounds grand,' I said. 'But I don't think I'll get up at six thirty to see it. And besides, isn't that just more bribery? How do we know what the guy's feeding him?' I may have been overly sensitive on the subject. My own programme of hand-feeding Como, as prescribed by Sarah, had not exactly been a raving success. When I remembered to do it, Como would dart over to snatch whatever I offered, down it and walk away. If it was making him like or even tolerate me more, the evidence was not exactly dramatic.

I tried to keep an open mind and stay optimistic about my relationship with the now firmly entrenched family dog. I looked for signs of progress and encouragement wherever I could find them. One positive development was the somewhat easier process of getting Como onto the leash. I didn't always have to take to my bed or the bathroom to capture him. But then when we did go out, another kind of puzzlement awaited.

Depending on his highly unpredictable mood, Como would sometimes want to scurry up the few blocks to do his business under a pine tree in the open land at Twelfth Avenue and quickly hustle back. But he was just as likely to treat his outing as a leisurely promenade. On those days, he'd stop to smell every tree trunk, bush, utility pole, scrap of paper and fragment of hardened chewing gum along the way. I don't know if all those fascinating scents unlocked his hidden gregarious side, but his curiosity extended to passing strangers as well. The dog who made no mistake of his need for solitude around me was suddenly the friendliest, most outgoing figure on the block. Women, children, a teenage girl chattering into her mobile, two boys deep in conversation about some rapper, even normally forbidding men striding along Lawton Street with their fists rammed into their pockets or rushing to catch a bus, snagged his interest. He'd veer across the pavement in their direction, his tail switching hopefully and his ears perked up and swivelling to receive any kind words.

Many people walked right by without noticing or stopping to return Como's overtures. Others paused to greet him, bending down and offering a hand to sniff. Mothers would ask first if it was okay for their young children to pet him. 'Oh, he won't bite,' I said. 'He's very gentle.' Then I'd stand and watch, a thin, polite smile frozen on my face, as Como chummed it up with someone he'd never met. I knew it was churlish and small-minded of me, but I couldn't help resenting it a little. How was it that the passing throng on the street, including some men as well as women, earned better treatment from him than I did? Could it really be, as it seemed, that he'd happily go home with almost anyone in preference to me? No man is ever more dishonoured, I thought, savouring the gall, than he is in his own house. Como was turning me into a brooding bar-stool philosopher.

One couple who lingered for a longer conversation wanted to know what breed he was, what we fed him and how many times a day he needed to go out. They were thinking of getting a dog and wanted to learn as much as they could.

'Don't do it,' I blurted. The woman looked a little startled, glanced down at Como and took a step back. I could see her wondering what kind of crank I might be.

'What do you mean?' her more persistent partner asked me.

'Oh, don't listen to me,' I said, deciding against getting into all the backstory. Como was a cute and apparently winning dog. He'd made them want to stop and talk. That was all. There was no reason to darken their sunny lives. 'You'll do great,' I said. 'You'll find a great dog and have a great time with him. You'll all have a great life. Dogs are wonderful.' At that point the man took his girlfriend's hand and started pulling her away. They'd got more – and also less – from me than they hoped. I really was acting like an idiot.

When we met other dogs on our walks, Como displayed an equally unpredictable range of responses. Sometimes he slunk by and paid them no attention whatsoever. Other times he cowered, his tail submissively tucked between his hind legs, and used me as a shield. When he did decide to either initiate or submit to a meeting, nose to nose or nose to tail, I was always on edge about the outcome.

According to the experts, that's exactly the wrong message to send. Because dogs are so acutely sensitive, they can feel nervousness in your tensed body, the pressure on the end of the leash, the slightest tonal stiffening in your voice. I was aware of all that but unable to stop myself from telegraphing my uncertainty. I never knew if Como might panic and get the two leashes hopelessly snagged, incite aggression with his sheepish manner, or issue one of his rare but alarming snarls and lunge away. As a result I tended to keep him at a distance from other dogs, even if it meant crossing the street in the middle of the block while pretending it had nothing to do with an approaching dog and owner. That's when Como's radar would go on high alert. Trotting along with me in one direction, he'd swivel his head back to keep the other dog in sight – and run smack into a curb or post box. Once he banged a Toyota hubcap so hard his tags made it ring like a cymbal. In another life he could have been a silent movie star, a scene-stealing sidekick for Charlie Chaplin, Buster Keaton, or Harold Lloyd.

In general I preferred it when Como entertained at home. In addition to Lizzy, who was probably his best and maybe only true dog friend, Como seemed to welcome visits by Jessie and Riley, the mother and son Welsh springer spaniels who lived next door. Arriving by the back steps, as they had in the days before we got Como, the two dogs brought a charge of unrestrained energy into the house. They looked enormous to us now, in comparison to our compact little terrier, but they didn't use their size to intimidate him. They'd greet Como with wagging tails and wiggling noses and head off in search of food or adventure elsewhere in the house. Como tagged along like a slightly awestruck younger cousin, ready to see what mischief Jessie and Riley might find for him. Sometimes we'd hear a little scuffling or something would get knocked over upstairs, followed by a quick flight of dogs away from the scene of the crime.

'What happened, Phoebe?' Sally or I would call out. 'You all right up there?'

'Nothing. We're fine.'

It was always nothing. In our daughter's view, dogs were blameless creatures. They brought only joy and gladness into the world. In the case of Riley, whom I'd learn to distinguish from his more decorous mother, I tended to agree. There was something about his lunk-headed, oafish qualities that was absolutely irresistible to me. Having a dog like him was so straightforwardly simple. All it seemed to require was putting plenty of food and water in front of him, keeping the pesto salad well out of range, and getting him outdoors a few times a day. In return you got the affection and devotion of an animal who lived entirely according to his appetites. Como, by comparison, was a dense psychological riddle, a confounding puzzle of phobias, impulses, sudden spasms, interludes of sociability and an overriding drive to escape whatever boundaries or limitations he encountered.

One morning, when the dogs next door were paying a visit, Phoebe came down from her room to find me wrestling with Riley in the living room. The dog was big and sturdy enough that I could wrap both my arms around his neck, muscle him back and forth, knock his feet out from under him, and hear a gratifying thud when he hit the floor. Riley, without fail, would bounce back up for more. Phoebe watched for a while from the doorway.

'Daddy, do you like Riley more than Como?' she asked.

I let Riley loose and stood up. 'No, of course not, sweetie,' I said. 'Why would you think that?'

'Well, you like playing with him more.'

'Como doesn't really like wrestling,' I said. 'Anyway, I'm just fooling around with this big lug.' Riley was staring up at me expectantly, a silver stream of drool dangling from his mouth. I thought about changing the subject, then decided this was one of those moments a parent shouldn't let pass. 'Sit down for a second, Skidge,' I said. She perched noncommittally on the arm of the couch. Riley stretched out on the rug to listen, too.

Trying not to overstate the case, I told Phoebe that it was sometimes hard for me when Como kept his distance. I reminded her what the people at the shelter had said about a man or more than one being mean to our adopted dog in the past and maybe even hurting him. 'But that doesn't mean I don't love him and want him to love me. I know he loves you and Mommy. It just may come a little slower for me. But hey, we've made lots of progress. He'll actually go for a walk with me now.'

Phoebe sat very still before she spoke. 'I hope you're really trying,' she said. 'I'd better go and see what Como and Jessie are doing. I think they might have found my Beanie Babies.'

Our daughter was no longer the carefree, dog-crazed child who wanted to grow up and be a vet and devote her entire life to caring for adorable little puppies. She had other interests – reading, piano, soccer. She did well in school but also liked shopping and talking with friends on her mobile or by e-mail and instant messaging. When she dressed up for one of her seventh-grade dances, with her hair pinned back and her lips lightly glossed and tinted pink, she seemed to vault into and even beyond her teenage years. I felt that sense of forward velocity in her as she walked upstairs to check on the dogs that day. She'd set me straight, clearly and directly and with no sulky impertinence. And she was absolutely right.

If Como and I were going to find a common path, it wouldn't happen by me trying to blindly assert my will and master him. He wasn't that kind of a dog, and I wasn't that kind of an owner. We were tangled up together, Como and I, his past and mine, and we'd have to sort it out together. I had to meet him halfway, and he'd have to do the same.

❋

Gradually, in the weeks and months that followed, things did start to improve – not just between Como and me but for all of us as we adjusted to life with a challenging dog. Como and I settled into leading our parallel lives in separate rooms, blessedly free of any major incidents, while Sally and Phoebe grew closer and closer to him. Docile and sweet-tempered when he felt at ease, our terrier liked being cuddled, picked up and held by the two of them, even cradled on his back in Phoebe's arms like an infant. In one of his most delightful quirks, he would ride around the house like that and react to his name being called by pitching his head straight back and looking at Sally or me upside down. He was like a child who got a kick out of seeing the world giddily up-ended.

When it came to feeding and walks, we established a reliably regular routine that seemed to make our sensitive dog feel more secure. He slept on Phoebe's bed at night – the one that Sally and I shared was off limits – and knew who was responsible for the various aspects of his care. When Sally's alarm went off in the morning, he hopped down from Phoebe's bed, jangled his tags with a full-body shake, and trotted into our room, knowing she would walk and feed him. The midday walk was my responsibility if I was working at home; Sally did it if I was gone. Phoebe took the dog out when she came home from school. He ate dinner an hour or so before we did. I handled the last walk at night.

After delaying any trips out of town, we finally decided to try a weekend away – to visit family and friends in Seattle – after Sally introduced Como to Marianna, a professional dog boarder and walker she had met in her book group at the Sunset branch of the San Francisco Public Library. Short, sunny and clearly gifted with dogs, Marianna took to Como right away, and he to her. Her own dog, an Australian shepherd named Uncle Indy, was a serenely tolerant, avuncular presence. No little terrier was about to faze the dog of a woman who had turned her snug little house out near Ocean Beach into a congenial dog motel. Our Seattle weekend was wonderful, even if did rain most of the time we were there.

It was only when we got home that we learned Como had got loose from Marianna at one point, dashed across busy Lincoln Boulevard, and disappeared into a heavily wooded stretch of Golden Gate Park. Marianna was remarkably sanguine about it all, explaining how she'd pursued Como with a container of smoked salmon in her hand and managed to track him down and reel him in. I wouldn't have been able to catch him with a smoked whale. Thank goodness for dog professionals, I thought, as I wrote out a cheque for Marianna's services plus a $12 cleaning fee for the carpet he had peed on. It must have all been business as usual in the dog boarding game, since Marianna told us how much she'd enjoyed having Como and hoped he would come to stay with her again soon.

By the summer of 2004, Sally and I were long overdue for some time to ourselves. I'd been lobbying for a husband-and-wife weekend in Napa or Sonoma, picturing good dinners, a fair amount of wine and a couple of terry-cloth robes for padding back to the room after a swim.

Sally countered with the idea of a dog-friendly Carmel

Valley inn that her friend Denise had recommended.

'We're taking Como?' I said, without concealing my disappointment.

'Marianna's booked,' she said defensively. 'And besides, I think it'll be fun. We'll do some hiking with him. He needs to get used to new places. Denise says they do a very good breakfast.'

'Did you really just say we're going down there for breakfast?' The wine-and-bathrobes weekend was vaporizing before my eyes, replaced by orange juice and quality-of-life enhancement for Como. Sally must have seen me droop. She made peace by offering a kiss that promised we'd be paying some close attention to each other, and not just the dog, on our trip.

We left on Friday afternoon, ran into traffic in San Jose, and arrived at the inn after all the restaurants in the area had closed. Como's dining needs were well met by a welcoming bowl of dog bones in the lobby and water and feeding dishes in the room. After a brief snit about going to bed hungry, I switched on the gas fire, pulled out my own bathrobe and began thinking about eggs and toast. Sally turned down the fire, got ready for bed and suggested that I dispense with my robe as she slipped in beside me. We slept soundly and so long, without any disturbance from the dog, that we nearly missed breakfast.

On Saturday afternoon, we drove to a trailhead and began winding our way onto a ridge above the valley. The trail ran through a flat pasture, crossed a creek bed and rose through cooler, sun-dappled woods. That's where Sally dropped Como's leash and let it drag behind him. The dog skittered ahead of us on the trail.

'What are you doing?' I said, rushing to stomp on the leash. Como's head jerked up from the clump of leaves he'd been inspecting.

'Let him go,' Sally said. 'He'll stay with us. Trust me.'

'It's not you I have to trust,' I said. 'It's him.' But somehow I couldn't work up much righteous conviction. We were having a lovely, placid weekend. A view of the valley sprawled out below us. A light breeze ruffled the dry grass at our feet when we came out on top of the ridge. A hawk drew a wide, languid circle overhead.

And Sally was right. Como might get ahead of us by fifty yards or so, momentarily vanishing around a bend or two in the trail, but he never strayed further than that and often walked right along with us. Sally and I chatted about the books we were reading, pondered our dinner choices, and wondered what Phoebe might be doing. For a while I forgot about Como altogether.

'So this is what it's like to have a normal dog,' I said.

'What do you mean?'

'That you don't have to be on guard every minute. That you can take him for granted a little.'

'Like you do me?' Sally teased, snaking an arm around my waist.

Como, as if on cue, was waiting politely for us when we came around the next bend. We picked up his leash when we got near the trailhead car park. Back at the inn, Sally dropped the leash again as we were unloading a few things from the boot. Contentedly tired after the hike, we'd fallen into a casual, weekend-away rhythm.

'Where is he?' I asked, when I had the car unloaded and was ready to go inside the room.

'I thought he was with you.' Sometimes our flawed communication had nothing to do with whether I'd heard, or misheard, her.

My stomach lurched as I looked past Sally and saw the dog slip out of the car park and across the street, his leash still dragging behind. Instinctively, we both took off running. Sally quickly called me off, sensing the dog's alarm and knowing I would only make things worse by giving chase. 'Stop!' she called. 'Let me do it.' I paced out to the street and watched her follow Como across a playground and up into a residential neighbourhood. Twenty minutes later, she walked him back into the car park. She didn't say anything about what had happened and didn't have to. Our make-believe time with a well-adjusted dog was over. For the rest of the weekend we kept Como on his leash.

A month or so later, we hit another all-too-familiar bump when Sally came home from the grocery store around dinnertime one evening. I heard her from upstairs, where I was changing clothes for the theatre. When I came down, Como scrambled away from me and headed for the door Sally had left open to get the bags of groceries inside.

'Hey! Watch out!' I tried to warn her. Too late. Como was out of the house and onto the front pavement. This was a rerun I definitely didn't want to be cast in, or even watch. It might have been her mistake to leave the door open, but it was a good thing Sally was there. With a little coaxing, and a few crisps she grabbed from one of the bags in the boot, she was able to snag Como by the curb.

'Wait,' I snapped when she carried him inside. 'Don't even *think* about putting him down until I come back.' I was like a drill sergeant giving orders to the troops. I went out to retrieve the rest of the groceries, marched back and shut and locked the door behind me.

'All clear to let him go, sir?' Sally deadpanned.

'Very funny. That could have been another disaster.'

As soon as she put him down, Como took off through the dining room and hid under the kitchen table. I followed to see what was bugging him. Could he have got a twig stuck in his paw during his brief getaway? Was he reliving a previous chase episode? Whatever it was, he sure didn't need me to find out. As I came around the butcher block towards the table, he ran in the other direction and disappeared upstairs.

'Oh, this is just great,' I said, collapsing on the padded bench by the kitchen table. 'Here we go all over again.' Sally finished putting away the groceries and pulled out a chair for herself. She offered me a sympathetic look and didn't argue with me. We sat in silence for a while. She was about to push back from the table and get started on a stack of papers she had to mark.

'Are those new?' she said, peering at the floor.

'What?'

'Your shoes,' she said. 'Have you ever worn them before?'

'No. Why?' We both looked down at the shiny black dress shoes I'd bought a few months ago and forgotten about until that night.

'That's what it could be,' Sally said. 'He's afraid of the shoes. They must remind him of something.'

After living with Como for close to a year, I didn't hesitate to test out her theory. I took off my shoes and went off to hunt out the dog. I found him in Phoebe's room, perched on the end of her bed in lookout mode. He saw me coming in sock feet and stayed put. I lay down beside him and cupped a hand on his haunch.

'Como, you are completely insane,' I said, rolling him over for a belly ruffle. 'Those shoes cost a hundred and forty dollars, and thanks to you, I got to wear them for five minutes total. Maybe I can take them back to the store and return them. Probably not. It's been too long.'

Como loves to have his tummy scratched, but for some reason lying on his back sometimes brings on a sneezing fit. He got off a few good ones, flipped over and jumped off the bed. I stayed where I was for a moment, taking in the chaos of scattered clothes, books and papers in Phoebe's room and lamenting the $140 I'd apparently wasted. There was no way to know it at the time, but soon enough the sum Como had just cost me would seem like nothing at all.

CHAPTER TWELVE

The Fugitive

The banging and rhythmic pounding began that morning just after eight o'clock. When the percussion let up for a moment, worse things took over – a motor's high-pitched snarl and deep grating rumbles, the screech of lath and plaster wrenched from wall studs, the thump of something heavy hitting the floor. Male banter ripe with four-letter words broke through intermittent showers of tinkling glass. A boom box added the running verbal soundtrack of combative talk radio.

It was January 11, 2005, sixteen months to the day after we'd adopted Como. The dog and I were holed up in my study with the door tightly shut. Down the hall, a crew of four was demolishing our bathroom and hauling the wreckage out to the street. We had hoped to start this remodelling project a year before, but deferred it during Como's long adjustment period. Sally, Phoebe and I all agreed enough time had passed and it was safe to proceed, assuming we took the proper precautions to keep Como out of harm's way. All this had been discussed with the contractor and the builders, a genial if remarkably loud group.

'We have to be sure the dog stays inside the house,' I told Manny, the burly foreman. 'That's the only thing that matters. He won't come near you, and we can handle him if he gets freaked out. But we *have* to make sure he doesn't get loose.'

Red-haired and red-faced Manny folded his big forearms, each of them about the size of Como, and tried to look concerned. This was the afternoon before work was to start. 'Not a problem,' he said, barely hiding his impatience about such a petty matter. Manny led me on a walk-through of the house and showed me where the barriers would be placed – one in the hallway near the study and another in the dining room doorway. 'This'll stay shut,' he said, reaching into the wall and yanking the living room pocket door closed. We'd used it so infrequently over the years I'd forgotten it was there. I approved the plan and told him I'd see them first thing the next morning.

Manny and company were true to their word. Large, paint-smeared sheets of plywood, high enough to thwart Como's leaps and thick enough to prevent him from tunnelling through, were installed as promised. The pocket door was pulled shut. But Como and I were taking no chances. After I'd carried him out to greet the men, we retreated to the study. Como did better with the noise and commotion than I thought he would. He took up a sentry's post by the door for a few moments, with that wide-eyed, four-alarm look of his, then slipped back under Sally's desk, turned around a few times and formed himself into a coil on one of the soft white dog beds we kept for him around the house. With a heavy sigh, he pretended to sleep. After a few minutes of answering e-mail and checking on him every so often, I picked up the phone for a scheduled interview with a theatre director on the East Coast.

The interview went on longer and proved more productive

than I had expected. Laughing with the director on the other end of the line, I forgot about the chaos in the bathroom and the dog playing possum under the desk. I should have known that the uproar in the house couldn't be going down as smoothly with Como as it seemed. I should have known that four strange men storming around and demolishing a whole room had to be jangling his nerves. I should have known to pull the study door shut behind me when I went out to the kitchen after the interview was over to make myself some tea. I should have known, I should have known, as I'd tell myself a hundred times by the end of the day. I knew Como. I should have known.

What I didn't know, as I stood waiting for the water to boil and listening to the racket, was that Como had made his stealthy way out of the study and was silently scouting the house. I also didn't know that Manny had come back through the house a few minutes before to tell me something about the skip out front, heard that I was on the phone, and gone back outside. I also didn't know that instead of pulling the pocket door completely shut, he or someone else had left a little opening between the heavy, baulky door and the frame. Nor did I know that the workmen had taken the front door of the house off its hinges in order to make carrying the debris out to the street easier.

Soon enough I would know all those crucial details and see how they fitted neatly together, each one a necessary part in the chain of events that was about to be set in motion. But at the moment I was staring into space and thinking about nothing else but the next phone call I was about to make. The water boiled. The electric teapot clicked off. Just then, as I was filling my cup, I felt it as clearly as if someone had placed a cold hand on the back of my neck. A sinking premonition seized me. It hit me that I had left the study door open. And I knew that wasn't good.

'Como,' I called out in my sunniest voice. Childish hope sprang up in me for an instant. If I called him sweetly enough, he'd come to me, he'd be fine. 'Como, where are you?' I crooned. 'Come on, boy.' A big metal tool clanked on the bathtub. Someone swore. Someone else laughed. The voice on the radio was railing about immigration. 'Como, Como? Here, Como. *CO-mo.*' I walked back through the open door to the study, my last faint hope fading that I would find him there. I checked under the kitchen and dining room tables and went out to the living room. A sliver of clear winter air sparkled from outside, through the missing front door and the not-quite-closed pocket door. That was Como's escape route.

I shoved open the pocket door and stepped out to see for myself. Just as he had on his first great break from the house, shortly after we got him, the dog was lingering on the front pavement. This time there was something hesitant in his expression and stance, a wistful air that seemed to say he regretted all the trouble he was about to cause, but really he had no choice in the matter. We'd filled the house with noise and mayhem and men. What else could he do but flee?

'That your dog?' Julio, the youngest workman, called out to me from the skip, where he was stomping down our bathroom's splintered remains. 'Let me grab him for you.' Dressed in a painter's white jumpsuit and perched up on the wreakage mountain, Julio did look like the construction-worker version of a delivering angel. For an instant I thought he might save us with a mighty leap down to seize Como. And maybe he could have. But I was trying to think rationally, factoring in the dog's foot speed and distrust of men. I'd have to do this myself.

'No! Don't do that!' I yelled back at Julio, who gave me an odd look. It could have been the sudden, stressed urgency in my voice that caused his double take. More likely it was what I was wearing as I stood there trying to master the situation from the front porch – a navy blue bathrobe and, as far as he could see, nothing else.

'You sure, amigo? I'm pretty good with dogs.'

'No!' I repeated and started down the steps in my bare feet, gingerly picking a path through the litter of wood scraps, linoleum bits and stray nails and screws. Como, I could see, still hadn't moved off very far. He was watching the action from under the tree in front of Pam and Cheryl's house.

'Como, whaddya say? Let's head back inside. I've got some good stuff in there for you.' It wasn't fully conscious, but I must have been trying to channel the jocular tone of the builders, make the dog feel part of the scene. It didn't work. His ears flipped up quizzically for a moment before he turned and headed for the corner.

It had been well over a year since we'd played this scene, but Como remembered his moves. He was going west, just as he had on that morning when the Good Samaritan and his Power-Bar came to the rescue. The dog saw me coming, crossed Tenth Avenue and picked up speed. Como may have been bent on a re-enactment, but I wasn't betting on another stroke of divine intervention. The sinking feeling I'd had inside the house struck again, and for a second time I considered taking Julio up on his offer. But when I glanced back, he was heading up the front steps to continue mauling our bathroom. I was on my own.

Determined to head Como off and short-circuit our old chase before it got started, I immediately crossed Lawton and ran to get ahead of him on the opposite side of the street. My hope was to shoot back over at some point and catch him by surprise. And if that didn't work, at least I'd be able to herd him back towards the house. I tried not to think about what I was wearing – or mostly wasn't wearing – as people filtered by me on their way to the bus stop and work.

Como, meanwhile, seemed to be in no particular hurry. He was catching up on the pavement smells and pausing at one point for a quick leg lift on a brick retaining wall. Before we reached Eleventh Avenue, I was several hundred feet ahead of him and ready to swoop in. Using the traffic as a cover, I darted behind a passing blue airport van to strike. Como saw me coming before I reached the curb, wheeled around and picked up his pacc in the other direction.

All at once I lost what little illusion of control I had left. The ambush had been my best shot, and it hadn't come close to working. 'Como! Como!' I shouted. 'Come back, Como.' Not a chance. He scooted on to the corner of Lawton and Tenth, where, instead of crossing over in the direction of the house (and a possible Julio miracle catch by the skip), the dog turned left and started down the hill towards Kirkham Street. It was new territory for him, an unfamiliar stretch full of people and cars in rush-hour mode. I broke into a run, my feet slamming into the gritty pavement. If Como couldn't hear me and my heaving breath, he could surely sense my panic – which, of course, only fed his own. The gulf between us widened. I sped up. He looked back. He sped up more.

'Como,' I pleaded between ragged breaths. 'Come here.' I could barely hear the sound of my own voice. It was like one of those dreams where you're trying to cry for help and nothing but a hoarse, strangled whisper comes out.

A row of identical red garage doors that I'd never noticed

before spooled by. I had a clear, awful certainty that I wasn't going to catch Como and that this couldn't end well. Giving up hope but still running as hard as I could on feet I could barely feel, I was struck by the absurdity and unreality of the repeating red doors. I saw myself against them as strangers across the street in their sensible work clothes would – a fifty-three-year-old man hurtling down the hill in a flapping bathrobe, shoeless and wild-haired, in pursuit of a harmless-looking small dog.

The moment passed; my brain clicked off. Como knifed around the corner onto Kirkham. He was heading west again.

'Help!' I screamed, when I rounded the corner behind him and saw people coming my way at the far end of the block. The dog was between us, running right at them. 'Help me get him. He's mine.' We were closing in on him from both directions, with the buildings on one side of us and a line of parked cars on the other. Someone – a man, a woman, I couldn't say – made a move at him. Como darted free and into the street.

The driver of the SUV never saw him, never had a chance. She hit him with her left front wheel. Como let out a sickening yelp, gave one mighty thrash and dropped on his side. It was over that fast. He was dead. I knew it. I darted out to him and couldn't bear to look. I'd chased him under a car. He was dead – or worse, painfully dying. It happened because I was lazy and careless and preoccupied with some stupid phone call. It happened because of Manny or whatever mindless idiot had left the pocket door open. Or because the dog really was afraid of me and I hadn't found a way to make him trust me after all these months. And he was right. Look at what I'd done. I thought about Phoebe and Sally – their faces, their tears – and forced that out of my mind. I had to stay focused. I had to do whatever was still possible. I couldn't lose it or lose myself in guilt and recrimination.

Como lay on his right side inches from the SUV's big black wheel. Somehow the driver had managed not to run over him completely. That, or she'd already backed up instinctively and run over him twice. Or bounced off him, somehow. I was trying to make sense of his being not directly under the wheel but a little way off from it. Some detached part of me was playing traffic cop or lawyer before the other part of me, the terrified and enraged and desperate part, caught up.

Como wasn't moving, his face pressed to the ground and one unblinking eye staring, fishlike, straight up. But he was still alive, breathing so quickly his side seemed to flutter. I reached out to put my hand there. He sprang up at my touch and bit me so fast and so many times – on my shin, my bathrobe, my right arm, the fleshy ball of my left thumb – that I never felt pain. If anything I felt a little flicker of gratitude and relief: at least his self-protective animal reflexes were intact. That was something, something to cling to.

I must have said more things and done more things as I knelt beside him in the street. Other people came out to me and offered help, asked me if I was all right, murmured sympathy, said they'd seen it all happen. Someone called the police on her mobile, as I learned much later. But I wasn't seeing or hearing much of that. All I knew then was that Como was still breathing. And that he was bleeding now as well, in this bizarre way, in little spots from his neck and shoulder and a place back near his tail. There was no time to waste, no time to think about whether an animal in shock should be moved or not. I wedged both hands under his body and lifted him up. He went limp and let me do it.

'Do you have a car?' I said to the first face I saw, a woman who'd been standing close and leaning over. She nodded and led me around to the passenger side of the SUV. Only when she came around and got in behind the wheel did I get it: she was the driver. We were sitting in the car that had hit Como. The dog was in my lap, lying motionless across my bare legs. He felt very warm.

'I'm so, so sorry. I never saw him. He ran right out in the street.'

I couldn't look at her. 'The vet on Ninth Avenue,' I said. 'Just off Lincoln.' She started up the car, and we sped away, with her apologizing some more. 'It's okay,' I said blankly, wanting silence for the rest of the short drive to the vet's, wanting the trip to be even shorter than it was. Then I heard it, or finally noticed – another small voice in the car.

'Where's the doggie? What's the matter with him?'

'He's up here, sweetie. He's in the man's lap.'

'Why?'

'Because he needs to go to the doggie doctor.'

'Why?'

We turned onto Lincoln. Como hadn't moved, and the child in his car seat behind us needed to know everything that had happened and what would happen next. We were half a block from the vet's. Finally I looked over at the woman who'd hit Como and was doing everything she could to help him and me. This was terrible for her. Her face was knitted shut. She leaned forward and gripped the wheel, silently urging the cars in front of her to hurry, hurry, hurry, let us get there. I'd done this to her, too. But I was too scared, too worried, too guilty to acknowledge that.

'Here,' I said, as we pulled onto Ninth, and I slid out with the dog cradled in my arms. I'd never put my seat belt on. I'd never thanked her or asked her name. The little boy in the back was asking another question as I slammed the car door shut.

I banged open the vet's door with my hip, trying to hold Como in front of me as still as I could. 'He was just hit by a car,' I announced, expecting the woman behind the counter to leap up instantly. She remained seated.

'Is your dog a patient here?' she asked. 'What's the dog's name?'

'Yes. What does it matter? He's been hit by a car.'

I had everyone's attention, including two customers who were paging through magazines with their dogs lying docilely under the chairs. I hated them both for being there ahead of me, for their dogs being healthy, for looking up from their magazines and observing me so calmly. A woman veterinarian in a white lab coat appeared in the waiting room and led me back past the counter. The receptionist kept her head down over some files on her desk.

'This way,' the doctor coached. 'Let's put him here on the table.' She took me by the elbow and showed me where she meant. As soon as I laid Como down and let go of him, the hot fear I'd been holding in check flooded out.

'He's going to die. Oh, my God, he's going to die.' A sob came out of me. I sucked in more air. 'He was hit by a car. He got run over. Look – he's bleeding all over.' I could see that the doctor didn't know whether to attend to the dog first or to me. 'I'm okay,' I assured her, lifting my hands up high and squaring my shoulders to prove it. 'I'm okay, I'm okay, I'm okay.' I took a big breath. Another vet, who must have heard the commotion, came into the examining room to help. Both of them were blonde. The second one gave my bathrobe-and-bare-feet look a quick once-over.

'Tell me his name,' the first doctor instructed, with her calm-down-the-crazy-person technique of looking me straight in the eye. The other one was bending over Como. It was tag-team medicine. I told her the dog's name and tried to crane around her to see what was happening on the table. Gently but firmly, Blonde Doctor Number One blocked my way. 'It's best if you wait outside. We've got it under control. Can you just wait outside?'

I went. I didn't want to. I didn't want to leave him in there with those two blondes he didn't know. Or maybe he did know them. Sally brought Como here for his vet appointments. I'd been in this surgery exactly once. There was nothing for me to do but pace. I didn't want him to die in there with me outside. I couldn't stand it, but I couldn't do anything else. So I paced.

I went into the other examining room, where Blonde Doctor Number Two must have been when she heard me, and looked at the stark white table and all the tools and glass jars and closed cabinet doors. I came back out and roamed the hallway and then the waiting room, where everyone studiously avoided looking at me. I went back towards the room where Como was and made myself not fling open the door. I paced across the linoleum – so smooth underfoot after the street – and wondered why a wall near the front desk was speckled red, with more dots and streaks on the floor.

What kind of place was this? Couldn't they even keep it clean? And why did they have that infuriating little tabletop fountain burbling away out front? Did they really think that would calm down anyone whose pet was sick or dying? I paced into the waiting room again, back to the open examining room, back and forth and back again. The receptionist met me on one return circuit and held out a handful of gauze.

'Do you know you're bleeding?' she said. 'Are you all right?'

I looked down at the place on my hand where Como had got me. A smeary patch of blood was caked there, and the wound was still open. So was the one on my shin. Those red speckles on the wall and the floor were mine. I was leaving a trail and stepping in it wherever I went. 'Oh, yes,' I muttered, and found a sink to clean up. That's where I was, looking for a place to dispose of the blood-soaked gauze, when Doctor Number Two came out with her first report.

'We've got Como sedated and stabilized,' she said. 'He's on an IV and resting comfortably. The good news is we're not finding any major internal organ damage right away. That's already pretty amazing, considering what he's been through.'

'But – ' I said, lurching ahead for the rest of the story.

'We don't know. We want to take an X-ray and see what else may be going on.'

'Which might be what?' I pressed. 'Is he going to make it?'

'Mr Winn,' she said. 'One thing at a time. We've got him stabilized. We're giving him fluids.'

'And what about all the bleeding?' I said.

'Internal? We don't know about that yet.'

'No. The blood on his neck and chest and all over.'

Number Two looked puzzled for a moment. 'Oh, that. That cleaned right off, and we couldn't find any wounds. We're not sure what that was.'

I understood then what it was. It was my own blood, which I'd apparently spilled on him after he bit me and then continued spattering around the office and, no doubt, the front seat of the SUV. 'I want to see him,' I told the doctor, slapping a wet paper towel on my thumb to prevent further red sprinkling.

'Please,' she said sternly, aiming me towards the waiting room. 'Let us do our job. We'll tell you just as soon as we know anything.'

This time I complied, collapsing on a couch by the window. There was no way to reach Sally, who was in class, and I definitely wasn't going to call Phoebe at her school and upset her. My mind was still whirring, as it had been all morning, but now with no place to go. The door beside me opened, and a woman carried a large grey cat inside. The phone rang. The fountain gurgled. One of the two people who had been in the waiting room when I arrived came out to settle her bill. Someone else came in to buy a bottle of aloe shampoo for his Pomeranian.

The normal, sane life of pet owners flowed around me as I sat motionless and stony-eyed, unconsciously flashing my underwear at the cat lady across from me. I finally noticed, stood up to refasten the belt on my robe, and sat back down. I realized, with a strange, flat detachment, that I hadn't once felt self-conscious about the way I looked. It was Como I kept seeing – under the tree in front of Pam and Cheryl's house; hightailing it down the hill ahead of me; lying motionless in the middle of Kirkham Street, his brown marble eye staring skyward.

'Mr Winn?' It was Doctor Number One, waving me back. I followed her into a small room I hadn't noticed while pacing. She clipped an X-ray sheet to a light box and switched off the overhead fluorescents. It felt as if a movie were about to begin, one I was both driven and frightened to see. 'Right here,' Number One was saying, 'you can see the breaks in several places.' Her hand moved across the ghostly brown image, pointing here and there. I came closer to the screen. We were looking at Como's pelvis, fractured in three or possibly four places. What ought to have been a slim but sturdy bone box looked more like a game of Pick Up Sticks, playfully scattered inside him.

'What does it mean?' I asked. 'Is he going to die? Will he ever walk?'

The doctor didn't try any happy-talk spin. 'I don't know,' she said. 'I honestly don't. He's not in immediate danger, as far as we know, but he'll need an operation. And we can't do it here.' She named a place across town that specialized in complicated surgeries and recommended it highly. Then she told me I needed to think about options and prospects. 'And about cost,' she added. 'It's a personal decision, of course.' The choice she was offering was to put Como down instead of putting him under the knife.

I thanked her and asked if I could see him. She switched off the X-ray and led me back through the maze. The dog spotted me from across the room and lifted up his head. They'd stowed him in a little cage lined with a blanket and heated by a small sun lamp. He was resting on his stomach with several plastic tubes coming off him. He looked surprisingly fine. I touched his cool nose and told him I was sorry and told him not to die. Then I turned and left him there. It only occurred to me later that he was shut inside a cage and, for once, not trying to get out.

I spent the next hour in a back office, dialling and redialling our home number, over and over, until Sally finally got home and picked up. I told her what had happened and where I was and asked her to come and meet me. She was there in less than five minutes. As soon as she walked in, I knew she would take over. She was nicely dressed. She'd been at work and out in the real world all morning, instead of careening around barefoot and half naked, spraying blood through the neighbourhood. She smoothed down my hair and tugged the sides of my bathrobe together.

'Which doctor is it?' she asked me. 'What's her name?'

'There's two of them,' I told her. 'I don't know their names. They're both blonde.'

Sally told me to sit down. She went up to the counter, where Number One came out to meet her and take her in to see Como. They were gone for quite a while. More dogs and cats and one parrot came in for appointments. When Sally came back out, she and Number One were talking and nodding. They looked over at me once and smiled. I could have been the patient myself, waiting for some test in my self-styled hospital gown. The doctor approached and gave me another of her direct looks.

'You should go home,' she said. 'Sally can take you home. Como is fine for now. You shouldn't worry. Go home and get some rest.'

I nodded and sat back down while they walked over to the counter, presumably to deal with more details and paperwork. They looked like old friends, chatting away. I felt miserable, bereft, and too steeped in guilt to even start working up a fury at the builders for leaving the pocket door open. My hand, I finally noticed, was throbbing, and my shin had started to hurt.

There was one last matter to address before we left Como in our vet's care and went off to decide what we would do next. To be absolutely safe and take no chances, Number One told us, we should consider having Como moved to the surgical hospital across town in a pet ambulance. I'd never heard of such a thing and asked what it would cost. It wasn't a funny number, but for the first time that day, I laughed.

CHAPTER THIRTEEN

Crossing Town

I t was close to one in the afternoon by the time we finally left the vet's. The pavements around Ninth Avenue and Irving Street were full of people on their way to or from lunch, busy with noontime errands, or heading to Golden Gate Park to enjoy the crystalline January sunlight. Being outside in our neighbourhood's midday bustle seemed surreally ordinary after the sustained drama I'd just been through, and I must have dawdled a little to take it in. When I turned to say something to Sally, she was a good thirty feet ahead of me on the street.

'What, you're embarrassed to be seen with me or something?' I said when I caught up with her at the corner.

She looked down at my bare feet, with their less-than-stellar toenails on full view, and bit her lip to suppress a smile as we waited for the light to change. 'Have you taken a look at your hair, by any chance?'

She asked me something else, which I didn't even try to catch. Whatever pride or self-righteousness I might have been holding on to about the events of the morning had long since drained away. I knew I looked ridiculous, and felt it myself now, without a fleeing or flattened dog to justify my breakfast-table attire. I also felt that I'd done just about everything wrong – letting Como out of the study, not giving the agile Julio a chance to grab him, chasing the dog back towards the house and then down Tenth Avenue into the traffic, forcing him out into the street when I called for help. If Como died – and no one had said he was sure to survive – it would be my fault.

'You know,' I said, when the light turned green, 'I just really want to get home now.'

'I know, dear,' she said, reaching down to squeeze my unbloodied hand. 'It must have been awful. I don't know what I would have done differently. You did great.' We knew that wasn't true, but it was good of her to say so. She loyally walked beside me the rest of the way to the car.

The front door was back on the hinges, and the builders, who were either on their lunch break or in hiding after the dog's escape, were nowhere to be found. I went upstairs to the unde-molished bathroom, dropping my bloodied and battle-scarred bathrobe in the laundry basket on the way. When I got out of the shower, Sally told me the vet had called to say that Como was still stable and that arrangements had been made to transfer him to the hospital later that afternoon. 'We can pick up Phoebe at school and tell her,' she said. 'Then we can all drive straight there. The timing should be about right.'

I'd thought about Phoebe a lot while I was pacing around the vet's surgery. I almost couldn't bear to imagine the look on her face if we'd had to tell her that her dog had been run over and killed or was going to die or couldn't walk again or spring up onto her bed when she was doing her homework. Now, it seemed, we'd have to tell her we didn't know what was going to happen. We'd have to go through this together, wherever it led.

After washing away the dried blood in the shower, I could see that two of the spots where Como had bitten me were still seeping. Sally insisted I go and have them looked at. I agreed, mostly to have something to do besides worry and stew for the next few hours, and assured her I was perfectly capable of driving myself. On the way over to Kaiser, I was flicking through the radio stations when I came upon something that almost made me stop dead in the middle of traffic. It was one of those moments that sometimes arrives in the midst of a crisis: with your system on high alert, you see something, hear something, notice something, that seems intended specifically, even exclusively, for you.

A plainspoken, gravel-voiced woman whose name I didn't catch was being interviewed by Terry Gross on the NPR programme *Fresh Air*. When I tuned in, she was talking about the associations and 'fear memories' a horse might get if he were treated badly by a man wearing a black hat. It wouldn't automatically be a fear of black hats. Then the woman, who turned out to be the well-known animal expert and author Temple Grandin, said this: 'Or a dog got hit by a car. You'd expect the dog to be afraid of the car. No, he was afraid of the piece of pavement he was staring at right at the time he got hit by the car.'

I'm not sure I'd thought about it consciously until then, with all the other things churning through my mind that day, but a gloomy sequence of worries had probably been nagging at me from the moment of the accident: how would Como remember it if he survived? What kind of indelible movie would be playing inside his head? Would he see me as the one who had somehow caused the SUV to materialize out of nowhere and run him over, permanently cementing me in his mind as the dangerous and perversely sinister presence in his environment, to be avoided at all costs? Were the chase scene and its awful climax imprinted as a grim two-person drama, a nightmarish replay of whatever terrible things some man had done to him in a past he could never escape?

Or maybe, just possibly, as this woman on the radio seemed to be confiding to me, that's not necessarily the way an animal's mind works. It could be that once he was out there in the street, with the big black wheel bearing down on him, Como may have forgotten about me entirely, freed me from any kind of cause-and-effect link. It might not be me he associated with the awful thud of pain he felt, but whatever it was his eye happened to light on at the moment of impact – the curbstone on the far side of Kirkham Street, the shiny chrome grille of the SUV, the tyre itself with its zigzag tread.

It wasn't just that I wanted to be let off the hook. I knew what I had done, and failed to do, and I felt plenty guilty about it. That wasn't going to change; in fact it might get much worse. But there must have been some little shimmer of hope I was carrying around with me. It had started when Como didn't die out there on the street. Then, when Blonde Number One and Blonde Number Two were able to keep him going in the vet's surgery, it glowed a little more brightly. And now, as I swooped up the hill on Masonic Avenue, sunlight bouncing off the bonnet of the car in a giddy display, I felt a fresh surge of provisional hope. Como, if he made it, might not blame or banish me for what had happened. We might find a way to each other after all. If. If. If he made it.

The *Fresh Air* interview turned back to the subject of horses and black hats. And then, just before I turned into the Kaiser clinic parking garage, Temple Grandin spoke directly to me once more. A dog could be afraid of Nike trainers, she specu-

lated, 'because that's what he saw when someone was whack-
ing him.' Those black shoes of mine that had terrified Como one
day – there was the explanation. As soon as I put them on, I had
stepped into some costume drama written and played out for
Como long before he and I ever met.

'You can desensitize, but you can never erase the fear
memory,' Grandin told Terry Gross. 'Nature will not let you
erase it. It will only allow you to put a lock on the file.'

The machine spat out my ticket for the garage. I drove
underground and parked, took the lift up to the fourth floor
and waited my turn. Dr Palacios looked briefly at the bites on
my shin and arm and spent more time with my left hand, flex-
ing the skin at the base of my thumb and asking if that hurt.

'You know, I can't really tell,' I said. 'I think I'm still in a
state of shock.' I gave him an abbreviated account of the
accident.

'Is this the same dog that may have had something to do
with that rash last year?' he asked, peering at my records on
his computer screen.

'Same dog,' I said.

'And you're sure he's up-to-date on all his shots?'

'I think so. Anyway, he's still at the vet's, so we can check
on it.'

Dr Palacios told me to keep the wounds clean and exposed
to air as much as possible and instructed me to come back if
Como's shots weren't current. He seemed satisfied there was
nothing to worry about. 'I hope that dog of yours is a lot of fun,'
he said, as I stood up to go, 'because he sure causes his share
of problems.'

An hour or so later, Sally and I drove past the vet's on the
way to pick up Phoebe at school. The pet ambulance, a sleekly

painted van, was parked out front. I wanted to stop and make sure that everything was okay.

'It *is* okay,' Sally said, patting my thigh and driving on. 'That's why the ambulance is there, right on schedule.' It seemed clear that it was her judgement we should trust from now on rather than mine. She parked a block and a half from school, and the two of us walked up the hill together.

'What's wrong? What happened?' Phoebe said as soon as she saw us. Both of us showing up in the school courtyard was enough to raise her suspicions. The look on my face must have ramped up her alarm. 'Is it Grandma?' she asked me. 'Is she okay?'

'She's fine,' I said, relieved to have a small piece of good non-news about my ailing mother to deliver first. 'There was an accident this morning,' I began, not knowing where I was going next. 'With Como.'

'Is he dead?' Phoebe cut in.

'No, sweetheart,' Sally said. 'He's on his way to a very good pet hospital where he has to have an operation on his pelvis. He got hit by a car.'

'I want to go there,' Phoebe said, and started out of the courtyard. One of her friends called out to her. Phoebe didn't answer or look up. She was on a mission. She had a purpose. She had to be with her dog.

We drove to the hospital, which is located in a warehouse district between the Mission and Potrero Hill, mostly in silence. Phoebe whimpered softly in the backseat but didn't ask anything more about the accident or what the vet had told us. In one way I was grateful for that: I didn't have to explain myself and go over the details again. But I was also a little concerned. Wasn't it better to talk things out with a child at a time like this and know what she was thinking and feeling? I glanced over at Sally and realized right away that hadn't crossed her mind. Silence was a natural, even desirable trait on her side of the family. It gave you room to think and let things sink in. Members of my family would never shut up, she'd pointed out to me more than once. We found the hospital and parked around the corner from the main entrance.

The receptionist was on the phone when we approached the front desk, a dramatic wooden form that looked like a boat's polished hull. Drawers and shelves of files rose against an exposed brick wall behind it. Men and women I took to be doctors, nurses, or vet orderlies, many of them dressed in blue or green scrubs, came and went through a door that apparently led to the examining and operating suites at the far end of the room. The staff all looked young and vitally engaged in their work; they could have been the ensemble cast of some hit medical show on TV. The phones chirped. Other people came in and stood beside us with their dogs and cats. The place was simultaneously bustling and soothing, with all the activity smoothly flowing through an open-plan space that had clearly benefited from the services of an interior designer.

'And whose family are you?' the receptionist asked us with a cordial smile when the phones finally let up.

'Como's,' said Phoebe, who understood the question faster than I did.

'Oh, yes. We're expecting him any time now,' the woman said. 'Please, have a seat.' We installed ourselves on two handsome striped couches in the waiting area alcove.

I was a little surprised that the ambulance hadn't arrived before we did. It had been parked at the vet's when we drove by on the way to Phoebe's school. That was close to forty-five minutes ago. Another fifteen minutes passed. And then another. I went over and asked the receptionist if there'd been any word about Como. She lifted her shoulders in a big, sympathetic shrug, then excused herself to do something in the back.

When the ambulance finally pulled up, I happened to be watching the street from the entryway. The driver and his companion took their time opening up the back and transferring Como onto the trolley. They thumped through the front doors and went straight to the desk, where paperwork got passed back and forth. Sally and Phoebe were busy watching Como, who lifted his head up at one point and looked around, before he was whisked by two scrubs-clad workers into the back. I hung around the desk, eavesdropping on the ambulance crew.

'We'da been here a whole lot sooner if we'd known where the hell this place was,' the driver said.

'Yeah, by the time we figured it out, we had to make an illegal left turn off Valencia to get here as soon as we did,' said his partner. 'What's the exact address here, anyway?'

It was all I could do to keep from snatching the invoice out of the receptionist's hand and demanding a rebate for ambulance crew incompetence. I walked away, telling myself that we had to do anything we could to ensure that Como got the best possible care. Alienating the all-powerful front desk people wouldn't be a good idea. I went back and sat down between Phoebe and Sally to wait.

The doctor who walked into the waiting area an hour later was an imposing figure. Tall, square-jawed and mightily built – the short sleeves of his green smock were stretched tight around his biceps – he told us his name and offered a quick, potent handshake. Then, in a ripe Australian accent, Dr Watt summarized Como's condition and laid out a plan of treatment. He led with the good news: there was no organ damage and, because Como was apparently able to move his legs a little, no major nerve damage, either. The pelvis breaks were serious but fixable.

Then came the caveats: Como had probably gone into shock after the accident, and his vital signs had dipped to a very low point (probably on that leisurely ambulance ride, I fumed). What Dr Watt was telling us, without quite saying so, was that we were far from out of the woods. Still, he hoped to get Como fully stabilized by the next morning and perform the surgery then. Sally, Phoebe and I shot each other quick, bright looks, then trained our attention back on the doctor to make sure we had good reason to feel hopeful.

'He's going to be a good little pie-shunt,' our saviour from Down Under told us, with a quick nod of noncommittal reassurance, and excused himself.

We took each other's hands when he was gone. I gripped Phoebe's almost as hard as the doctor had gripped mine. 'Ow,' Phoebe said with a grin, glancing over my shoulder in the direction Dr Watt had gone. Sally read our thirteen-and-a-half-year-old daughter instantly.

'He *is* awfully handsome,' she agreed. Blushing, Phoebe turned away. She was in her final year of middle school and now an inch taller than her mother. She would be in high school by the end of the calendar year. I had this sudden, dizzy sense that everything was speeding up and slipping away. It had been, in every way, a day of high velocity.

'Don't you think it's a little more important that he's a good surgeon?' I said, sounding as stuffy to myself as I must have to Phoebe. 'Anyway, let's go home and get some dinner.'

With Como sedated, Dr Watt had told us, there was no reason to see him until after the surgery the next morning. We were pulling on our coats to leave when one of the women from the front desk approached with a clipboard in hand. It held an 'estimate of services' we needed to pay in advance. I scanned down a dauntingly long list that included Transfusion Administration ($35), Surgical Consumables – Major ($200), Fentanyl Patch (Duragesic) 25mcg ($48), Metacam 32 ml Bottle ($58) and Biohazard Fee ($4).

'Now look at that,' I said, pointing out that last item. 'It's a real bargain. Four bucks for a biohazard.'

'Not funny, Daddy,' Phoebe informed me. She and Sally went out to the car while I stayed behind to start assaulting our MasterCard account. We drove home through the Castro and up Eighteenth Street, with the spires of the Sutro radio tower on Twin Peaks poised above us like a steel ship's masts. It was a reassuring sight, those twinkly beacon lights up there in the sky.

After dinner, Phoebe and I went to see her godmother, Jean, receive a writing award at the sleek new Jewish Community Center on California Street. I was glad we went, not only to share in Jean's big moment but also to take our minds off Como for at least a little while. Sally stayed at home to field any possible calls from the hospital. As soon as the ceremony was over, Phoebe wanted to call and check in on her dog. We were put on hold for several minutes before someone came on the line to say there had been no change. Pleading homework, Phoebe asked to go home instead of out somewhere to celebrate with Jean. A close friend of the family, and therefore of our dog, she understood.

'I'll be thinking of him tomorrow, Phoebity Phawb,' said

Jean, working one of her many affectionate variations on her goddaughter's name. 'Get some sleep.'

As it happened, that was a whole lot easier said than done. Thinking about where Como was and what he was facing the next day, we all had trouble settling down. Phoebe came into our room sometime after midnight and said she couldn't sleep without Como at the end of her bed. Sally suggested she put Dakta, her prized stuffed husky, in his place. That, or maybe it was just collective exhaustion, finally worked.

Wednesday was a school day for Sally and Phoebe. I begged off on a work assignment to camp out at the hospital. Manny and his crew still hadn't shown up by the time I was leaving the house around ten. I glanced in at the desolate, neatly swept shell of our bathroom and wished we had never decided to remodel. What was so terrible about our old brown and yellow tiles and bath-towel racks that sagged off the wall? I thought nostalgically about our semi-brittle shower curtain, which was probably wadded up inside the skip out front.

At noon, when I went out to move the car from its one-hour parking zone near the hospital and grab some lunch from the taco van parked across the street, there was still no news about Como. What little information I could glean when I approached the ship-hull front desk was all of the wait-and-see variety. Only by pretending to read some notices tacked to a wall, while actually listening in on staff chatter nearby, did I gather that Dr Watt was performing some complicated emergency surgery. Our dog getting run over and breaking his pelvis in three places didn't count as an emergency? I wanted to ask, once again restraining myself. Medical settings of any kind tend to make me simultaneously resentful and grateful for any attention I get, a trait I think I inherited from both my parents. It was only because I'd been so batty after Como's accident that I'd managed to assert myself with the doctors at our vet's surgery the day before. Now that I was fully dressed and had stopped bleeding, my normal hospital intimidation mode had resumed.

Sally showed up around two. Several minutes later, as if summoned from his emergency duties by her arrival, Dr Watt came out to give us what sounded like an ominous report. Just before they were ready to put Como out, pre-op X-rays showed some bleeding in his lungs. They'd put him on plasma and would have to wait until Friday or Saturday to do the surgery. 'Don't worry,' he told us. 'You can come back and visit him now if you like.'

Sally and I followed the doctor into what turned out to be a large, chaotically noisy room, with big tables in the middle and ranks of cages occupied by dogs, cats and other animals along the walls. There was plenty of barking, howling and mewling, with human voices raised to be heard above the racket. Como was in a cage at about eye level in one relatively placid corner. He was lying on his stomach when we approached and lifted his head at the sound of Sally's voice.

'Hi, Como pup,' Sally purred at him. 'How you doing in there? Hmm? What's going on?' His tail rustled once, and then he put his head back down and stared up at us vacantly.

'Oh, God, Steven,' Sally whispered to me, making sure that Como couldn't hear. 'He looks terrible.'

'You should have seen him when he first got hit,' I said. 'This is much better.' But not a whole lot better, I added to myself. If it's possible for an animal who is covered in white-and-cream-toned fur to lose colour, Como had. He looked pallid and listless.

It felt as if we were standing over Phoebe's bed when she ran a high temperature as an infant or was squalling in some toddler agony she couldn't or wouldn't describe to us. We were powerless, frightened, frustrated. Instinctively, we looked around for someone – anyone – to offer us a crumb of good news and pull us out of the doldrums. Two staff members were attending to a greyhound stretched out on one of the tables. Everyone else was busy with other animals, lab samples, or supplies.

'We should go,' I said after another few minutes of trying to coax a response out of Como. 'He probably needs to rest.' I exchanged a doleful look with the greyhound on the way out.

We brought Phoebe back that night, but weren't allowed in to see Como. Another, unspecified emergency had closed down the room he was in to all visitors. Phoebe held it together while we waited around for an hour in the alcove, then started wailing in the car. She cried all the way home, refused ice cream and television, and eventually cried herself to sleep. Sally and I both tried to console her, but neither of us had much energy left to see ourselves, much less each other, through this.

Sally went to the hospital as soon as her classes were over on Thursday. Como's back end had been shaved that morning in preparation for his scheduled surgery the next day. Sally called to describe it to me. I couldn't quite picture the way he looked, nor could I tell if she was alarmed or amused by his appearance. It was probably a little of both. I stayed in my study working that morning, pointedly avoiding any contact with the workmen. I was afraid of what I might say to Manny or any of the others if they asked what had happened to the dog.

Sally was still at the hospital when I showed up. As soon as we saw Como together, we both started giggling. With the back half of him shaved down to his bare grey flesh and the furry front half and untouched tail looking luxuriant by comparison, he was comically imbalanced. Sally was calling him 'Frankenpup', as if he were the monster pet of Frankenstein. I thought he looked more like some mad Russian count who'd ventured out in the dead of winter with nothing on but a white fox coat pulled up around his neck. It helped that Como was in his liveliest spirits yet, standing up on his spindly back legs and even wagging his tail. We told each other we were laughing with him, not at him. I think we just needed to release some of the tension.

Dr Watt strolled over and stood beside us. 'He does have that "Tike me 'ome" look about him,' he said.

'If only we could,' I said. 'But he seems ready for his big day tomorrow.'

'That he does,' said the doctor. 'That he does.'

We saw Dr Watt one more time that day, when we brought Phoebe over for a final pre-op visit. Before we got in to see Como, our surgeon marched past the front desk and straight out the door with a full-grown Doberman pinscher tucked under his arm. The massive dog looked like a small pug or toy poodle in Dr Watt's casually jaw-dropping grasp.

'There he goes,' Phoebe said, 'the Aussie Muscle Man.' At that, Sally and I had our second big laugh of the day. It was a master coinage.

Como's good showing of the afternoon continued. Once again he stood up and wagged his tail. At one point he got so frisky I thought he might yank the IV line out of his front paw, now shaved to match his back paws. He also did a fair amount of melodramatic whining and had to be hand-fed from the container of boiled chicken we brought him from Gordo's. Phoebe did most of the feeding honours. As someone who's seen his share of hammy acting over the years, I'd have given Como four stars for his performance. We went home in high spirits. I chose a route this time that took us past the large Victorian buildings, some of them decked out in exuberant rainbow colour schemes, that line the Golden Gate Park Panhandle.

The phone call came at ten thirty the next morning. Someone at the hospital whose name I didn't catch and don't remember meeting said the surgery hadn't happened after all. 'Como wasn't handling the anaesthesia well, so Dr Watt decided it was best not to proceed. He said to let you know he'd call you himself later on today and talk more about it. He's performing another surgery at the moment, but wanted to let you know Como is fine. Como is fine now.' She said a few more things, answered what questions I managed to think of on the spot, and hung up.

The most telling word in that brief conversation was 'now' – 'Como is fine now.' It would be a while until we learned it, but before Como was fine, he was anything but. When our dog was knocked out and about to go under Dr Watt's knife on Friday morning, his lungs once again filled with blood. By then, setting his shattered pelvis was the last thing on anyone's mind. Back in some little operating room, Dr Watt and his assistants worked as quickly and efficiently as they could to clear Como's lungs. They had to keep him breathing even as his own blood tried to smother him.

Meanwhile, as Dr Watt knew, the longer the surgery was delayed, the harder it would be, as Como's muscles and nerves began to tighten around the broken pelvis and made a repair all the more precarious, even impossible. Time, even another few days, was the enemy.

But never mind that. Time was measured in seconds just then. His lungs were full of blood. Como was right there on the brink, as close to dying as he'd ever been.

CHAPTER FOURTEEN

The Magic Kingdom

Phoebe did a startling thing when I picked her up from school that Friday afternoon: she announced that she was going to Disneyland. This wasn't some out-of-the-blue scheme, exactly; the weekend bus excursion to southern California had been planned as a church youth group activity months before, and Phoebe had wavered back and forth about going. But no one had mentioned the trip since Como's accident. It certainly hadn't crossed my mind again, and if it had, I would have been willing to bet Phoebe wouldn't opt to leave town with her dog facing surgery.

Not for the first time (or the last), I underestimated our daughter's instincts. Faced with the prospect of waiting around for untold hours on those striped couches at the hospital, knowing there was nothing she could do for Como anyway as he went through the operation, and placing her full trust in the Aussie Muscle Man's formidable hands, she realized the smartest, sanest thing to do was spend seven hours on an overnight bus ride with her friends; devote all day Saturday to the Matterhorn Bobsleds, Big Thunder Mountain Railroad and Pirates of the Caribbean; then return home, exhausted, on another overnight bus.

Disneyland may no longer have been the shining paradise it was to Phoebe when Sally and I first took her there for her sixth birthday. But given the circumstances, she knew it was the best, maybe the only, place to be for the next few days. If Como made it through the surgery, Disneyland would have been a kind of charmed talisman. If he didn't, she would have tucked herself away, temporarily shielded from any painful news, in Fantasyland. Sally and I gave her our blessings and dropped her off in front of the church after dinner.

Unable to connect with Dr Watt after his morning call about postponing the surgery, we drove straight from church to the hospital. The Muscle Man was off duty for once, and the place was frantically busy in his absence. Apparently twenty-four-hour vet hospitals, like human A&E departments, heat up on weekend nights. Do animals also kick back and get wild and crazy when Friday rolls around? I wondered. Just as Phoebe seemed to have anticipated, we spent the better part of an hour waiting for even a scrap of information or a chance to go back and visit Como. When we did, we found him fitted with a white plastic cone around his neck. A young woman informed us he had been chewing on his IV line. Now his sci-fi Frankenpup look was complete.

'Co-*MO*,' Sally said, stretching out his name in an affectionate scold, before slipping him a hunk of chicken from a container she had squirrelled away in her bag.

The dog resumed his confusing behaviour of alternately wagging his tail and whimpering. Sally didn't seem to mind, but it was beginning to get to me. Several hospital staffers had told us he only did that when we were around. They also told us he didn't eat enough unless we, specifically Sally and Phoebe, hand-fed him. So there we were, trapped in some strange but crucially nourishing psychodrama with him. Sally and I hung out near his cage until it was clear, from the pointed looks coming our way, that we had outstayed our welcome amid all the other animals that needed attention.

We spent the weekend in a state of suspended animation, fixing and eating our meals, going to the gym, waiting in vain for Phoebe to check in from Disneyland, half listening to each other, and paying our chicken-enhanced social calls on Como. After one of our trips to the hospital, we stopped by the SPCA a few blocks away. Como had been scheduled to begin an agility class in another week, his first post-graduate course since Basic Training over a year before. The receptionist was gracious and understanding when we explained the circumstances and credited a full refund of the deposit back to our beleaguered MasterCard.

'I hope it all turns out for the best,' she said, looking a little doubtful about it.

'We do, too,' said Sally, who suggested on the way back to the car that we go out for a nice dinner somewhere. 'I sort of need a break from all this.'

Finding a table in restaurant-crazed San Francisco on a Saturday night can be a feat, and sometimes all but impossible at the last minute. But luck was with us that night. We called a Basque place we like; they'd just had a cancellation. Half an hour later we were ordering. We tried to behave as if this were one of those romantically scripted married-couple dates, with our daughter out of town and even no dog to walk when we got home. But we couldn't stop fretting about Como, comparing notes about our impressions of him and our predictions about the timing and length of the surgery. When we finally gave that up, we started speculating on whether Phoebe was still in Frontierland or Tomorrowland or back on the bus yet. We passed on dessert, left some wine in our glasses, asked for the bill, and drove back to the hospital to check on Como one last time. As if to confirm our worries, he looked terrible – listless and woebegone inside his big plastic ice-cream-cone helmet. Sally and I had trouble getting to sleep.

Early Sunday morning I drove through a rainy and deserted Golden Gate Park to the church. Sleepy-looking parents, mostly fathers, were holding cardboard cups of coffee and waiting for the bus in a basement meeting room. It was a congenial group, allied by the odd duty of picking up adolescent children after an all-night bus ride. I smiled along gamely, but couldn't get into the spirit. Five days after the accident, the gloom and foreboding I felt followed me around like a shadow.

Phoebe looked rejuvenated when she got off the bus and slung her backpack into the boot. She was full of stories about the 'awesome' rides, her weekend junk-food consumption and the complex social interactions of the other kids. Getting virtually no sleep for thirty-six hours seemed to have been just the thing she needed. She asked a few questions about Como, seemed satisfied by my minimal information, and went straight to bed when we got home. We all decided to take a day off from visiting Como, to preserve our sanity, if nothing else. At dinner that night we joined hands to send him our strongest healing prayers for Monday's surgery.

Sally and I had decided not to tell Phoebe about Dr Watt's warnings that the operation had to happen very soon if Como was going to have any hope of a repaired pelvis and normal mobility. If his lungs filled up with blood again and he couldn't have the surgery and couldn't walk . . . Sally and I hadn't even talked about that. We didn't have to. We knew it meant he would have to be put down. Such a dreadful phrase, part benign euphemism and part unvarnished reality. A 'put-down' was an insult, after all, in this case the ultimate one.

Manny and his crew showed up first thing Monday morning. I finally stopped avoiding them and filled them in on what had happened to Como. Once he could see I wasn't going to try to hold him responsible for the dog getting loose and then run over, Manny acted officially, politely concerned. 'I'm sure he'll be fine,' the foreman said, in such a bland, empty way that I wanted to tell him I'd changed my mind and decided to take up the matter of his negligence with the contractor. But I let it go; I was on my way to the hospital to wait out Como's scheduled operation. Julio, who had overheard the exchange, followed me out to the street.

'Mister,' he said, with a genuine, searching look that made his forgetting my last name not matter. 'So sorry about your dog. I know, too. My son, Angelo, he see our dog get hit by a car in the street, by our house. I run out to get him. Too late. He die in my arms.'

I stood there dumbly for a moment, too stunned to respond. I felt awful for Julio and his little boy and wondered how old Angelo was when he had to watch his dog die. I felt a stab of guilt that Como had lived and that his dog hadn't. Then – and this made me glance away before I looked back at Julio's wide brown eyes – I saw that I should have let him jump down from the skip and grab Como when he got loose. He would have caught him; I had no doubt of it. He would have done what he couldn't with his own dog.

'Julio, that's terrible,' I finally managed to say. 'I'm really sorry to hear that. How's your son doing?' He hadn't told me when this happened. Very recently? A month ago? A year or more?

Julio shrugged and looked over his shoulder at the house. It was time to get back to work. Things happen. Dogs die – and sometimes they don't, or at least not right away. People get over it. Or anyway, they keep going. Those were the thoughts that came along with me, swirling and slowly dissipating, like a vapour, as I started the car and drove over Twin Peaks and down through the Castro and the Mission on the way to the hospital. The striped couches were empty when I arrived. I let the people at the front desk know I was there for Como's surgery, and sat down to wait.

As with many things that seem like they will never arrive – Christmas when you're a child, turning eighteen or twenty-one, getting married and having a child – the dog's operation was suddenly, abruptly over. One minute I was paging through a back issue of *Cat Fancy*, and the next Dr Watt was looming over me and telling me everything had gone smoothly.

'No problem with the anaesthetic. No blood in the lungs this time. No problem with the pelvis. The brikes were nice and clean, set with pins and screws. Looks very solid.'

All this telegraphic good news. I wanted him to keep going before he got to the 'buts'. As it turned out, there were only two stipulations our Aussie surgeon had to offer. First, he said that Como would be feeling some 'pine' for a while; painkillers would help with that. Then he informed me the dog would have to be 'immobilized' for the next four to six weeks while the fractures healed.

'You'll 'ave to kaij him to make sure he doesn't run or joomp or anything like that. It's very, very important.'

I'd never had any trouble understanding Dr Watt. In fact I quite enjoyed the cadence of his accent and the jaunty tilt it gave certain words. But this time my comprehension came up short.

'Kaij?' I repeated, then immediately realized why it hadn't registered. *Cage*, given our dog's history, was not a word I was eager to hear in connection with Como. 'Oh, yes, of course,' I muttered. 'We'll do that for sure.' I couldn't possibly tell Dr Watt that there wasn't a cage this side of Alcatraz that could hold our pet. He'd just snatched Como back from the brink, and he was making an altogether reasonable request that was clearly in the interests of the dog's recovery and long-term health. And besides, Como had just been through some pretty heavy-duty surgery. That ought to be enough, I hoped, to tamp down his aversion to being locked up. I thanked Dr Watt profusely for all he had done and told him we'd all be back to visit the patient later, when the anaesthetic had worn off.

I greeted Sally with the good news when she got home from school. She looked more relieved than happy. 'I thought he was going to die on the table,' she said.

'Me too,' I confessed, not realizing until I said it how well I'd kept that fear from rising to the surface. Sometimes the vein of fatalism Sally inherited from her family is cleansing. We clung to each other in a short, tight hug. When we pulled back, I told her about the four to six weeks Como would have to spend in a cage.

'You're kidding,' she said.

'The Muscle Man's orders,' I said. 'I'm not about to cross him.'

'We'd better get on it,' she agreed. 'When did they say he might come home?'

'I forgot to ask. Maybe we'll find out when we go and see him tonight. But yes, we have to be ready.'

Recalling the pet store manager with the dyed black hair and his snide remarks about Como's teeth when we tried to return the ruined plastic crate, I suggested we look somewhere else first. We drove to a place at the Stonestown mall, which turned out to have a full selection of wire cages, all of them on offer without any attitude from the staff. We had a reasonably sized one picked out, with a plan to pad it with blankets and towels.

'What about this one?' Sally said, as I was pulling out my credit card to pay for the one we'd already chosen. She had her hand on a monster cage that came up above her waist and was long and wide enough to house a good-size ape along with half the dogs on our street.

'We've stayed in smaller hotel rooms,' I said. 'What are you thinking?'

'I'm thinking how much Como *hates* cages,' she said. 'We have to make this as easy on him as we can. The bigger the better.'

I put up a mild protest, pointing out that the idea was to restrict his movements, not give him the run of a spacious suite. But, seeing that Sally had made up her mind, I relented. It took two assistants twenty minutes to collapse the giant structure into a pile of wire walls. Even at that we had to leave our Honda's hatchback open to haul the thing home. We reassembled the cage in our bedroom, figuring that Como might not find confinement so terrible if he knew we were nearby. Phoebe's room, which has a low, sloping ceiling, was too small to accommodate the thing.

Our daughter was waiting on the pavement in front of her school that afternoon right after the last bell. When we gave her the thumbs-up sign for Como's successful surgery, she wanted to go straight to the hospital. 'Not till tonight,' I told her, repeating the Muscle Man's recuperation orders and telling her about the cage. 'Or "kaij", as he says.'

'Dad, don't make fun of him. That's the way Australians talk. I like it.'

'I do, too,' I said. 'Dr Watt's the hero of the day. Of the year.'

'He's mine,' she replied, sounding shyly brave about saying it out loud.

'Mine, too,' said Sally. We celebrated with snacks all round and a Diet Pepsi refill for me at the Chevron station.

After dinner we picked up Phoebe's friend Jeanne to pay our first post-surgical visit to Como. He was in amazingly good spirits, cone and all, and glad to see us. It was just as well that his view of his shaved back end was blocked. With an ugly-looking incision held shut by surgical staples and extensive purple bruising in the area, he looked a whole lot more brutalized than he had right after the SUV hit him.

Phoebe and Jeanne glanced briefly at the damage and concentrated instead on wriggling their fingers through the openings of the cage and petting Como's cone-framed face. He'd had enough of it after a few minutes and started in on his hospital-issue whimpering. With Dr Watt off for the night, we asked around to see if anyone else knew when Como might come home.

'The Aussie Muscle Man's probably out celebrating,' said Phoebe, as we made our way back to the front desk. 'He saved a life today. Maybe more than one.'

'Is he married?' Jeanne wanted to know, at which point the girls began whispering to each other.

No one could tell us about Como's discharge plans. But there was another bill for us to pay, while we were there. I was trying not to add up the charges as they mounted.

🐾

The house was quiet the next morning. Manny and the builders were off, waiting for a noon inspection before they could proceed with the next phase of work on the bathroom. I stood looking at the bare studs and wiring and wondered how we'd ever pay off this loan and the dog's medical expenses as well. I'd just sat down at my desk to get some work done when Dr Watt called to say Como would be released late that afternoon.

'Today?' I marvelled, thinking about the staples and bruises.

'He's doin' groit,' the doctor insisted. 'And he'll do even better when he's back at 'ome.' He reminded me about the importance of keeping Como inactive while his remade pelvic bones set. 'They'll be stronger than ever,' he said, 'but only if he goes noice'n easy on 'em.'

I wanted to keep Dr Watt on the phone, thinking that some of his miracle touch might seep through the line and clinch a swift recovery for Como. But our doc was always brisk and businesslike. More operations to do, more Dobermans to pluck up one-handed. I told him we'd be there before five.

Como was in a sorry state at discharge time. The operation, not to mention spending six days cooped up in a tiny cage with an IV line in his paw, had left him drained. As for the pain medications he was still taking, they were draining him from the far end. We had to keep a towel pressed under his tail to prevent him from leaking on the floor. The diarrhoea could continue for another day or so, one of the nurses told us as she walked us out to the front, where I handed over my credit card once again. Phoebe was carrying the dog and doing her best to keep his makeshift nappy in place. Como did some first-class whining on the ride home.

Even with a thick carpet of blankets, towels and an old quilt we retrieved from the basement, the cage looked dangerously big to me when Como went inside. Phoebe crawled in after him to help settle him down. The dog could barely stand up, but that didn't stop him from trying. He wobbled around, falling to one side and then the other in the hills and folds of the blankets. It made us nervous, but it was also pretty comical to watch. He was like an actor playing a drunk scene.

'See if he'll lie down,' Sally said, watching from the bed and stifling a laugh.

'It's not funny, Mom,' Phoebe snapped. 'He's got to be really, really careful, or his bones will break all over again.' Sally and I shot a mock-chastened look at each other.

Our vigilant daughter stayed inside the cage for the better part of an hour, nestling and snuggling with Como as he plopped down and then almost immediately grew restless. It must have been very hard for him, the poor half-shaved guy, to get comfortable. Eventually Phoebe was going to have to come out and go to bed, but we let her stay in there as long as we could. Around nine, Sally said she was going to take Como out-side to do what he needed to. That involved using a towel as a sling around his belly to keep the weight off his back legs.

'He did it!' Sally exulted when she carried the dog back upstairs. 'He peed!' It reminded me of the day Phoebe came home from the hospital right after she was born, and what a victory it was to change her first few nappies. Some of our proudest triumphs come in our humbler moments.

It was a rough night. Como turned in a sustained performance of operatic wailing, huffy whimpers and some distressingly human-sounding sobs. For the first few hours, Sally and I took turns getting up to murmur soothing nonsense at him and readjust the towels and blankets in his cage. Eventually, when his vocal concert grew more strenuous, I got Como out and held him in my lap in the rocking chair. It really was a throwback to our sleep-deprived nights with a newborn. Sally slept for a while. Then the silence got to her as much as the whimpering had.

'My turn,' she said, wobbling over to the rocking chair and sending me back to bed. We were like bleary night watchmen on a rotating shift.

When the sun rose and we finally gave up, Sally figured we'd slept about three hours total. I thought it was more like forty-five minutes. She and Phoebe got up and dressed for school while Como, wrung out from his night's exertion, finally slept, and I went back to bed to stare at the ceiling. Cleared by the inspector to resume work, Manny and the gang arrived a little after eight, radio blaring and nail guns firing away. It felt as if they were shooting tiny pointed slugs directly into my skull.

My editor, who had recently acquired a demandingly athletic Australian shepherd puppy and was newly attuned to all things dog-related, let me off the hook for an assignment. 'Take as much time as you need,' he said, as if we'd had a death in the family. I shamelessly played Como's needs for all they were worth, hoping I could get some more sleep out of the deal. Unfortunately, my editor couldn't do anything about the banging and clatter in the bathroom; going back to bed was out of the question. I spent the morning carrying Como around the house in a towel. I tried to think of it as quality time for the two of us.

When Sally got home, she looked grim. On top of teaching after a night of very little sleep and then a 'mindless meeting' she'd had to attend, she was coming down with a cold. 'I *can't* have another night like that,' she said, pacing around the kitchen while more or less ignoring the dog in my arms. She didn't seem to notice, or care, that Como's previously limp tail had sprung to life and started switching as soon as she walked in the door.

'Maybe Phoebe could get in the cage and sleep with him tonight,' I suggested. 'That would probably keep him still. And she might even like it. It would be like a camp-out.'

'I'm not putting my daughter in a cage!' Sally cried, at a near screech. I motioned for her to keep her voice down, sensing that the bathroom workmen might be overhearing us. Sally, audible to a fault for once, was too desperate to mind. 'Look,' she said, 'we're just letting him manipulate us. You heard what they said at the hospital about how he never whined unless we were there. I say we go completely the other direction. Put the cage downstairs and make him figure it out himself. It's the only way we're going to get through this. That *he's* going to get through this,' she corrected herself.

But she really did mean how all of us were going to manage. Terrible as the accident and the scary delays before the surgery had been, the prospect of weeks and weeks of sleepless nights and days spent keeping the dog from doing something to re-injure himself did seem very daunting. Como's recuperation loomed as a threat to our collective sanity. Even so, I was startled to hear Sally take such a hard line, after all the anguish and tenderness she'd expended on Como.

'Well, I guess we could try that,' I said tentatively. 'But what about him bouncing around in there and breaking his pelvis again?'

'Already thought of that,' she said, leading the way upstairs to the big wicker linen basket at the foot of our bed. Every blanket and quilt that we owned, aside from the ones on our bed and Phoebe's, were soon piled on the floor.

'Okay,' I said, and began breaking down the cage to transport it downstairs. I decided not to mention that the dog's diarrhoea hadn't fully cleared up yet. If we ended up having to replace our entire stock of bedding, I could see that Sally would have gladly made that trade for a decent night's sleep.

We all hung out in the living room after dinner, with Como roaming around inside his well-upholstered lair and the rest of us reading and chatting as if nothing unusual were afoot. Sally and Phoebe took the dog out for his last sling-assisted visit to the garden and returned him to the cage. Then, agreeing not to establish eye contact with him, the three of us went upstairs. I turned on some music in the bedroom to continue the show of normality (and mask any potentially unsettling noises from below). Como waited until all the lights in the house were off before he got to work.

The first things we heard were a few intermittent light thuds. I tried to give our invalid the benefit of the doubt, thinking he was just trying to get comfortable against one side of the cage and then another. But those relatively mild bumps soon gave way to a more sustained and purposeful wrenching, a groaning sound of metal straining to do something it didn't want to do. It went on for quite a while, followed by a brief intermission, and started up again.

Sally and I were making a point of not acknowledging the racket. She was trying to prove that her plan to ignore him would work, and I was going along with her. At one point I thought she might have actually fallen asleep. But when I whispered her name, she replied immediately.

'What?' she said, her voice flattened out in defeat. 'What do you want me to say?'

'Nothing,' I assured her. 'I'll go and check on him.'

When I did, Como was staring at me through the wires of his hut. 'What?' I said to him, adopting Sally's exhausted tone. 'Lie down. Go to sleep.' This all felt very familiar. Sixteen months before, I'd stood down here and attempted to talk our new dog out of thrashing around inside his plastic crate. That was before we knew he could gnaw his way out of it, and before he'd escaped from the house and escaped again and run under the wheels of an SUV. I trudged back upstairs, knowing the night was probably young.

And so it was. When Como altered his strategy and began to do something else that made the cage rock and shudder and thump the floor, Sally and I both got out of bed. I followed her down to the living room, where we caught him in the act. He was gripping a spot near the cage's lower door hinge with his teeth and yanking as hard as he could. His mouth was open so wide to do it that he must not have seen us come down. From the streetlight coming in through the windows, we could see his jaws working and the dark, determined pit of his throat. The blankets and quilts were heaped up against one edge of the cage, and the wire floor laid bare where he stood.

'Como. Stop,' Sally said in a hoarse whisper, trying not to wake Phoebe. 'Stop that right now.' It was more a plea than a command. We both knew he wouldn't stop, couldn't stop. All he knew was that he was trapped inside something, and that he had to get out.

'I'll call the hospital and see if they have any ideas,' I said. Sally nodded and went to get Como out of the cage. Before I could dial, she called me back to see something. The area around the hinge had been bent and twisted as if someone pretty strong had done it with pliers. Two of the wire struts were nearly chewed through. That black-haired store manager was right: Como's teeth were off the charts. Still, this was a shocker, and for an instant I felt something hollow out in my stomach. But I also felt a small, shivery thrill. This dog was too strong, too driven, too manically determined not to survive. It shouldn't have been a surprise, but Como wasn't going to follow any conventional course of recuperation.

'I guess he's not going to stay in there,' I said.

'No, I guess not,' Sally said. I went back to the phone.

The all-nighters at the hospital told us to bring him in and they would see what they could do. We woke up Phoebe so she wouldn't be alone in the house; still semi-asleep, she rode with her dog in the backseat. Como was given half a tranquillizer at the hospital and the other half plus a few extras to take home. We were told to give him the other half of the knockout drug 'only if he's really, really wired. These things are pretty potent.'

Neither half made a dent. When we finally got back to bed, a little after two a.m., Como was wide awake. 'Settle down,' Sally said, stroking the dog's unshaved head and neck. 'Settle down now. It's time to sleep.' And then to me, stretched out on the other side of him, she offered a weary 'G'night.'

Como had pulled off an impressive double feat. I had to hand it to him. Not only had he found a way out of the hated cage downstairs, he had also broken down our ironclad rule and wormed his way into our bed for the night. All in all, I thought, this was his most impressive escape yet. Instead of leading me around the neighbourhood or darting disastrously into traffic, he'd worn us down to the point of total surrender. The warmest, cosiest spot in the house was his, even if it did mean sleeping next to me. With a deep, snuffling sigh, Como nestled his head down in the covers and closed his eyes.

CHAPTER FIFTEEN

Cage-Free

Early the next morning, Como and I were back in Dr
Watt's office. Most of his appointments are scheduled
days if not weeks ahead, but between our midnight
visit for drugs the night before and my wheedling on the phone,
the receptionist gave in. 'Can you be here in half an hour?' she
said. 'That's his only opening.'

'We'll be there,' I said, and gathered up Como to go. His fragile pelvis did provide one advantage: he could make only half-
hearted attempts to evade me.

The Muscle Man perched on the edge of his desk and listened to my account of our post-surgical trials. I sat in a chair
with the dog in my lap. When I got to the attack on the cage
bars, Dr Watt came over and popped open Como's mouth with
his fingers. He didn't say anything, but I did see his eyebrows
briefly crest. Then he went back to his desk. When I was done
with my story, the doctor plucked a towel from a pile behind
him and spread it out on the floor.

'Go ahead and put 'im down. Let's 'ave a look.'

I gingerly placed Como on the centre of the towel. He stood
still and warily stiff-legged at first, as if the towel might be a

magic carpet that was about to lift off and sail away. But then he started wobbling around. When he ventured off the towel, his back legs gave way and dropped him to the floor. He got up again and went weaving across the room.

'Is this okay for him to do?' I asked. 'I mean, if he's supposed to be immobilized.'

Dr Watt was busy studying Como's movements and didn't reply right away. He watched a while longer, then reached down to scoop the dog up and examine his surgical handiwork up close. It was hard not to wince as he flexed Como's back legs wide open, scissored them together and probed the stapled incision with his thumb. The doctor stood up and gave me a hard look that made me feel as if I were being examined, too.

'It's not recommended,' he told me, 'but let's give it a try without the kaij. The mine thing is no sudden movements, no joomping up on the furniture, no stairs. Everything nice and slow. One step at a time.'

I let out a big sigh and said we'd do our best. Then, surprisingly, Dr Watt sat back down, his expression softening, and said he had a favour to ask: would we mind if he discussed Como's surgery at an upcoming veterinary conference? He wanted to use some X-rays and photographs and apparently needed our consent.

'Of course,' I said. 'Use anything you like. But I'm curious: what's so special about this case?'

His answer was both vague and too technical for me to grasp. But when Dr Watt told me things were 'touch'n'go there for a bit', he more or less confirmed what we'd already thought. Como, after his lungs filled up twice with blood, had been snatched from the brink. He had come back to life, back to us.

I felt a pulse of gratitude for that, and with it, a new sense of responsibility for this rescued life.

The Muscle Man had one last piece of advice before we left. 'That back side's pretty bare. You might want to find a sweater to keep him warm.' I promised to do it and carried Como back to the car. We got home in time to watch the second-term inauguration of George W. Bush. Some of it I actually heard, whenever breaks in the bathroom racket permitted. Como dozed through it all in my lap.

The patient had his first get-well visitors that afternoon, when his poodle pal Lizzy and her family stopped by with a card and a bouquet of helium balloons. Phoebe had to hold on tight to Como, who was dying to get down on the floor and take some high-speed laps with Lizzy. From a dog's point of view, we must have seemed like neurotically overprotective parents. Why couldn't we just let him run free?

The bigger question was how to prevent him from indulging in dangerous behaviours when he wasn't secured in someone's lap. After storing the now very-used cage in the garage, I retrieved the baby gates, which had failed us completely when we first brought Como home from the shelter, and used them to block off the stairs. Both bedroom doors were to be kept shut at all times. We turned the dining room chairs upside down on the living room sofa and inverted the kitchen chairs on the banquette to prevent 'joomping' up on any inviting soft surfaces. With all that added to the bathroom chaos, the house looked as if we were getting ready either to exterminate pests, shampoo the carpets, or move out.

Sally's dog-loving friend Denise solved the sleeping dilemma. Put Phoebe's mattress on the floor and push it up against the wall, she suggested. 'If he sleeps with you two, he might try to get down or back up in the night. This way he's at ground level.' It worked perfectly, with the added bonus of putting Phoebe in charge of the dog's well-being for the night. She took her duties seriously, constructing a little fort in her covers and taking on the manner of a drill sergeant as she got Como settled in. 'Get in here now. Right away,' she'd command. 'That's it. Lights out.' When Sally and I came in to wish them good night, the dog would look up at us from the little enclosure Phoebe made with her knees pushed up against the wall at one end and her head and arms at the other. This was one place where Como didn't seem to mind being trapped.

Sally brought a dog sweater home the next afternoon, a stylish black cable-knit that covered Como's shaved half and came up high on his neck. When she pulled it on him the first time, his head popped through with a wild-haired, wind-swirled look. It was a ludicrous, delightful sight.

'Einstein!' Sally declared with a hoot. She was right. The combination of Como's dishevelled white head and a crewneck sweater conjured photographs of the famous physicist. It also clinched a new nickname. 'Frankenpup' had become 'Einstein', our own private relativity theorist.

'We ought to get him panting,' I said. 'Remember that shot of Einstein with his tongue hanging out?'

'I do. Yes.'

We were both enjoying ourselves, with Como as the unwitting butt of the joke. His ears perked up quizzically, which got us roaring. It was about time we had a few laughs; they'd been few and far between since the accident.

'Wait till Phoebe sees,' said Sally.

'Do you think she even knows who Einstein is?' I asked.

Our daughter's eighth-grade maths was already beyond us, but there was still so very much for Phoebe to learn. It was pleasing to think of all the classes and school years to come, all the growing up that was ahead of her. I put a hand on Como's head and ruffled up his fur some more, to enhance his mad-scientist look. Sally grabbed her camera and snapped a few pictures.

None of us were laughing later that night, when we noticed some bleeding around Como's incision. It looked as if one or more of the staples had pulled loose. Sally called the hospital and had to wait for someone to come on the line. The blood on her dog's back was beginning to upset Phoebe and make Sally and me a little nervous as well. Sally was finally told to apply some light pressure and make sure the dog didn't bite at the staples. That meant putting him back in the cone they'd sent home with him. If the bleeding didn't stop, Sally reported after hanging up the phone, we should bring the dog in to be seen. Phoebe and Como's sleepover was a downer that night. He was an unhappy Einstein in his inside-out dunce cap, and she had trouble getting comfortable herself with a big piece of plastic in the bed.

🐾

Como made slow but steady progress in the days and weeks ahead. In some ways we viewed it from a no-news-is-good-news perspective. As long as he didn't do anything to rebreak his pelvis – like, say, attempting to vault over one of the stair gates or springing loose and running under another SUV – we were doing well. But there were also some clearly positive improvements in his condition.

A week or so into Como's recuperation, we no longer had to support him with a sling when he went outside for his constitutionals. True, he sometimes toppled over when he began taking three-point stances on his own, but he's a small dog and doesn't have far to fall from a standing position. Once he started seeming more confident, we gradually stretched out the distance and duration of his walks. The first time Sally and I got him all the way to the corner of Twelfth and Lawton, where he peed without collapsing, we both responded with cheers and applause. A woman pushing a baby buggy up the hill looked alarmed and took a wide turn around us on the pavement.

'Do you think we've gone round the bend?' I asked Sally.

'No question about it,' she said. 'We have a round-the-bend kind of dog.'

It helped our spirits that the weather was getting warmer and the camellias and rhododendrons in the garden were starting to show their first blooms. A bathroom that was beginning to look like a bathroom contributed as well to the upbeat mood. By early February the walls and a shiny new bathtub were in place and the new cabinets installed. For the first time I began to think that we might wind up feeling all right about a home improvement project that had, however indirectly, nearly finished off our dog. Not that we were getting too cocky about anything. We still locked Como in our bedroom whenever we left the house, with a big hand-written sign taped to the door: DOG INSIDE. DO NOT OPEN. Happily, Como's carpet-shredding and door-clawing days seemed to be behind him.

Dr Watt was still seeing the dog for regular checkups. At one of them, the surgeon showed up with a broken arm. The cast, somehow, made him seem more formidable than ever, with a bulkier-than-ever Popeye forearm. Our Aussie Muscle Man was in a chatty mood, discussing several surgeries he had coming up in the next few days.

'You can operate with that?' I asked, nodding at the cast.

He modestly declined to answer, which only affirmed my sense of his superhuman powers. He surely meant that he'd be supervising the surgeries and of course wouldn't attempt anything he couldn't handle. But I couldn't help seeing him as a doctor who could literally perform a complex operation one-handed.

Dr Watt continued to be positive about the progress of Como's healing. But he also made sure I understood some of the long-term possibilities. Watching Como amble around his office, he pointed out the way the dog favoured his back right leg. That could indicate some permanent nerve damage, he explained. It also might lead to arthritis as the dog aged. Dr Watt had mentioned these things before, but they'd never quite sunk in. For a long time we were all fixated on whether Como would live or walk again. I thanked him and told him I hoped his own healing went well.

'What a nuisance,' he said, giving his cast a thump with his free hand. For a moment I thought he might karate-chop the thing off right there in front of me.

Before we left, it registered on me that Como never flinched or shied away when the doctor touched him, picked him up, or poked at him. I wouldn't have said that Como felt warmly towards his doctor, in the way he did toward Sally and Phoebe or some other people he had come to greet with an eagerly wagging tail and playful stance – Phoebe's friends Jeanne and Marlena and Hallie; Lizzy's 'mother', Margene; even our expatriate friend Leana, who made infrequent visits from her home in Nicaragua and always got an ecstatic reception from the dog when she arrived. Dr Watt, after all, was a member of Como's less preferred gender, and a decidedly male male at that. Still,

Como had shown none of the terrorized avoidance behaviour with the Muscle Man that he had with me and with most other men he encountered. That, it seemed to me, was surprising, illogical, and, as Phoebe would say, 'totally weird'.

As far as Como knew, Dr Watt was the man who'd kept him caged up for six days, knocked him out with drugs more than once, splayed him out on an operating table, and finally sliced him open to rewire his skeleton with metal pins and screws. He'd caused him all kinds of pain – 'pine', in Muscle Man parlance. Why didn't Como despise this big burly guy with the green scrubs and peculiar accent and want nothing to do with him?

Walking Como back to the car, I recalled the radio interview with author Temple Grandin I'd heard on the day of the accident. Animals don't necessarily form the same chain of cause-and-effect associations around traumatic events that people do, Grandin had said. So just as Como may have 'blamed' the pavement or the SUV's tyre instead of me for getting run over, he could have held his IV line or the smell of some other dog responsible for the suffering he'd endured in the hospital.

If that was true, if Dr Watt was off Como's bad-guy hook for the ordeal of the operation, maybe there was a way for Como and me to move beyond our thorny past and find some common new ground. It was already a blessing that he didn't seem to link me to the accident. Our dealings with each other certainly hadn't got any worse in the past month. In some ways, they had even improved. While it may well have had something to do with his own impaired mobility, Como was more willing to let me approach and handle him now, to put him on the leash, to pick him up and carry him around, to hold him in my lap and lace my fingers through his wild hair. Nurturing is not a notable strength of mine: I'm neither particularly patient nor intuitive about their needs when Sally or Phoebe is sick, and the empathy I'd shown for my ageing parents over the years tended to be more dutiful than deeply engaged.

But now, perhaps, in the gradually calming wake of that turbulent morning when Como slipped out of the house and I came charging after him in my bathrobe and bare feet, I was uncovering some new aspect of myself, some capacity to be more responsive and fully present for another being. I reached down to gather up his leash and lift Como onto the passenger seat. All this had come over me unexpectedly, after a routine trip to the vet, and it was a lot to think about. As I drove up Sixteenth Street towards Market, swerving around Muni buses and those boxy brown UPS trucks, one of them double-parked on every block, it seemed, my mind shuttled from Phoebe's full-on love for Como to Julio and his son watching their dog get run over and killed. I thought about the two dogs my sister had had – Ralph and Sebby – and how wrenching it was for her when Ralph died prematurely and Sebby entered his excruciatingly prolonged old age.

Out of nowhere, I remembered a tiny, wirehaired dog, brown and white and yipping madly, who rushed down a pavement one afternoon when I was ten. The surprise of it panicked me, and I ran all the way home, my lunch box banging against my leg and my school books and three-ring binder nearly slipping from my arm. I was so scared by then – my startled overreaction scared me more than the dog had – I don't think I would have stopped to pick up anything I dropped. I ran straight upstairs, flung myself onto my bed and sobbed uncontrollably. I'd terrified myself, but I also felt ashamed at my reaction to a small, probably harmless dog who was only protecting his turf and saw me as a threat. It took my mother a long time to calm me down (she finally managed by cajoling me downstairs for a TV dinner). I couldn't tell her or anyone else what had happened, since I didn't understand it myself. I loved dogs. I wanted a dog. But I was also frightened by their speed and sound, by their ropy muscles and sharp teeth, by the sheer animal energy packed into their nimble, charging forms.

I reached over to switch on the radio and glanced down at Como on the seat beside me. He was sitting in a characteristic off-kilter way of his that always amuses me, his rear end pitched off to one side and both back legs carelessly flung out like paddles in the opposite direction. His supporting front legs, meanwhile, were straight and held close together. The total effect was simultaneously slovenly (the slouchy rear end and back-leg paddles) and decorously polite (the prim front paws). The half-shaved look only heightened the comic effect.

'So which way is it, Como?' I asked him. 'At ease or at attention?' His ears flipped up at the sound of his name, then rotated back and flattened out when a Mozart string quartet poured out of the speakers. I had the volume up too loud. 'Sorry about that,' I said, turning it down. 'You'd probably like something else anyway. A little jazz? Sports talk? Easy listening? That's kind of an easy-listening pose you've got going there.'

One of the underrated adult pleasures of having a dog, as I'd come to appreciate, was the cover it gives you for talking freely and fluidly to yourself. Having another body around, especially one who reacts to the sound of your voice – and won't take you on about the content – was far more appealing and comforting than I'd expected. When Como and I were home alone, which was often the case for long stretches during the weekdays, I'd sometimes keep up a pretty steady stream of banal narrative and unanswered questions with him. Did he think it was time to do the dishes? I'd wonder. And what about a couple of ginger snaps with my tea? Didn't that sound like a fine idea? And by the way, what the hell did that editor mean about a different ending for that Sunday piece I'd just submitted? Did anyone but us understand the concept, Como? Anyone but the two of us?

We passed the University of California medical complex on Parnassus and drifted down the hill towards our part of town. I stopped at the little grocery store on Kirkham, a block from where the accident had happened, and got a sandwich while Como waited in the car. When I returned, he'd coiled himself up and gone to sleep on the driver's seat. Shifting the sandwich bag to my other hand and reaching in my pocket for the keys, I didn't notice him there until I got the door open and almost sat down on him. Apparently, having claimed the seat, he had no intention of giving it up. For all the trips we'd taken in the car, this was a first.

A year or even six months before, it might have put me on guard. Was this another one of his tactics to challenge or defy me? I might have wondered. Was he making a point about my irrelevance? Was he, by refusing to move, denying that we existed on the same physical plane? Or could it be some sly cat-and-mouse game to lull me into carelessness so he could spring into action and escape through the open car door?

But now, as I nudged him on his hairless haunch and got him to shift over sleepily to the passenger side, those possibilities receded. Maybe my side was sunnier. Maybe it seemed softer and more inviting. Maybe he just liked being where I had been, drawn to whatever familiar human smell and warmth I'd left behind. 'Thanks, Como,' I said, drawing my seat belt across my chest. I put the sandwich on the backseat, out of his curious reach, and started the car. 'Let's go home now.'

🐾

Before dinner one Thursday evening in February, our neighbour Pam phoned and asked us to come and say good-bye that night. She and Cheryl were both big travellers, but this farewell wasn't for either of them. It was for Riley.

We'd known for several months that the younger of our next-door neighbours' two Welsh springer spaniels had been diagnosed with a brain tumour. For a long time that was easy to ignore or forget. With his big craggy head and glossy brown-and-white coat, his impulsive energy that could turn a routine walk into a championship-calibre tug-of-war, and an unquenchable enthusiasm for anyone who paid him attention or for anything even remotely edible, Riley seemed indestructible. I remember thinking, when I saw him out on the pavement one morning just after Como's accident, that if Riley had been hit by an SUV – or a petrol tanker, for that matter – he would have bounced up wagging his tail, eager for another playful knockdown.

For a while the symptoms of the tumour weren't apparent. Riley still ate as much and as fast as ever (Phoebe and I once timed his full-bowl start-to-finish mealtime at thirty-seven seconds), lunged down the steps for his walks, and let out his double bass barks that echoed off the houses across the street. But then he began to slow down. His trips in and out of the house grew more laboured. His tail didn't fan the air so rapidly. His expressions grew more plaintive than avid when a snack or a romp was in the offing. One day, and it seemed to come all of a sudden, we saw Cheryl gather Riley in her arms to carry him up steps he could no longer manage on his own. The end, when it came, came quickly. He would be at the vet's the next morning for a final injection.

Sally, Phoebe and I walked over to pay our last respects around eight. At first it seemed like a normal visit. Riley and his mother, Jessie, brayed when we rang the bell and met us with their customary happy writhing when we came inside. Almost immediately, as the dogs' own behaviour made clear, the rules of the game had changed. As Jessie hurried away to the kitchen, her claws briskly ticking, Riley slumped into a sitting position before sliding all the way to the floor in an awkward heap. Phoebe got down with him and wrapped her arms around the loose flesh of his neck.

'It's all right, Riley. We're here now, boy.'

Cheryl, who has a quick and sometimes lancing sense of humour, looked at Sally and me and blinked back her tears. 'I'll get Pam,' she said, and went upstairs. Sally and I sat down on the floor with Phoebe.

'Hey, Riley pup,' Sally said, stroking his long, soft ears. 'Hey, boy. What do you say? Hmm? Whaddya say?'

I propped my back against the front door to have some face-to-face time with him.

'Riles, my friend, this is a very bad deal.' He cranked his head around to look at me. Flattered by his effort and attention, I felt a spear of grief when I looked into his sallow eyes. The fact that I was no one special to Riley, that I was simply included in his indiscriminate love of the universe, didn't dim the pleasure I'd taken in his company over the years. He liked me, with no conditions. He liked us all. He liked everything. And tomorrow he would be gone. We stood up when Pam came down, with Cheryl right behind her.

'This is so hard,' said Sally, who is not always a natural

conversationalist but knows just what to say at times like this. 'He's a great spirit.' That set off a round of hugs.

'Thanks for coming,' said Pam, the indefatigable good hostess.

'Of course,' I said, and then didn't know what else to say. We all sat on the floor, crowding the front hall around Riley. After some petting and fussing over him, the respectful silence lifted. Pam started replaying the course of the dog's illness. Cheryl offered a few tactful corrections to her story.

'That was before they offered chemo,' she said.

'Was it?' Pam wondered back. Riley, as he was about to depart, was becoming a part of their history, and ours as well.

Then a wave came over us, and the sadness lifted. We all had stories to tell about Riley's antics and couldn't seem to tell them quickly enough, getting them all in. Sally and I talked about how much we had loved having Riley and Jessie both plough through our house on their many visits. Cheryl remembered Riley as an eight-week-old puppy, incorrigible even then. Pam named several dog walkers who had been worn down by his sheer, bull-headed strength. Like Como, we learned, Riley had got loose on several occasions and even run into traffic once. Characteristically, he was unharmed. Phoebe told our neighbours the story, for the first time, of the purloined pesto salad – '*Riley's* Pesto Salad,' she emphasized. 'We thought you might be mad that we let him eat so much,' she said. Pam, who hadn't cried yet, let the tears loose now in laughter.

At that, Riley hoisted his head and thumped the floor a few times with his tail. Pam sucked in her breath. 'Look at him,' she said, seizing up with fresh, hot tears. 'He'll be like this, almost normal for a few minutes, and I'll think: how can we *do* this? What are we *doing*?' Cheryl gripped Pam around her shoulder and pulled her close. Riley's head sank back to the floor.

We stayed a few minutes more, remarking both on Riley's unforgettable stunts and his ravaged body, how thin he was, how bony his back and sides were. 'It's the right thing to do,' Cheryl said quietly.

'It's time,' said Sally.

While we were standing at the door, my hand on the brass knob, Cheryl asked about Como's recovery. 'So how's he doing?'

Once again words collided and abandoned me. It seemed all wrong to be celebrating Como's close call and recovery just as Riley, too young at ten years, was about to go. Cheryl could see me fumbling for a way to put it. Her ready sense of humour rescued me.

'Nobody's keeping score here,' she said. 'It wouldn't have saved Riley if Como hadn't made it. One live dog is better than none.' I took my hand off the doorknob and stepped past Riley into Cheryl's good-night hug.

CHAPTER SIXTEEN

Z

Como, after his ordeal, wasn't only Como to us anymore. I don't mean that he was a fundamentally different dog following his accident and surgery and continuing recuperation. He still met every knock at the door and visitor's arrival, every leash-waggling suggestion of a walk or signal that his morning or evening meal was coming with high-alert ears, saucer-eyed astonishment and poised-to-bolt body language. He still greeted Phoebe and Sally with a mixture of exultation and relief that another period of male-only company with me was over. And he remained, in my mind, at least, a perpetual escape risk. My own exits and entrances through the front door were still made as quickly as possible, and through the narrowest possible opening.

But as life gradually returned to normal, we began to see Como in new ways as his place in the family evolved. Part of that had to do with the simple fact of his survival. By making it through a trial that might well have finished off a normally constituted terrier, he showed us that his willful mind-set about certain things (cages, men, me) had another side to it. The very qualities that had made him seem like a crisis waiting to happen for the first year and a half we had him were the things that made him so resilient. He was too driven, too compulsive, too hypervigilant and hypercharged to respond to a genuine, life-changing emergency with anything but his own kinetic momentum. A plastic crate or a pair of black shoes might have sent him into a full-blown panic, but he wasn't about to let a run-in with an SUV keep him down. It made perfect sense that his recovery from a severely broken pelvis defied all medical logic and advice. Como couldn't afford to be incapacitated for even a few days, much less six weeks. He never knew when circumstances might demand that he spring into action for an instant getaway.

Yet strangely, the very things that ought to have made Como even more remarkable to us in truth made him less so. His accident and its aftermath convinced us, as nothing else quite had, that Como was simply wired in a particular way that was never going to change. And just as we might have done with a cranky in-law who was never satisfied with the way his bread was toasted, a nosy neighbour who was always dropping in at the most inconvenient times, or a child who worshipped ice skating to the exclusion of anything else, we got used to it. We got used to Como's fixations and eccentricities, his flair for drama and innate ability to entertain us, his eggbeater hairdo when he got up from a nap, and his habit of vaulting across the bare floor between the living room and dining room rugs, as if he were still clearing those gates we'd once futilely placed to contain him. We got used to his unpredictable quirks on walks that could be devoted entirely to the minute investigation of each and every telegraph pole on the block (while ignoring all people and dogs he encountered) or might play out instead as complex, inscrutable social rituals of snubbing anyone who was friendly to him but wagging his tail hopefully at those who walked on by. We didn't pretend to understand a lot of what he did, but we got used to it.

As we genuinely began to accept Como as he came, he gradually stopped seeming so exceptional to us. Having an odd dog was part of who we were as a family, an integral, essential, necessary component. Phoebe was more right than she ever could have imagined when she campaigned so steadfastly for this dog. Her growing up would have been lonelier, narrower and more constrained without this wonderfully peculiar dog to both keep her company and measure her resourcefulness and reservoirs of love. Early on, when our daughter would cradle Como in her arms and coo into his snout as if she were comforting an infant, I sometimes felt uncomfortable about her tendency to anthropomorphize the dog, to turn him into the younger sibling she never had. She routinely referred to Como as her brother. But soon enough I got used to that, too, and began to find it both comical and ineffably sweet. Watching her stroll into the living room with her furry bundle was a little like whooshing through a time tunnel. There was our thirteen-year-old as a young mother, at some future date ten or twenty years hence, beaming down at her own first child.

Sally and I, too, were better off for all the disruption the dog had caused in our lives. Our marriage was better off. Yes, we might have got more sleep on those many nights when Como's antics kept us awake. But then we would have missed all those murmurous, meandering conversations that had us whispering together, night after helpless night, in the velvety darkness of the bedroom. We would have saved a heap of money if Como had never been around to run up those staggering vet bills after his accident. But that would have meant missing out on the superheroics of the Aussie Muscle Man and the equally astonishing course of Como's I'll-Do-It-My-Way recovery.

We probably would have travelled more, if Como's flighty, high-anxiety style hadn't made us feel we couldn't venture far from his sight. And then again, if we hadn't had a dog – hadn't had *this* dog – we probably wouldn't have met those dual yellow Lab Methusalehs of Twelfth Avenue, Max and Willie, and their sublimely wise owner, who was guiding them gently through their final years. We wouldn't have witnessed the synchronized hairpin turns that Como and Lizzy executed whenever they got together for their Olympic-calibre sprints. Sally and Como would never have befriended the tottering old treat-bearing Russian man and his steadfast canine companion on their mutual early-morning walks. We might not have been there, and certainly wouldn't have identified so strongly with what our neighbours were going through, on Riley's last night with Pam and Cheryl.

Like a lot of couples who have a child later in life – Sally was thirty-seven when Phoebe was born, and I was forty – we were enmeshed in our careers and obligations, often too busy, distracted, overburdened and weary to take in the full spectrum of raising a daughter. Too often we were pressed for time and simply getting by, getting through the day and all the demands it presented. Getting Phoebe off to school in the morning and getting our own work done. Getting to a class or an interview or a meeting and then getting back to an in-box freshly padded with e-mails. Coordinating pickups at school, soccer practice, playdates and piano lessons. Getting dinner on the table, getting our daughter and ourselves to bed, and getting ready to do it all the next day.

Como didn't change any of that. In some ways he only complicated matters, with his walks and feedings and of course his unscheduled and eventful forays out of the house on his own. But he also pulled us out of our speeding orbits and into his own. He, quite literally, made us look down and watch where we were going. He reminded us, with everything from his rapturous writhing at the sight of his food dish to his lolling contentment in a patch of sunlight in the upstairs hallway to his violent distress at being confined anywhere for any reason, that we are all fellow residents of the physical world. Even at his most maddening or wrenching moments, Como was fully alert to the pleasures and perils of being alive. It was a little baffling and at times pretty ridiculous, but it was also undeniably true: the scraggly, scared terrier we'd found in a shelter cage one afternoon had made us tune in more closely – to him, to each other, to the lurching ride of our life together.

One of the moments I recall most keenly from the days Como spent in the hospital came on a night when Phoebe and I were waiting for news on the striped couches in the waiting area. I was in a particularly wretched state of mind at the moment, staring down at the floor and thinking that the dog was surely going to die, when I felt Phoebe's eyes on me.

'Daddy,' she began, her voice an inquisitive hush, 'what exactly happened?'

'What do you mean?'

'You know, when he got hit by the car.'

My heart sank even lower. 'Sweetie, I told you how he got out of the house. It was just an accident. It was nobody's fault.'

Phoebe shook her head. 'I don't mean that. I mean when he actually got hit. Did the tyre *actually* go over him? Or did it, like, push him forward?'

It was as if she were back there at the scene of the accident with me, peering down at Como as he lay on his side in the street, lungs heaving, his eye staring up. Those were the very questions that had darted through my mind as I ran out and reached down to touch him. Phoebe needed to know every precise detail of it, to live it again herself, as if that might somehow cast a protective spell over her dog.

I had been there and seen what happened when he ran from the curb – or seen what I was able to see. Phoebe had not, but she wanted desperately to be there. She wanted to go through it with him. She wanted to be there with Como in the moment – to smooth the fur on his head, to lift him and hold him in her arms, to do whatever she could. It made me ache to see the tensed apprehension and pressing curiosity in her face. It made me love her, too, and love the dog who had knitted us together, my daughter and me, both of us hurting and yearning and hoping with all our might that Como really would make it.

❖

When Sally and I first began dating, it took a while before she adjusted to the nicknames my friends and I handed around like playing cards. It was another of those things – like the fact that my family talked constantly and hers recognized the merits of silence, or that I loved Sondheim and she adored Springsteen – that we had to puzzle out about each other. Falling in love is glorious. It's also pretty easy. Figuring out how to live with another person and make sense of his or her unique and at times seemingly alien place in the world is a lifelong, perpetually unfinished undertaking.

Sally's friends and family members, sensibly enough, tend to call one another by their given first names. I've never much gone in for that. Ever since I was little I've renamed people, often in a chain of freely associated nicknames, spun out in search of some elusive bonding essence. It's not something I consciously try to do or can even control once it gets going. It's just one way – and maybe more revealing of my character than I realize – that I relate to the people I care about. Calling people by their actual birth-certificate name often seems dry and formal after I've got to know them. It lacks the intimacy and specificity, the history and stories and laughs we've shared.

Take my friend Judi, for example. Drawn to each other by our love of French food, Charles Dickens and Handel operas, as well as a strong aversion to several of our graduate school professors, we started spending time together as soon as we met. Several months later, with no premeditation, I called her 'GooGoo' one night at dinner. As soon as I explained the source – I had known an endearingly ditzy Judith in college – the newly deemed GooGoo sighed but graciously assented. The point, as she saw, was not how much she shared with her namesake, but rather how little. Serious, scholarly-minded GooGoo was one of the least goo-goo people I knew.

But that didn't stop me and other mutual friends from picking up the nickname and playing with it like a free-for-all Scrabble game. GooGoo soon became 'Googlers', 'Gogglers', 'Gagglers', 'Gigglers'. When the inevitable reduction to 'GG' occurred, our grad school friend Jim (nickname Measie, short for 'The Measle') quickly dubbed her 'G^2', or 'G-Squared'. After Judi objected to having an exponent in her nickname, the double-G possibilities opened up and migrated towards the food-and-drink realm that was dear to her. GooGoo became 'Green Goddess' and 'Gin Gimlets'. Later, in a nonsensical development that would require a team of linguists to reconstruct, Judi answered to the name 'Crab Cutlets'. Now and then, for old time's sake, we revert to the simple and classic 'GooGoo'.

Como presented a special set of circumstances. First, of course, he was a dog and could not participate in the origins and derivations of any nicknames. Then there was the problem of the various actual names he'd already had. After stripping him of his shelter name, Gandalf, Sally, Phoebe and I had run through a gamut of Italian options – from Prosecco to Pavarotti to Palladio – before settling on Como. Before all that, as Sally pointed out, he could have been called any number of things. Among the mysteries our dog's past presented was what names he might have had prior to his days as Gandalf. We didn't know that any more than we knew what had happened to him out on the streets of Santa Clara County (and wherever else he might have been) that had made him who he was.

The nicknames, more like pet names, for our pet started early. In an endearment that may have signalled her slight regret that she hadn't got the very young animal she once imagined, Phoebe often called her new dog Como Pup. Sally, who has got over her initial nickname resistance in the years we've been married, turned it into a more stately title. To her he was 'Como Pup the Como Dog'. That rolled off the tongue so pleasantly that it invited an impromptu ditty (sung to the tune of 'The Muffin Man') that we all launched into for a while:

He's Como Pup the Como Dog,
Como Pup the Como Dog,
Oh, he's Como Pup the Como Dog,
Yeah! Como Pup the Dog!

One clear compensation for all the difficulties Como caused us was the chance to be shamelessly silly about him. Sally and I may have enjoyed it – and needed it – even more than Phoebe did.

Once lengthened, like a stretchy rubber band, his new name longed to snap back to something shorter. 'Como Pup the Como Dog' became 'The Pup' or 'Hims Pup'. Then, in some further tightening, he was simply 'Hims'.

That suited him, somehow. Seated in the middle of the living room floor, patiently awaiting a round of petting or a treat, he had a kind of comic dignity. With his ears tilting asymmetrically at the sound of our voices, or of dry food tumbling into his metal dish, he looked compact and self-contained, contented, happy to be precisely where he was. He was ours. He was home. He was Hims.

And then he ran out in the street one day and nearly got killed, after which he was shaved and saved and fitted out with a sweater that earned him his post-traumatic names of 'Frankenpup' and 'Einstein'. Those were passing handles of the moment, emergency measures with natural expiration dates built into them. As his recuperation continued and his fur grew in, he went back to being Hims.

If the dog happened to be in the living room with Sally or Phoebe when I came home with my briefcase under my arm, I'd offer a respectful greeting: 'Good evening, Hims.' He'd remain seated and look back at me, polite but noncommittal, like someone sizing me up in a prospective business deal. We were in an ongoing negotiation, Como and I, and that new name we had for him, at once formal and frivolous, seemed to help. We were serious about getting along, but then again not taking it too seriously. 'Nice to see you, Hims,' I'd say, setting down my briefcase or gym bag and stepping past him to peck my wife on the cheek. 'Thanks for stopping by tonight.'

Soon enough, the dog's gradual return to his pre-accident buoyancy led to a bouncier version of what we called him. 'Hims', at some point, morphed into 'Himsie'. Then musical wordplay took over. We began, for nothing but the fun of it, stressing the second syllable: 'Him-SIE'. Phoebe, with her younger, fresher ears, heard that less literally than I did. In what I later came to regard as a pivotal piece of family correspondence, she left me a note on the kitchen counter one day about whether or not she had walked the dog at noon. She spelled his name 'Him-Z'.

It was one of those accidental breakthroughs that seems like a preordained act of genius. The next step was obvious, blazingly self-evident. I couldn't wait until Phoebe got home from Jeanne's house.

'You've done it, Skidge,' I trumpeted as soon as she walked in the door.

'What? What did I do?' Her eyes shifted nervously, making me wonder for a moment what she was hiding. But I was too pleased to think very hard about that.

'You found it,' I said. 'You found his name: "Z". The last letter. The last word in dogdom. The ultimate animal. Z! Z! The Mysterious, Amazing Z! The Masked Man! The mark of Zorro!'

Phoebe gave me a guarded half smile. I could see she was glad to have delighted me, even if she didn't quite know what she'd done or how she'd done it. Now that I thought of it, I wasn't altogether sure she knew who Zorro was. 'Let me go change my clothes and put my stuff away,' Phoebe said, and came downstairs a few minutes later with the dog in her arms.

'Z,' I said gratefully. It seemed even better now that he was there in the room with us. There was something Zen about it, the single letter he'd unknowingly aspired to be. After *X*, it was the oddest, zingiest, zaniest letter in the alphabet. It was him, filed down to his elusive, zigzagging, antic essence. Phoebe turned around to look straight into her dog's newly christened face.

'Z,' she repeated. 'Little Dog Z.'

'Exactly,' I said. 'Z.'

His name went through a few temporary elaborations in the months ahead. After a friend of Phoebe's returned from a trip to the Mexican state of Guerrero, we briefly celebrated that fact by recasting 'Z' as 'The Zihuatenejan'. 'Too hard to remember,' Sally declared. 'Or spell.' She was right on both counts.

Then there was that drive home from an overnight trip to Point Reyes. Phoebe and I were sitting in the front seat; Sally, worn out from our hike to a wind-battered beach, was asleep in the back. Missing Como, who was bunking with his sitter, Marianna, Phoebe and I began picturing our dog in exotic period costumes. We imagined Como as a Victorian explorer, an Egyptian pharaoh, a musketeer with a great plumed hat, and a pirate with a patch over one eye and a hook affixed to his paw. That one had us laughing so hard I nearly had to pull off the road.

The whole thing was a nostalgic riff on *Wishbone*, a 1990s PBS show about a Jack Russell terrier who appeared, dressed up, as a character in condensed versions of classics such as *Robin Hood* and *Don Quixote*. With a dog as its hero, *Wishbone* had been a particular favourite of Phoebe's when she was six and seven. Threading through the green hills along Highway 1, we were re-imagining the show now with Como as the star. Phoebe conjured him as a sailor in a smart navy blue jacket with brass buttons and a captain's hat festooned with gold cord.

'He's Z, Z, the Man of the High Seas,' I cried out. That had Phoebe doubled over and laughing so hard it woke up Sally.

'What's so funny?' she asked groggily from the back.

'I'm not really sure,' I said, trying to hold the wheel steady through a curve.

'Z,' Phoebe exclaimed, 'the Man of the High Seas.' At which point both of us lost it completely, and I really did have to pull over until the ocean swells of laughter passed.

'You guys,' Sally said. 'I fall asleep, and all hell breaks loose.' She slumped back against the window and waited until we were able to drive on.

❧

Phoebe started high school in the autumn of 2005. Sally and I couldn't quite believe that our shy and soft-spoken daughter was leaving the security of the school she'd attended from kindergarten through to eighth grade to take on the autonomy, responsibility and uncertainty that the freshman year entailed. She'd have to navigate a whole new group of classmates, teachers and academic expectations; find her way to classes that operated on a bewildering schedule that changed from one day to the next; and roam around halls filled with eighteen-year-old senior boys who could drive and presumably perform all sorts of other adult feats.

The halls, it turned out, were the least of our concerns about Phoebe's whereabouts during the day. Located in the city's grittily colourful Haight-Ashbury District, scene of the Summer of Love revolution that had bedazzled Sally and me from a distance when we were her age, Phoebe's new school had an open campus policy that allowed students to leave the building and walk up and down Haight Street at lunchtime and during breaks between classes. Sally and I, who are not coffee drinkers, listened with cowed attention when Phoebe breezily mentioned stopping in at the People's Café, Squat & Gobble, or Coffee to the People for a mid-morning mocha or cappuccino. Even more noteworthy were some of the new friends and acquaintances she was making. Along with new classmates Jonah, Nora, Sam, Oona, Jacob, Alexanna and Alan, we heard in passing about a man at the corner of Haight and Masonic who grinned and called our daughter 'Baby Doll' and 'Sugar Bun'.

'What man?' Sally asked. She was sitting next to me on the living room couch and holding Como in her lap. Phoebe, who had shot up five inches since eighth grade, loomed over us, shifting her weight impatiently from one foot to the other.

'No one,' she said. 'Just some guy.'

'How old a guy?' I asked.

'Dad. What do you think? That I ask everybody I meet how old they are? He's just a guy.'

'A school-age guy or a grown-up guy?' I pressed.

'Grown-up.'

'Does he work in one of the stores on the street?' I went on.

Phoebe responded with one of those faint, pitying smiles she seemed to have mastered overnight, as a way of signalling the absolute cluelessness of her parents. 'I really don't think so,' she said.

'So he's a homeless person,' Sally said. 'This guy.'

Phoebe shrugged. 'I've got a ton of homework. C'mon, Z. Let's go.' The dog hopped off the couch and followed her up to her room.

Como was spending a lot of time up there. As soon as she came home from school, Phoebe would disappear into her room, taking the dog and a snack along with her. They'd emerge for dinner, then vanish back into her lair for the rest of the evening. All those 'tons' of homework were the overt reason for her bedroom vigils, but as the sounds of music, the pattering of her laptop keyboard for e-mail and instant messaging, and her bleating mobile affirmed, she was also busy pursuing her twenty-first-century electronic social life behind her closed door.

Stretched out at the foot of her bed, Como kept her loyal company. With his fur fully grown back in and his recovery from the surgery seemingly complete, the dog had taken on a new self-sufficiency. He went where he wanted and when he wanted, sometimes at a casual, lordly amble and occasionally, when the spirit moved him, at a dead run. His destination, more often than not, was Phoebe's room. It was as if the two of them had entered a new phase together, one that relegated Sally and me to secondary status. I was used to being snubbed by Como, so I didn't much notice or mind his absence. Sally did.

'Where's Z?' she'd say, after finishing the dinner dishes or running through a pile of student papers.

'Where he always is,' I'd say.

'I know it. I just miss him.'

What we both knew, beyond Phoebe and Como's where-abouts, was what it meant about the few short years ahead. Phoebe's retreat to her room was the first in an inevitable series of tactical moves that would lead to her leaving home for college. High school, homeless guys who called her 'Sugar Bun', and her closed bedroom door were steps in the same direction.

Fortunately, as hopeless as she found us to be, Phoebe still consented to going out with us – to dinner or a movie – and to travelling with us on vacations. In the spring term of her freshman year, we all went to Nicaragua to visit our friend Leana. We booked Como with Marianna for his longest stay yet – a full week. The trip, from Leana's small village to sprawling Managua, the gorgeous colonial city of Granada, an actively steaming volcano and a cliffside beach resort, was sensational. Phoebe impressed us all by using her Spanish to communicate with waiters and shopkeepers. We loved the people, the food, the murals in Esteli.

Desperate to see Como when we got back to San Francisco, Phoebe pleaded with us to have the cabdriver stop at Marianna's house on the way in from the airport. Dusty from his communal dog walks but apparently no worse for wear, Z slathered Phoebe and Sally with tongue-lapping kisses and even tossed a few my way in the general spirit of euphoria. The next morning he threw up on the stairs, had diarrhoea on his walk, and hid out for most of the day under the kitchen table. When Sally came home from school we took him to the vet – the very one I had charged into after Como was run over.

'Why don't you take him in?' I said, pulling up in front of the building. 'I'll go and find a place to park and meet you back here.' Well over a year had passed, but I still wasn't eager to revisit the place I had last graced in my bathrobe. I could still picture, all too clearly, that softly bubbling fountain on the counter and the red speckles of blood I'd left on the walls and floor.

Sally came outside forty minutes later with the dog under her arm. They'd checked him over thoroughly, 'hydrated' him with an injection of water under the skin on his upper back, and prescribed a two-week course of pills for a possible stomach virus. The bill was two hundred and sixty dollars.

'That's perfect,' I said. 'We go to a Central American country for a week, and none of us gets sick. We come home, and he's the one with the stomach crud.'

Z looked at me balefully from his perch in Sally's arms. He may have settled into our lives and our hearts, but our dog clearly wasn't done surprising us.

CHAPTER SEVENTEEN

The Lake, the Beach and the Bluff

In a new spirit of optimism and social engagement, I started taking Como for longer and more ambitious walks. Instead of just marching him up to the corner of Twelfth and Lawton and back, I decided to devote longer chunks of time for forays to Stow Lake in Golden Gate Park, Ocean Beach and the cliffside dog mecca at Fort Funston. All three locations are a short drive from our house.

Part of my motivation was selfless, or at least semi-selfless. Dogs need more exercise than Como was getting, and it was about time for me to do something about it. Sally was already doing her part, by taking him for longer weekend rambles through our hilly neighbourhood and down to the baseball fields in the park. Como, speedily and pretty miraculously up to full strength after his surgery, was more than ready for me to pitch in. Whenever I waved the leash at him and asked him if he wanted to go to the lake or the beach – he appeared to understand the offers – Como ramped up the enthusiasm.

'All right, Z. Slow down. We'll get there.' He'd wriggle around so much at my feet, it was often hard to clip on the leash. On other occasions, he'd remember he was still suspicious of me and wriggle out of range altogether.

The car ride was a torment of anticipation for him. Propped up beside me, with his back legs on the backseat and his front legs fixed on the console, he'd peer out of the windscreen with more focus and intensity than I ever had as a driver. If I'd turned over the wheel to him, I sometimes thought, he could have got us there as safely as, and probably more quickly than, I did. As we approached our destination – he seemed to have a built-in global positioning system for distance and parking places – he'd whimper and pace from side to side in the backseat. We couldn't get there, get out of the car and get going fast enough for him.

His basic dog identity did seem to come into fuller bloom out there in nature. On the paths and lawns around Stow Lake, the seaweed-strewn sand at the beach, or cypress-studded dunes at Fort Funston, Como moved with a revitalized sense of purpose. His dutiful pavement plodding was replaced by a darting, propulsive drive. So many things to sniff and so little time to sniff them – bushes, flowers, driftwood, crab carcasses, other dogs (he was less standoffish and inhibited on these field trips), people, rocks, rubbish. No sooner did he find something of transfixing interest than something a few feet or a hundred yards away demanded his immediate attention. Off he'd go, with me lashed behind and trying to keep up. So many places to lift his leg and leave his mark. So many popcorn kernels, bread crusts, wads of hardened gum and God knows what else to gobble up on the run. Even the air itself seemed to excite him – in bright sunlight, wet fog, winter, spring: it didn't matter. He was a happier, more fulfilled dog on these jaunts. So much so, in fact, that I'd sometimes watch him straining at the far end of the leash and think I should just let him go, let him loose into the wide open world he'd come from and yearned to rejoin.

Gratifying as it was to see Como excited by all this fresh terrain, our expanded walks weren't only for him. One of the reasons I'd let Phoebe talk us into getting a dog in the first place had to do with my own tendencies towards isolation. Because I worked at home a lot, because I was over fifty and conscious of a constrained social circle that wasn't likely to get a whole lot bigger in the years ahead, because an empty nest loomed when our only child went off to college, I had envisioned a dog as at least a partial hedge against all that. I had imagined myself walking and visiting with fellow dog owners, meeting strangers on the street with our politely sniffing pups as the icebreaker, frequenting the congenial dog parks and runs I'd noticed around the city, stopping on a picturesque path for a soulful moment of communion with my affectionate and devoted pet. All that was going to be Ecstasy, I once thought – both the dog of that name and the heightened state of feeling and belonging she'd represent.

When the fates dealt Como to us instead, those rosy-hued film clips flickered out of view, replaced by the long-running reality series of dealing with a panic-stricken dog who devoted a good deal of his energy to evading me, behaving erratically in public and plotting his next potentially disastrous escape. To put it mildly, having a dog in the house hadn't worked out the way I thought it would.

But then what does? Being a husband and a father; working for the same newspaper for over twenty-five years; making and keeping the friends I had, while losing track of others along the way; witnessing my father's death and my mother's decline into the tightening grip of Parkinson's disease – none of it had played out according to whatever naively simplistic scenarios I might have pictured. Como was another chapter in the unexpected and the unpredictable, the perpetually unfinished story of disappointment and resilience, menace and consolation, desolation and love, that life serves up in its unforeseeable way.

Our dog's innocence of all those things, his total absorption in the moment – panting in the heat, prowling for a dropped chocolate drop in the grass at the park, whimpering like an opera diva in his cage at the hospital, quivering with joy when Sally comes up the steps and opens the door – both focused my self-awareness and invited me to be a little freer of it. Z, by being so thoroughly who he was, opened a route out of myself and into a more immediate, vivid and connected world. When Como popped his head up at the merest hint of a walk and stared at me full on with his deep brown, shag-fringed eyes, he made me want to be nowhere else but outside somewhere with him. In making me want exactly what he wanted with all his powers of wanting, he bypassed my analytical default mode and retapped my own drives and desires. He rerooted me. In his sheer unadulterated dogginess, he helped make me more human.

Of the three new routes for our walks, the one at Stow Lake is the most overtly social. The path that runs around the man-made, paddle-boat-filled attraction near the arboretum in Golden Gate Park is heavily used from early morning until sunset. While dogs are plentifully represented, it's the constant variety of people that makes the place so alluring, especially in a setting that includes a Chinese pavilion, a double-arched stone bridge and a handsomely devised waterfall. On a half-hour stroll around the perimeter of this picturesque lake, it would be surprising not to hear a multitude of other languages, including but by no means limited to Spanish, Mandarin, Cantonese, Vietnamese, Hindi, Russian, Czech, Tagalog, Italian, Polish, Farsi and French. Walk a few hundred yards, and you're the citizen of a larger world.

For a while Como and I went there alone, just the two of us threading our way through the rambling international bazaar. After a few trips all that avid, incomprehensible socializing on the paths and benches made me crave some human company, too. I invited my friend Mark and his dog, Oreo, a pleasantly puffy, sensibly socialized black-and-white shih tzu, to join us. The experiment promptly turned into a tradition, repeated once a month or so.

Mark and I have known each other for years, ever since our wives met in a mother-and-baby group at Kaiser in 1991. Emily, Mark and Barbara's first child, was born the same month that Phoebe was. Besides having teenage daughters, Mark and I have other things in common, not least of which is a love of baseball that borders on obsession. Sally and Barbara can't quite fathom how much there could be to say about the Giants' bullpen, the Phillies' infield, or our precise memories of outfielder Kevin Mitchell catching a fly ball bare-handed.

For all its appearance of bonding and bonhomie, male friendship can be a tenuous, even treacherous thing. Mark and I are often at our best, our most companionable and forthcoming, when our dogs are tugging us around Stow Lake. There's something about the distracting punctuation the dogs supply – 'Como! Don't eat that!' 'Have you got an extra plastic bag?' 'I think that's about the twenty-third time he's peed today' – that allows our conversation to flow from topic to topic with an unforced ease. Our kids and their well-hidden social lives, work, money worries, local politics and of course baseball come and go like the gulls, ducks, geese and occasional egrets and herons that swoop across the lake.

Mark and I always take the same route. We meet at the boathouse, cross one of the lake's two bridges to Strawberry Hill, climb the path to the top, descend the steep steps beside the waterfall and circle slowly back to the cars. This unspoken agreement is a means of convergence for us, a predictable shared space we might not have found in our busy schedules if our dogs hadn't given us the excuse we needed.

We're very different people. Mark, who grew up in San Francisco and seems to have liked everyone he ever met, is more outgoing and gregarious than I am. It's a rare occurrence when we *don't* meet someone he knows. I've run into an acquaintance of mine on our walks exactly once. Our dogs are distinctive, too. While Como zips back and forth across the path, head down and often oblivious to the crowd, Oreo trots along with his eye out for meet-and-greets with other dogs and people. When Como decides to participate, promptly tangling the leashes, Mark steps in to sort out the mess. He's a grade-school head, and it's easy to see how skilled he must be with young students, overworked teachers and demanding parents.

I love hearing about the complex negotiations Mark has to make in his job, and he's always keen to know what I'm writing. We may not come to any ringing conclusions about ourselves, our daughters, or our futures as we make our way around the glossy, rippling waters of Stow Lake, but I always feel we've made a little music together, the four of us. Mark lets Oreo off his leash when we get to the little patch of lawn near the cars, and his dog responds by racing around in big loops and circles. Como joins in, briefly, at times, bobbing and weaving on the end of his leash. But he's just as likely to sit it out in the dwindling late-afternoon light and enjoy the spectacle of a dog who's just not like him.

'We'll see you next time,' I say to Mark and Oreo, leading Como over to the car and popping open the back door. He hops up and has himself in position, front paws on the console, when I come around and get in. Side by side, we drive home. 'Well done, Z,' I say when we pull into the driveway. 'Couldn't have done it without you.'

Phoebe was zipping through high school, loving her classes (well, most of them), her new friends, social freedoms and mobility. With a Muni Fast Pass plucked from her wallet, she could get anywhere she wanted to go on San Francisco's abundant bus and streetcar lines. The car rides to Jeanne's house, the Stonestown mall, Mel's Drive-In, or downtown to a movie that Sally and I sometimes grumbled about giving were now rarely requested. Even Berkeley and Oakland were within easy striking range on the BART trains that speed under San Francisco Bay. One afternoon I picked up the phone and heard a staticky blur of teenage chatter, laughter and some oddly distinct and inventive swearing. The sound of glasses was also involved.

'Phoebe? Is that you?' She'd developed the maddening habit of placing these check-in calls to us on her mobile and then, apparently regarding the duty as such an empty obligation, falling into conversation with a friend and neglecting to respond when we answered. 'Phoebe? Phoebe!'

'Dad. For God's sake, stop yelling. Jeesh.'

'Well, you're not talking to me.'

'I'm talking now. What do you want me to say?' It was

amazing, almost impressive, how quickly she could be annoyed by Sally or me, as if our very existence were an affront to her.

'Where are you?'

'Jack's.'

'Who's Jack?'

'You know. Jack.' I didn't know, but decided not to pursue it.

'When are you coming home?'

'Wait. Hold on.' The background rabble was muffled as she held the phone to her arm or shoulder (I'd seen her do it) and spoke to someone else. 'What?' she said, returning to the line with that master teenage touch of stalling for time before abruptly cutting it short. 'I don't know. I'll call you later. Bye.'

'What was that?' Sally called out from the kitchen. 'Was that our girl? What did she say?'

'Nothing,' I said. 'Really nothing. I'm taking Como to the beach.'

Unlike the scheduled Stow Lake walks with Mark and Oreo, my trips to Ocean Beach with Como tend to be spontaneous. Sometimes I take him first thing in the morning, often as a procrastination tactic if I have a writing assignment. Late afternoons are also good, when the sun becomes a glowing brass disc dropping into the Pacific Ocean like a precious coin. Thick fogs are frequent on the city's western edge, but when the mood is right, a blurry wet scrim gives the surf an enticingly eerie appeal. There's something about ruminating when you can't see ten feet in front of you that can make even the most insubstantial thought seem broodingly profound.

Como hopped down from the backseat primed to hit the sand. 'Hold on,' I nagged, pulling him closer to my side. Crossing the Great Highway always makes me a little edgy. After the accident, Como and cars became and remained an unwelcome combination. 'Go for it, Z,' I said, when the roadway cleared and the green Walk sign came on. Slapping along in my sandals, I raced him down the soft slope and onto the expansive plane of Ocean Beach sand that stretches from the Cliff House at the north end to Fort Funston at the south.

Como and I have distinct but workably parallel ideas of what a walk on the beach entails. I like to shed my sandals or shoes and splash along in ankle-deep water. He prefers not to get his paws wet. Linked by a twenty-six-foot retractable leash, we can each have our way. I just have to make sure the leash doesn't trip anyone walking or jogging along the shoreline and that I spot Como before he rolls in some foul-smelling seaborne gunk and yank him away. Otherwise I'm free to let my mind wander and forget how far we've walked. Off the city's grid of streets and blocks and tightly spaced buildings, distance and time open out.

For the first few hundred yards that day, I replayed my phone call with Phoebe, coached myself on not getting frazzled and worried that we were losing touch with her. Then I reminded myself that nothing Sally and I thought about Phoebe one minute was necessarily true the next. Yes, she could be shockingly dismissive and rude to us. But she was also tender and affectionate, needy and kind. Approaching fifteen, she still nuzzled in between Sally and me on our bed to watch television, and still liked to be tucked in at night – at least on the nights when she hadn't slammed her door on us earlier in the evening. She still showed us her English and history papers (sometimes) and cared what we thought. She still called us 'Mommy' and 'Daddy' – if she wasn't whispering some other names under her breath.

Sally and I had wanted a second child. Our failure to

conceive again and our decision not to adopt pried open some painful, wrenching fissures in the early years of our marriage. We were disappointed in ourselves and in our biological bad luck. We blamed the doctors when the fertility treatments didn't work. We blamed each other – privately and sometimes not – for waiting too long, for not having got together sooner, for our ambivalence about adoption and for the guilt we felt about it. Then, when it really was too late, we gradually stopped blaming and started being more thankful for what we had – in each other, in our delightful and exasperating daughter, our friends, our families, our work lives. Our anxious, ambivalent dog, who didn't die.

I felt a tug on the leash. Como had his feet planted in the sand to scrutinize an impressive sand castle fitted out with sand-dollar shields around its base and surrounded by a sagging moat. Usually it was something either repulsive and smelly or mysteriously inconsequential that snagged his attention. This time he'd found something of genuine, general interest.

'Hey, that's pretty cool,' someone said. It was a surfer heading out towards the breakers. 'Did he build it himself?'

'He wouldn't let me help,' I said, playing along. 'He's very particular.'

The surfer nodded. 'What's his name?'

'Como,' I said. 'But we call him Z.'

No explanation was required by the man in the shiny black wetsuit. There's a free-floating, come-what-may feel to things out at the beach. Encounters that might seem peculiar elsewhere come off as perfectly natural here. 'Later,' said the surfer, who turned and sprinted into the water with his board tucked under his arm. Como looked up from the castle and watched him go.

Z and I have had a number of similar chance meetings on the beach. A shell collector stopped to remark on how much Como resembles a dog she once had in Ireland. A tiny, wide-eyed child got down on his knees in the wet sand and waited patiently for my wary dog to come close enough to be petted, while his father and I talked about preschools. An old man ignored Como altogether and speculated on the contents of a container ship on the horizon.

'What breed is he? Or she?' a woman dressed in a hooded sweatshirt and red-and-white-striped leggings asked me one morning. Her large black sheepdog mix circled around us.

'He,' I said. 'Terrier mutt.'

'Don't ever say that,' the woman scolded me. 'Mutt is a horrible, insensitive, mean thing to call any dog.' Off she stalked with her sheepadoodle, or whatever his precise and proper designation was.

You have to take it all as it comes. People are nutty, nostalgic, reverent, obsessive, occasionally cruel, adoring and doctrinaire when it comes to dogs. Somehow that's all so plainly, bracingly apparent out there on the beach, whether it's some serious runner charging along with a leash held firmly in hand, a couple fussing over their beagle, or a boy flinging a dripping-wet tennis ball as far as he can and a German shepherd vaulting over the foam-lipped waves in pursuit.

I'd walked further than I meant to that day. 'Come on, Z,' I said, reversing directions and checking my watch. As we started the trek back to the car, I realized that these trips to Ocean Beach weren't really what I thought they were. I always came out planning to be alone with my thoughts and more often than not wound up feeling a little less alone. We were about to start back up the slope to recross the Great Highway when Como found a long strand of bright green kelp, as thick and slimy as a snake.

I was in a hurry. I had work to do. But I caught myself before I pulled him away. 'Go for it, Z,' I told him. 'That may be the shiniest, best piece of kelp you ever find.'

🐾

Phoebe was silent the afternoon I drove her straight from school to the hospital in November 2006. No matter how much we had assured her in advance that Sally's abdominal surgery was routine, she wouldn't be satisfied until she saw for herself that her mother had made it through safely. A devoted fan of the TV programme *Gray's Anatomy*, Phoebe regarded medical events of any kind as inherently dramatic. My first few attempts at chirpy conversation, as we parked in the Kaiser garage and took the lift to the sixth floor, went unanswered.

'Can you believe this is the same building where you were born?' I asked, waiting for the lift doors to slide open.

That did it. Phoebe couldn't let such an apparent inanity stand. 'Well, Father,' she replied, 'I don't exactly remember that.'

'No,' I agreed, 'I guess you wouldn't.' At least I'd induced her to speak.

Phoebe held back and made it clear she wanted me to go in first when we got to Sally's room. The patient was propped up and grinning, if a little tepidly, at the sound of our voices.

'Get in here, you,' she called to her daughter. Phoebe rushed past me and stood as close to Sally's bed as she could without getting into it.

'Mommy, are you all right? How did it go? How do you feel?'

'I'm fine, sweetie. It went fine. And I feel great seeing you.'

'That's more than I could get out of her,' I put in. 'All she told me this morning – what I could hear of it, anyway – was how thirsty she was. The Ice Chip Man Cometh.' That remark was ignored, sensibly enough, as Sally shot me one of her tenderly lethal looks and went back to revelling in Phoebe's bedside attention. The truth was, my attempt at theatrical humour masked the near-teary gratitude and relief I'd been feeling ever since Sally was wheeled into the recovery room and her doctor gave me the thumbs-up sign. Like Phoebe, I didn't fully believe this surgery was 'routine' until it was over.

Phoebe and I spent several hours in the hospital that afternoon. Sally ate some soup and lime jelly while we were there and laughed when Phoebe deemed the meal 'disgusting'. Sally was definitely on the mend. A day and a half later she was installed on the living room couch at home, with Como as her constant companion. He was like a spoiled pasha, lolling on the blanket with her, his eyes heavily, dreamily lidded. After several days his lassitude started getting to me. I was also growing a little weary, I had to admit, of my nursing duties and all that surgical bonding on the couch. Both she and Como, as Sally said, smoothing his fur, had now had pelvic reconstructions.

'He needs a big walk,' I told her one afternoon. 'I thought I'd take him to Fort Funston. You going to be okay?' I figured, correctly, that she'd approve the dog-exercise plan and therefore not object to me abandoning her for a few hours. Como looked a little reluctant to get off the couch, but wagged his tail at the sight of his leash.

Fort Funston, which occupies a dramatic bluff over the Pacific, is San Francisco's ultimate dog paradise. Everywhere you go, from the paved paths to the grassy dunes to the beach itself, dogs gallop free and cavort with one another. The owners convene in the shade, doling out treats and roughhouse pats to the friendly, roving pack. A brisk ocean breeze adds to the general air of vigour and well-being.

I always feel a little awestruck here at first, both by the scenery and the jolt of canine liberation. But after we've walked a way, I stop feeling self-conscious about having my dog on a leash and begin to enjoy the formless flow of the place. There are various routes to take and no purposeful runners or power walkers. Everyone seems to have all the time in the world. I always stay longer than I expect.

The sweeping sea vistas from the bluff seem to encourage long-distance thinking, both backwards and forwards in time. As the waves shimmered in the sunlight and Como trotted along beside me, my thoughts turned that day from Sally and Phoebe and our futures to my father. I don't think about him a lot, at least not consciously, but certain activities and settings, a particular frame of mind, summon him up clearly. Being outdoors and alone with Como, especially with Sally safe and freshly home from the hospital, was a powerful trigger.

Austere and all but mute about his own feelings, my father kept duty and principle at the forefront of his life. He was a small-town Missouri boy who had worked extremely hard to achieve what he did in academia and banking, and he took a steady, grindstone approach to everything from his job to gardening to his expectations of others. Even on the tennis court he exuded a determined and largely joyless demeanour, thwacking the ball and frowning as he laboured back into position for a return shot. I'm sure he loved my mother, who had a series of trying medical crises in their marriage, and my sister and me. But sometimes, especially when I was growing up in the cone of paternal silence, that wasn't always obvious.

Gengy, our family dog, unlocked my father. From the moment that temperamental animal came into the house, Dad was lavish, almost foolishly forthcoming with his affection, babbling baby talk, protectiveness and pride. Nothing was too good for Gengy – lean ham from the table; a shiny patent leather Christmas collar; the prime riding spot, right behind my father's neck, on the front seat of the car. It was baffling and even a little hurtful. My sister, Judy, and I used to ask each other, in all seriousness, if we thought our father cared about Gengy more than us. But in later years, long after Gengy and then our father were gone, we've taken to marvelling at how dogs and young children were the keys that flung open a door that often remained fearfully or defensively shut. Behind it lay the room where Dad felt free to let loose and giggle, make silly faces and talk nonsense and pour forth all the love that would pour right back to him without qualifications or conditions. Walking along in the California sunlight with Como, I felt a surge of fondness, maybe for the first time, for my father's devotion to a not-very-likable miniature dachshund. Life is too short to be jealous of a dog, especially one who's been dead for decades.

My parents moved from Philadelphia to Cleveland after my sister and I had both gone off to college. That's where Gengy died, quite unexpectedly, in 1972. He turned listless one day and wouldn't eat. Two days later, ravaged by tumours, he was put to sleep. My father never said a word to Judy or me about it. It took my mother, who was also pretty broken up, several months to tell us the full story – the trip to the vet, the awful news, the ashes they took home in a coffee jar to bury in the garden.

The detail I remember most, the sound I never heard but go on hearing, is the sobbing my mother described. For three nights running, my father sat doubled over on the side of the bed, his head in his hands as he wept for the loss of Gengy. The thought of it, of his raw, raking voice in that darkened Ohio bedroom, makes him as present to me as almost anything does. That was the defenseless, openhearted father I saw in fleeting glimpses at a distance, the one whom only dogs and babies knew straight on. He died in 2002, a year and a half before we adopted Como.

'Let's go, Z,' I said, turning away from the bluff and starting along the path that runs through the dry white sand to the car park. 'It's time to go home.'

The Dog at the Door

On September 11, 2008, we celebrated Como's sixth birthday in the traditional manner at home – a hamburger with a splash of A.1. Steak Sauce for the guest of honour and a carrot cake with the appropriate number of candles after dinner for us. Actually we had no idea if that was our dog's real birthday. We marked it every year on the anniversary of the date in 2003 that we had adopted him as a purportedly one-year-old stray, who went by the name of Gandalf at the time.

'Here's to Z,' I said, draining the Prosecco from my glass. The Italian sparkling wine was customary, too. It was a nod to Venice, where, on Phoebe's twelfth birthday, Sally and I told our daughter she could have a dog.

'To Z,' echoed Sally, who put down her glass, lifted Como into her lap at the table, and proceeded to feed him cake crumbs from her plate. As recently as a year or two ago, that wouldn't have happened, even on his birthday. One standard of dog discipline after another had fallen over time, including the policy that excluded him from our bed. Sally had got especially sneaky about this one, smuggling the dog under the covers when I wasn't watching. Her lame defence when my knee bumped into Como's midsection between the sheets: 'He's keeping me warm.'

Our birthday dinner table conversation touched, as it usually did, on some of Como's past highlights, lowlights and recent stunts. We replayed the day we first found him and the day he got run over. Sally invoked Needle Nose, the savvy, sharp-featured young woman who had introduced us to our dog-to-be at the shelter, and Sarah, Como's tough but kind Basic Training teacher at the SPCA.

'Remember Jake?' I asked. 'And his pounds of smoked turkey?'

'You should talk,' Sally said. 'You're just as bad with your Shredded Wheat.' She was right about that. A month or so ago, after dropping a piece of my cereal on the floor one morning (to the dog's twitching delight), I'd taken to slipping him a single bite-size piece every day. Soon enough, when I got up in the morning, Como would be sitting at attention, like a loyal retainer, by my side of the bed. Sally and I had both caved in to him.

Phoebe, who had listened to our recollections and made minimal contributions of her own, licked the last smear of cream cheese icing off her fork and fiddled with something in her lap.

'Can I have the car?' she said. The fiddling must have been a text message exchange.

'Where are you going?' asked Sally.

'Nora's.' Pause to see if we'd require more information. 'And then maybe to Jonah's later. I'll call you.' She stood up. I handed over the keys.

'Home by ten,' Sally said.

'Ten-thirty,' Phoebe called back at us.

'Ten,' Sally repeated.

'Ten,' I echoed. The front door banged shut and rattled in its frame.

Phoebe was a senior in high school and growing more independent and self-assured by the day. She was a full four inches taller than her mother and possessed of a quick, withering wit that could instantly expose our ignorance of pop music, parking, boys, bus routes, or the *only* Asian chicken salad in the West Portal neighbourhood worth knowing about. You didn't need a psychology degree to know that Sally and I were feeling the distinct advance warnings of what our life would be like in another year, when our only child was off at college. Phoebe was talking a lot about schools in New England and elsewhere on the East Coast – three thousand miles away from us. It was no real mystery why we were hauling Como into bed and buying his affection with breakfast cereal.

Sally and I both knew we were behaving a little nuttily about the dog. But we also counted our blessings that Phoebe hadn't written us off (yet) as totally hopeless anachronisms. She still filled us in, albeit selectively, on her classes and social life at school. She didn't object to being seen with us on city streets, or even at a restaurant or movie theatre where a classmate of hers might conceivably spot her in the potentially humiliating company of her mother and father. We were, in Phoebe's phrase, the 'Parental Units'. It was a label with a healthy measure of reductive mockery that nonetheless stopped well short of derision. We were glad, even grateful, to settle for it.

One point of sustained newspaper-reading and television-watching tangency that summer and autumn was the extraordinary political events that culminated in the election of Barack

Obama. We sent out for pizza on election night and let out a three-way chorus of whoops at eight p.m., when the network and cable anchors acknowledged officially what we already knew: with the closing of the polls in our state, California could be 'called' officially for Obama, thereby delivering him to the White House. Phoebe, who had spent the day as a poll worker, said she couldn't believe how long it had taken the country to elect a black president. Sally and I said we couldn't believe how soon it had happened. All three of us had tears in our eyes. Pepperoni had never smelled that good.

Three days later we watched Obama's first press conference together and whooped all over again when the new president was asked about the dog he and his wife, Michelle, had promised their daughters, Malia and Sasha. Connecting his own mixed heritage to his family's preference for adopting a dog, Obama remarked that 'obviously, a lot of shelter dogs are mutts like me.'

Phoebe plucked Como off the floor and danced him around the butcher block in our kitchen. 'Z!' she exulted. 'You're positively presidential. The First Mutt. But don't worry. The Obamas can't have you. We found you first.' Our daughter went on dancing with her dog, his eyes wide and hers dreamily half closed.

March 2009. A foggy weekday afternoon. Phoebe, after nervously checking the post for college news (there's none today), is off to the gym. Sally is shopping. I'm hunkered down in the study with something to write and too little time to finish it. In my typical, irrational response to the problem, I'm finding as many things as I can to distract myself and not face the deadline that's ticking away at me. I play a little computer pinball, hunt around on Google for nothing in particular, pick up the phone for the sixth time in the last half hour to see if I might have missed a message, which is all but impossible, since I've been sitting here listening to the phone not ring all that time.

My thumb provides another diversion, specifically the meaty base of it on my left hand. That's where Como bit me when he was lying in the middle of Kirkham Street right after the SUV hit him a little over five years ago. I can go weeks, maybe a month or more, without noticing or thinking anything about the little white scar that remains there. It doesn't hurt, and it's hardly noticeable unless you know to look for it.

But every so often – when I'm driving and happen to glance at my left hand on the wheel, when I'm chopping celery with a freshly sharpened knife and suddenly imagine how a slip might bring blood springing to the surface of my skin, when I'm killing time under the swing-arm lamp on my desk – I'll see it, that little comma-shaped mark that Como left behind with his desperate, reflexive strike right after the accident. I know he wasn't really biting *me* – I knew it at the moment it happened. But I was there with him, I was the one bending close when he'd been sent into shock by the tyre ramming into him and shattering his pelvis. He bit me because his instincts made him do it, because he had no choice, because I was there.

The scar is plainly tooth-shaped. I can see where Como's sharp canine entered and left a nearly perfect imprint, wider at the base and curving up to a point. Halfway up, two small scar branches flare out to either side. If I tilt my hand and look at it in a certain way, the tooth mark becomes a tree, a tiny tropical palm bending in an ocean breeze, its imaginary fronds rustling in the sunlight. I'm carried away. I may never get my assignment done.

Como has aged since we adopted him. The nerve damage and arthritis that his muscle-man surgeon, Dr Watt, warned us about haven't cropped up. But Como is a little slower, a little less nimble, than he was in his first few manic years with us. He's a little heavier, thicker in the middle and shaggier all around. He's started making an odd, guttural, throat-clearing sound from time to time, like an old man muttering to himself. His dog world has changed, too. His best friend, the dynamo poodle Lizzy, moved away to Denver with her family. Max and Willie, those sublimely ancient yellow Labs that never made a menacing move towards our easily spooked dog, both died. So did Jessie, our next-door neighbours' older dog, who followed her son, Riley, into the great beyond of Welsh springer spaniels.

It's not all about departure and loss. Pam and Cheryl, after a suitable grieving period for Riley and Jessie, found a pretty new springer spaniel named Clancy, who greets Como with a busily wagging tail. A feisty, friendly Jack Russell terrier named Rocky moved in up the street. We've had some spirited encounters with him on our walks, with Como proving to be cautious but no pushover for Rocky's bully-boy tactics. Lizzy, along with her new and larger poodle 'brother' Rufus, comes back from Denver to visit once or twice a year.

When Como does show some real and possibly difficult symptoms of ageing, Phoebe will be gone. Sally and I will have to handle whatever comes on our own. It's an odd thing to consider, but this thought does occur to me from time to time: when he is gone, some day, Como will leave at least one tangible piece of himself behind – that toothy little palm tree he planted on my thumb down the hill on Kirkham Street.

Como has never been a barker. Days can pass sometimes

when we may not hear a sound, save for a little muttering, come out of him. So it's a bit of a puzzle when he starts barking out in the front hall. I ignore it for a while, thinking that a deliveryman has come and gone from the porch or that the dog has heard a motorcycle or particularly noisy truck out on the street. I keep pecking away at my keyboard. Finally, as the barking continues and grows more expressive, with some longer, lower yowls and higher staccato yips worked in, I get up and open the study door.

'Z,' I begin, then see and feel it simultaneously: the open front door, with foggy grey air blowing in on Como and, down the hall, on me. I freeze in place and begin to panic. My mind lunges ahead and tries to head this off, to deny it, to make it not happen. Not again, I think. Not another horrible doomed run from the house and down the front steps and out into the streets. We can't do this again. We can't. We just can't. And who left the door open? Was it Phoebe, when she went to the gym? Had Sally come home and left it open a minute while she carried something into the house? Had I done it myself, somehow tempted fate by not shutting and locking the door so it would blow open with a gust of wind?

We can't do it. We can't. Not again.

And Como, it seems, knows that better than I do. Shooting a pensive look back over his shoulder at me and then at the wet air and shuddering tree leaves outside, he's barking for me. He's been trying to tell me for several minutes now, ever since the door came open, however it did, and left him standing there in front of it, on full sentry duty with his tail raised. He backs up a few steps, in my direction, still barking but less urgently now. He's got my attention at last. He's warned me. He's made me listen.

Don't let me go out there, Como is telling me. Don't let me go this time. Don't let me go.

Neither one of us makes another sound. I walk straight at him and pass him in the hall. He holds his ground, craning up to watch me as I shut the door.

Acknowledgements

This book would never have come to be if my friend Wendy Miller hadn't taken me to lunch. I thought we were just passing the time, back in 2003, when I told her about the torments the newly adopted Como was putting me and my family through. Wendy, an instinctive and supremely gifted editor who was working at the *San Francisco Chronicle* at the time, knew better. In what I recall as a single, fluid movement, she put down her fork, picked up her mobile, and called features editor Carolyn White. Club sandwich in hand, I listened mutely as Wendy and Carolyn decided to have me write about Como for the paper. (I was a deliberative arts critic, unaccustomed to lightning bolts.) Wendy edited the first set of what would eventually become a ten-part series in her cheerfully remorseless way. My debt to her is unrepayably large. She did what any great editor does: she made my work the very best it could possibly be, without once trying to make it her own.

The *Chronicle* family did the same, with grace, talent, kindness and a sustaining generosity of spirit. My own editor, David Wiegand, encouraged and supported me from the start. Lynette Evans shepherded the stories into print and made them live and breathe in her 'Home & Garden' section. Lance Jackson drew the colour portrait of Como that made such a stunning impression when the first instalment ran; a framed original print of it hangs on Phoebe's bedroom wall. Liz Hafalia took the photographs that both captured and brightened the tone of the series. The response of *Chronicle* readers – empathetic, informed, indignant, warmhearted, intimate and blunt – was an enlivening force throughout.

Over the years, many have counselled, goaded, cheered and solved problems that stumped me. At the risk of excluding others, and in no discernible order, I offer my deep gratitude to Sydney Goldstein, Leslie Anne Sullivan, Jerry Nachman, Jean Gonick, Rodger Broadley, Judy Winn, Louise Kollenbaum, Jeffrey Hirsch, Linda Ronstadt, Barbara Graham, Hugh Delehanty, Marianna Monaco, Chuck Breyer, Meredith White, Arthur Solomon, David Thomson and Joel Selvin.

My two editors at HarperCollins, Lisa Sharkey and Nancy Miller, were both sensitive and sharp-eyed, enthusiastic and creative, judicious and insightful. They improved the book in more ways, I'm sure, than I realize. Amy Kaplan and Bruce Nichols were early and committed HarperCollins stalwarts.

As for my agent, Amy Rennert, 'agent' comes nowhere near defining her role. Amy envisioned a book long before I did. She's got the ticket stubs from a 2006 San Francisco Giants game, where we first discussed the idea, to prove it. She waited patiently for me to catch on. Her perseverance, tact, wisdom, editorial acuity and breadth of vision have enlarged *Come Back, Como* beyond anything I thought possible. Amy's associate, Robyn Russell, added an enthusiastic boost. Every writer should be so fortunate and so blessed.

My family put up with a lot and bore up well while I was writing. Whether they can endure the results remains to be seen. With love, I beg their indulgence for whatever omissions or distortions I have committed here.

The dog in our family is one of millions whose life was saved by an animal shelter committed to a no-kill policy. It's richly gratifying to think of the enormous, collective umbrella these shelters provide for the animals and families united by their brave and steadfast work.

Como, who has a flair for being saved, remains an endless source of renewal in our house. Six years after we adopted him, he still looks astonished every time I walk into the room. The feeling is entirely mutual.

what's next?

Tell us the name of an author you love

Steven Winn   Go ▶

and we'll find your next great book